COMPUTER DATA
MANAGEMENT AND
DATA BASE
TECHNOLOGY

COMPUTER SCIENCE SERIES

COMPUTER SCIENCE SERIES

COMPUTER DATA MANAGEMENT AND DATA BASE TECHNOLOGY

HARRY KATZAN, Jr.
Chairman, Computer Science Department
Pratt Institute

VAN NOSTRAND REINHOLD COMPANY
New York   Cincinnati   Toronto   London   Melbourne

Van Nostrand Reinhold Company Regional Offices:
New York   Cincinnati   Chicago   Millbrae   Dallas

Van Nostrand Reinhold Company International Offices:
London   Toronto   Melbourne

Library of Congress Catalog Card Number: 74–31147
ISBN: 0-442-24263-8

Manufactured in the United States of America

Published by Van Nostrand Reinhold Company
450 West 33rd Street, New York, N.Y. 10001

Published simultaneously in Canada by Van Nostrand Reinhold Ltd.

15 14 13 12 11 10 9 8 7 6 5 4 3 2 1

Library of Congress Cataloging in Publication Data

Katzan, Harry.
    Computer data management and data base technology.

    (Computer science series)
    Includes bibliographies and index.
    1. Data base management.   I. Title.
QA76.K342   001.6'42   74-31147
ISBN 0-442-24263-8

PREFACE

In recent years, there has been an increasing interest in the technical aspects of data base management systems. In fact, many people regularly attend seminars on the subject costing hundreds of dollars. Because of the importance of data base technology and its impact on the computer industry and on enterprises that use computers, basic knowledge of the subject matter should not be limited to those that have the financial means to attend expensive seminars. This is only one reason for this book. Another reason is that the concepts are sophisticated and the methodology complex; they should be recorded in book form for study and reference. Lastly, the topic has academic value since our older concept of data and storage structures has slowly evolved to a consideration of what we actually do with the methodology we have developed.

Thus, the objective of the book is to explore data base technology. In order to fully appreciate the concepts, however, a general background in data management is required—hence the more general title *Computer Data Management and Data Base Technology*. The book is self-contained and only the barest familiarity with computers and data processing is needed. The subject matter is intended and organized for executives, managers, and technical people.

The book is composed of three parts:

I. Fundamentals
II. Data management concepts
III. Data base technology

The first chapter in Part I is an introduction to the concepts of information and knowledge, and how they are used. It sets the tone for the book and is recommended for all readers. Chapters 2 through 4 cover Computer Systems, Computer Software, and Data and Storage Structures, respectively. These chapters reflect the latest concepts in computer technology, and represent the most widely used systems. They can be used to review basic concepts or to refresh one's terminology.

Part II of the book is an introduction to computer data management. Again, the subject matter reflects the latest concepts and includes the following topics: data management concepts and facilities, input and output operations in a data management enviroment, input and output supervision, file organization concepts, and virtual storage access methods.

Part III of the book concerns data base technology and covers: foundations of data base technology, data base structures and representation, descriptive techniques, the DBTG report, the GUIDE/SHARE data base management system requirements, a relational data base model, Integrated Data Store (IDS), and Information Management Systems (IMS).

Lastly, the appendices supplement the text by giving DBTG, IDS, and IMS programs. Appendix A provides a comparison of IDS and DBTG programs; they are reproduced with permission of Mr. Sven Eriksen and the *Honeywell Computer Journal*. Appendix B provides a sample IMS program; it is reproduced with permission of the IBM Corporation.

The book is an outgrowth of a graduate seminar on data base technology given by the author at Pratt Institute. Most of the attendees were practicing professionals, and as a result, the subject matter covered reflects areas of data base technology that are currently of the greatest professional interest.

It is a pleasure to acknowledge the assistance of my wife Margaret who typed the manuscript and provided a liberal amount of assistance.

HARRY KATZAN, JR.

CONTENTS

PART **I** # FUNDAMENTALS

1 | **INTRODUCTION**

DATA AND REALITY

A well-known computer advertisement reads somewhat as follows: "Not just data. Reality." The implication is powerful. The objective of a computer system is not solely to replace routine clerical tasks—although this is indeed an important function. An equally important function of the computer is to provide insight into the processes of problem solving, decision making, and data analysis. Insight requires information and this fact relates to another important aspect of computer utilization. The computer can be used to store large amounts of data and make it available to a user at a moment's notice. Most computer applications involve a combination of computational and data management operations.

A computer system is deterministic in the sense that the manner in which the system responds to input conditions can be predicted. The set of possible responses is necessarily dependent upon the logical circuitry of the computer and the programs used to control it. Similarly, the data used by the computer during processing operations must be organized and accessed in a well-defined manner. Computer people can be generally grouped into two classes: users and specialists. The user normally utilizes the computer through a language, system, or special hardware device and need not necessarily know the precise details of the structure and operation of the computer system. The engineer, scientist, or analyst that uses the computer with an easy-to-learn language, such as BASIC or FORTRAN, might fall into the "user" category. Two other examples of users

3

are the information specialist that can retrieve information from a data bank with the aid of a query language via a remote terminal, and the retail clerk that uses a point-of-sale device that is connected to a central computer. But because a computer system is deterministic and data must be organized and accessed in a precise manner, someone must know exactly what the computer is doing and this is the role of the specialist. There are specialists in different areas, such as hardware, software, and data management, and there are varying degrees of specialization.

The subject matter of this book is concerned with the specialized topic of data base technology. Before data base technology can be studied, however, a thorough background is needed in computer systems, computer software, and data management. The first two parts of the book are designed to satisfy these basic needs. This review material should provide an introduction to information technology for people who have not had the opportunity of previously being exposed to one or more of the topics. Experienced people can simply omit topics with which they are familiar.

THE NATURE OF INFORMATION

In a society such as ours, one that benefits greatly from the use of mass communications and computer facilities, information is a valuable commodity. In fact, people concerned with the social aspects of computing emphasize that "information is power," and that it can be used as a control mechanism to influence the behavior of individuals. However, major problems arise in information-based societies when information is not up-to-date. The "currency" of information is a problem addressed by data management and data base systems.

In journalism, yesterday's events are without news value. The same philosophy holds true, to some extent, in computer based systems. As depicted in Figure 1.1, the value of information changes with age, where value is generally considered to be a multidimensional attribute. Two major components of the value of information are "quantity" and "quality." The *quantity of information* is measured in terms of volume, completeness, and accessibility. The *volume* of information refers to the capacity of the system and the amount of information that is available for use by a user of the information system. There is a natural limit to the volume of information that a system can store and a user can reference. As shown in Figure 1.1, this limit is reached when the cost of storing and maintaining the information exceeds its value. Some information systems utilize a storage hierarchy concept wherein infrequently used information can be migrated to a relatively inexpensive storage facility.

The capacity of an information system is also related to the efficiency of the system or the accessibility of information, since there exists a relationship between the volume of a storage medium and the speed of access. *Completeness*

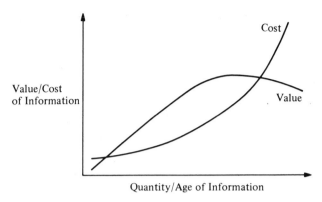

Figure 1.1 The value and cost of information is related to the quantity and age of information, measured in terms of volume, completeness, and accessibility.

refers to the degree to which an information system satisfies the information needs of a user. Completeness can also be transformed into an economic variable since complete information is obviously of greater value than incomplete information but is more costly to maintain. The last attribute of the quantity of information is *accessibility*, which denotes the response time of the system and the facilities available for using it. Systems that provide immediate response to large amounts of information and are also easy to use are naturally more valuable and more costly than systems that provide a lesser degree of accessibility. To sum up, the quantity of information is not an absolute measure, but rather, is a design "trade off" between the value and cost of information.

The *quality of information* implicitly relates to how information can be used and the degree of confidence that can be placed on it. The attributes of quality are timeliness, relevance, accuracy, reliability, and flexibility. It should be noted that these attributes are closely related and both can be used to describe information itself and the information system that makes it available to meet the needs of the user. *Timeliness* refers to the process of collecting, storing, and processing of data and the time factors involved. The key point is that systems that permit informational changes to be made to stored data as related events occur are inherently more timely than systems that require special update procedures.

The *relevance* of information is the measure of how well the information system meets the needs of the user. It can be a measure of the completeness of information or the "degree of preciseness" provided by the query system. *Accuracy* refers to errors in the collecting, storing, and processing of data, and may refer to explicit inaccuracies caused by faulty data or implicit inaccuracies caused by information that is out of date. *Reliability* is an operational characteristic that measures the degree of confidence that the user can place on the information system and the information that it contains. A reliable system provides information that is more timely, relevant, and accurate than an unreliable system. *Flexibility* is the last attribute of information and of an information system, and indicates the diversity of applications for which a given information set can be used. Data that can be used by several users, in several programs, or in making several decisions, is more flexible than data that can be used in a single application. Thus, if data from several applications can be integrated, the quantity and quality of information or of an information system is increased.

The "components of information" given here are not definitive characteristics and should be used to place the subject of information systems in perspective. The various attributes are of greatest value when they are used to describe a particular system or to compare competitive systems.

KNOWLEDGE, INFORMATION, AND DATA

One of the puzzling aspects of our modern computerized society is the fact that even though we are practically submerged in information, we are notably inept at using it effectively.

The world is filled with information. It is inherent in the design of buildings and automobiles, the structure of organizations, and the operations of groups and teams. Yet to a computer or an information scientist, it becomes *data* only when it is recorded on a medium of some kind. It is immaterial whether the media be a notched stick as ancient cave men used to count their wives or sheep, or a modern device such as a punched card or magnetic tape. Informally, *information* may be regarded as raw or processed data used for making decisions, although an information scientist would regard it as that which is generated by a change in a unit of storage. Either definition is satisfactory since the notion is rather well-defined anyway. *Knowledge* implies organization and is defined as the systematic organization of information and concepts. Knowledge can also be defined as the assignment of meaning to information—and therein lies the difficulty for organizations using computer-based information systems.

What is meaning? Clearly, it is a process of naming and identification. But it is more than that. It is also the identification of an object or event by name as a result of a common, agreed upon correspondence between an *event* metaphor and a *name* metaphor. It follows that the meaning that we assign to an event metaphor is implicit in our response to it.

One might inquire at this point what all of these definitions have to do with information systems. The answer is, essentially, that intelligence is a behavioral property and that an information system which we can use intelligently is one which takes account of the context in which it operates. One might also state that this type of information system must be adaptive and this is certainly true. But the basis of an effective information system is deeper than that. *Intelligent behavior,* on the part of a man, a machine, or both, *is the detection of the change of meaning brought about by a shift of context.* Therein lies the foundation of a useful man-machine information system.

This latter point must be amplified. Many information systems store data and a subset of this data is eventually used for making decisions or preparing reports. For the most part, however, data is single-purpose in that it is collected and used with a small number of objectives in mind. In a large organization, like the City of New York, a significant amount of data is required to support its diverse activities and much of it is redundant. Using the notion of intelligent behavior given previously, a minimal amount of data would be stored with its specific meaning being dependent upon the context in which it is used. An accepted name for this would be a *common data base.*

SYSTEMS CONCEPTS

The preceding discussion of knowledge, information, and data emphasizes the fact that before a data item can be made usable, a relationship must be established between it and an independent entity, such as a user, an operational environment, or another data item. This is the process that ascribes meaning to data.

Essentially, we are talking about a system. In his book *A Methodology for for Systems Engineering,* Arthur D. Hall defines a system as follows:

> A *system* is a set of objects with relationships between the objects and between their attributes.

Objects are the components or parts of the system and in a general sense are unlimited in scope and variety. In actual practice, however, the objects of which a system is synthesized give the system its structure, and implicitly determine the practical limits on its functional operability. Attributes are properties of objects, such as the resistance of a wire or the age of an individual, and normally correspond to data stored in an information system. Relationships connect the system together, so they can be regarded as a single entity, and can take the form of a physical connection, a logical similarity, a casual rule, and so forth. In information systems, relationships are used to connect data items to form data aggregates.

Systems exist with the support of an environment, and in most cases, the environment determines the nature of the system itself. The *environment* of a system exists as the objects outside of a system, whose attributes affect the system or are changed by the operation of the system. Open systems interface or exchange information with their environment; closed systems do not interface with their environments and there is no exchange of energy between them. In the same manner that objects possess attributes, systems do also. Systems have been variously classed as being adaptive, probablistic, deterministic, stable, and possessing a feedback mechanism.

The nature of the existence of systems is referred to as *systems ontology,* which establishes a distinction between real systems, conceptual systems, and abstract systems. The existence of real systems can be perceived or inferred from observation and exist independently of the observer. Conceptual systems utilize logical or mathematical constructs to model a system's operation. Abstracted systems form a subset of conceptual systems and exist as conceptual systems with a real counterpart.

Systems ontology plays an important role in the computer and information sciences, wherein an abstract system is provided as a conceptual model of a computer or an informational facility.

THE CONCEPT OF AN INFORMATION SPACE

A *data base* is a centralized collection of data stored for use in one or more applications. Two aspects of a data base are of prime concern: the nature of data, and the manner in which it must be structured to model the existing data relationships in an enterprise. In a general sense, there is very little doubt about what data is; it is simply recorded information. The notion of a data base, however, requires a more fundamental approach to the subject.

First, an enterprise is a collection of people and artifacts, organized to serve a set of goals. An enterprise can be a business, a school, a government, or any sort of social group. Events take place in the history of an interprise that must be recorded; yet as discussed previously, the event itself cannot be stored in the computer. Thus, a data item is created, replaced, or altered to symbolically represent the event.

Something about which we record operational data is termed an *entity*. An entity can be a person, place, or thing—real or abstract. A unit of operational data is simply a fact, as in the assertion: "Employee with social security number 123-45-6789 has the job title programmer." In this example, "employee" is the entity and the property "job title" is a fact recorded symbolically about the entity "employee." The title "programmer" is a value of the property "job title." One of the defining characteristics of a data base environment is that properties can also be entities, about which facts are recorded. Thus for the property "job title," we might record the facts: qualifications, pay range, career path, bonus type, and so forth. A property is simply a characteristic, and so a fact may be a property of more than one entity. For example, a particular female entity may be one entity's "mother," another entity's "wife," and a third entity's "sister." Similarly, a specific value for the property "price" might be the cost of several commodities.

A collection of similar entities that have the same properties is known as an *entity set*. Typical entity sets are: a set of employees, a set of bank accounts, a set of automobiles, a set of driver's licenses, and a set of dependents. The entities in an entity set possess at least one property that distinguishes them from other entities in the set. These unique properties are known as **identifiers**.

In a payroll application, for example, the entity set consists of employees with the unique identifier "social security number." Other identifiers might be the part number for an entity set of parts, or the name for an entity set of dependents.

It is obvious that we are talking about three different things: elements of the real world, units of information, and data itself. In the real world, we use the terms "entity" and "property." When dealing with units of information, we use the terms "entity" and "attribute." When dealing with units of data, we use the terms "data element" and "data item." Thus, to record the fact that an entity has a specific characteristic involves establishing a property class, referred to as an attribute, and assigning a value to that attribute. This information is represented as data by associating a symbolic data item to a data element associated with the attribute. In a conventional computer file, data items are normally represented by fields within a record or by some kind of logical association with other records. For example, the attribute "social security number" in a personnel file would normally be a field in an employee's personnel record. The attribute "job title" could be stored as a field in the same record or by association with a record for the entity "job title."

The whole notion of information can be reduced to three concepts: entities, attributes, and values. An entity may possess several attributes; entities with the same attributes form an entity set. A specific entity is determined by specific values for the attributes that describe it. In fact, an attribute/value pair is occasionally referred to as a "descriptor." For example, an entity that exists as a specific insurance policy might be described by the following descriptors:

Attribute	Value	
Owner (policy holder)	John Brown	
Policy number	12345	
Policy class	Automobile	
Policy type	Liability/Collision	
Deduction class	100	
Policy value-P	100	(personal liability)
Policy value-O	300	(each occurrence)
Policy value-D	50	(property damage)
Rider-J	Yes	

Obviously, there are other descriptors that would apply, such as age, address, accident record, and so forth. One of the above descriptors is unique, i.e., policy number, and it serves as an identifier for the entity—i.e., the insurance policy.

An element of information can be conveniently depicted as a point in a three-dimensional space, as shown in Figure 1.2. The axes represent a set of entities, a set of attributes, and a set of values. The intersection of an entity, an attribute,

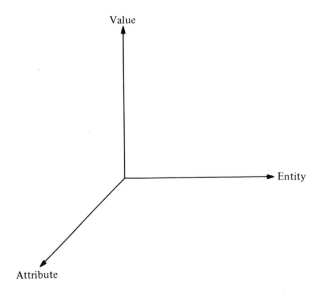

Figure 1.2 An element of information can be represented as a
point in a three-dimensional space, where the axes
are: the entity about which information is represented, the attribute used to describe the entity, and
the specific value for that attribute.

and a value determines an item of information. It should be recognized that the information space applies to all entities—i.e., insurance policies.

Any descriptor that concerns policy class involves a point that lies in the "policy class" plane that runs parallel to the value and entity axes (see Figure 1.3). Similarly, any descriptor that concerns the value "automobile" lies on the "automobile" plane that runs parallel to the attribute and entity axes (see Figure 1.4). The intersection of the "policy class" and "automobile" planes (see Figure 1.5) is a line representing the descriptor "automobile policy," which applies to a wide class of entities, not necessarily related to insurance. In an analogous fashion, the value "automobile" can apply to several attributes and its value is not restricted to the attribute "policy class." (The attributes "deduction class" and "policy value-P" in the preceding example that both have the value 100 is evidence of this fact.)

The entity plane runs parallel to the attribute and value axes and represents the descriptors for a single entity, so that the intersection of the three planes (entity, attribute, and value), as in Figure 1.6, represents a single item of information. Thus, the information space represents all possible triplets of the form (⟨entity⟩, ⟨attribute⟩, ⟨value⟩). Many points in the information space are not relevant to an enterprise—hence the concept of a data base.

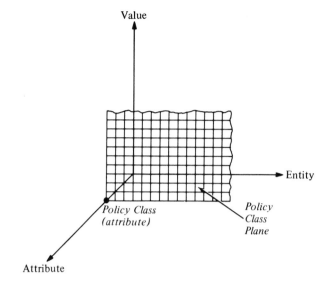

Figure 1.3 Any descriptor involving the attribute "policy class" lies in the "policy class" plane.

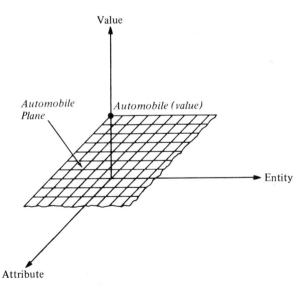

Figure 1.4 Any descriptor involving the "automobile" value lies in the "automobile" plane.

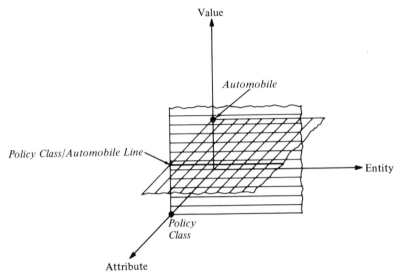

Figure 1.5   The intersection of the "policy class" and "automobile" planes is a line representing all entities with the "automobile policy" descriptor.

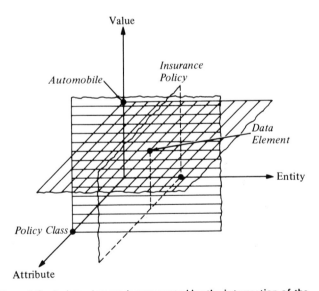

Figure 1.6   A data element is represented by the intersection of the entity, attribute, and value planes.

THE CONCEPT OF A DATA BASE

A subset of the points in the total information space is known as a *data base*. It must be defined for a given enterprise and its description is referred to as a *schema*. Thus, a schema is a definition of a data base for a particular enterprise. In actual practice, schemas are usually developed for a specified class of computer applications.

In a data base application, the user is concerned with the descriptors for a particular entity set—such as the data records that correspond to an insurance policy file. A policy record, using the above example, would then be a subset of the points in the data base that lie in the plane of the entity corresponding to a particular policy. A description of the points corresponding to the points of the data base corresponding to a single entity is known as a *subschema*. Thus, a subschema is a definition of a data record for an entity set. The number of records in a file defined over the data base normally corresponds to the number of points along the entity axis.

The attributes of interest to a computer application are dependent upon the schema and subschema, and are independent of the total attribute set of the data base. However, the meaning of a particular value, represented as the data item corresponding to a data element in a subschema, is dependent upon its associated attribute.

Data base design involves the mapping of one subset of the information space to another subset of the information space, and establishing paths between the points in a subset.

A data base is used in a fashion similar to file processing. Consider a file of insurance policies (i.e., entities) sorted by the unique identifier "policy number." The process of reading the file is analogous to traversing the length of the entity axis.   Similarly, the process of searching the file for automobile policies is equivalent to traversing the line corresponding to the line formed by the intersection of the "policy class" and "automobile" planes.

A good data base design is a minimum subset of the information space with sufficient mapping to allow efficient file processing.

DATA BASE MANAGEMENT

Data base management is a concept that permits a data base to be utilized through a combination of hardware and software facilities and operational conventions.   A simplified view of a data base management system is given in Figure 1.7.   Several system components and operating conventions are needed:

1. *A Data Base Description Language* (DBDL) is used by the user and a data base administrator (i.e., a person) to define data files.
2. *A data base manager* (i.e., a set of hardware and software components) is

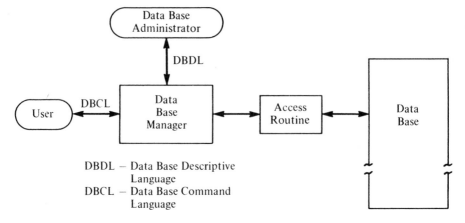

Figure 1.7 Simplified view of a data base management system.

required to establish and store the relationship between a data file and the subset of the information space known as the data base.
3. *A Data Base Command Language* (DBCL) is needed so that the user can access his data file in the data base.
4. *Access routines* are needed so that the data base can be accessed; and lastly, a *data base* itself is needed to store information.

The functions performed by the data base administrator are:

1. To describe data.
2. To define relationships.
3. To define mapping.
4. To define security.
5. To specify performance measurement.

The hardware and software components of the data base manager are designed to serve as the focal point of the data base system. Functions defined for the data base manager are:

1. To manipulate data (open, read, write, etc.).
2. To enforce data security.
3. To insure data integrity.
4. To record system performance data.

In actual practice, many computer scientists feel that a data base system augments data management facilities, but does not replace them. Although most data, both structured as a data file and unstructured as textual information or program libraries, can logically be placed in the domain of a data base; it is generally felt that "other data," such as private data checkpoints or pages of a virtual memory, justify the need for data management facilities.

AN IMPORTANT COMMENT

Data base technology is a complex subject that requires a thorough familiarization with computer systems, software, and data management. The next few chapters are concerned with the necessary prerequisites. In actual practice, no specific knowledge is needed to study data base technology. It is the "overall" knowledge of information processing that is needed to place the concepts in proper perspective.

REFERENCES

Burch, J. G., Jr., and Felix R. Strater, Jr., *Information Systems: Theory and Practice*, Santa Barbara, California, Hamilton Publishing Company, 1974.

Dippel, B., and W. C. House, *Information Systems: Data Processing and Evaluation*, Glenview, Illinois, Scot, Foresman, and Company, 1969.

Hall, A. D., *A Methodology for Systems Engineering*, New York, Van Nostrand Reinhold Company, 1962.

Joint GUIDE-SHARE Data Base Requirements Group, *Data Base Management System Requirements*, New York, Share Inc., November 11, 1970.

Katzan, H., *Information Technology: The Human Use of Computers*, New York, Petrocelli Books, 1974.

Klir, G. J. (editor), *Trends in General Systems Theory*, New York, John Wiley and Sons, Inc., 1972.

Lyon, J. K., *An Introduction to Data Base Design*, New York, John Wiley and Sons, Inc., 1971.

Meadow, C. T., *The Analysis of Information Systems*, New York, John Wiley and Sons, Inc., 1967.

Meltzer, H. M., *Data Base Concepts and Architecture for Data Base Systems*, IBM Corporation, Presented to the SHARE Information Systems Research Project, New York, Share Inc., August 20, 1969.

2 | COMPUTER SYSTEMS CONCEPTS

A simplified diagram of a computer is given in Figure 2.1. The *storage unit* holds both the instructions and data, and the *processing unit* performs the arithmetic and control functions. It is important to recognize that the input and output functions do not involve the processing unit so that input, output, and computing can take place simultaneously. The storage unit is used to hold instructions and data during computing; it is not a mass storage device. The processing unit is composed of a "control unit" and an "arithmetic/logic unit." The *control unit* keeps track of the program address (explained later), fetches instructions from the storage unit, decodes them, and passes control signals to the arithmetic/logic unit to have the instructions executed. The *arithmetic/logic unit* contains the registers and circuitry necessary to execute the computer instructions. The instruction repertoire of a computer is reflected in the complexity of the arithmetic/logic unit. A more detailed (but still conceptual) diagram of a computer is given in Figure 2.2.

The main function of the *storage unit* is to hold machine instructions, data, intermediate values, and results before output. Each of these quantities is located at a specific place in the storage unit and that location is termed its *storage address*. The manner in which storage is organized determines how a specific location is addressed. When storage is organized on a *word basis*, each word is assigned a physical address; a word can hold a numeric value, an instruction, or a series of characters—such as those from a punched card. When storage

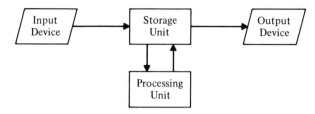

Figure 2.1   Simplified diagram of a computer.

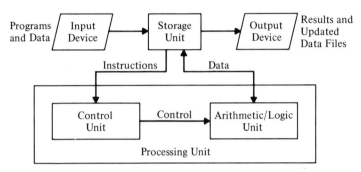

Figure 2.2   Expanded diagram of a computer.

is organized on a byte basis, each byte is assigned a physical address. A byte can hold a character or be a subunit of either an instruction or a numeric field. Thus, instructions and data are usually composed of several bytes. The amount of data used during the execution of an instruction depends upon the instruction itself; some instructions operate on bytes, others on words, and so forth.

As mentioned, instructions are stored in the storage unit along with data. The programmer insures that instructions are not inadvertently treated as data, and vice versa. An instruction is usually composed of an operation field and one or more operand fields or modifier fields. The *operation field* is interpreted by the control unit of the processing unit and tells the computer what operation to perform. The *modifier field* augments the operation field and the operand fields specify the data on which the operation is to be performed. Figure 2.3 depicts a typical symbolic computer operation, a machine form of the same instruction, and an example of how it is executed.

Before an instruction is executed, an effective address is computed, as depicted in Figure 2.3. An effective address specifies the storage locations that are accessed and incorporates any indexing operations or address arithmetic. When two or more programs reside in the storage unit, one program can access or modify one of the other programs, either inadvertently as the result of a programming error, or on a planned basis to destroy or obtain information from

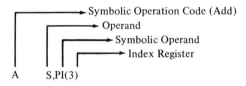

(a)   Symbolic Form of an Instruction

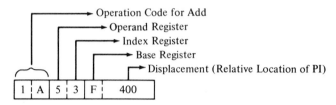

(b)   Machine Language Form in Hexadecimal

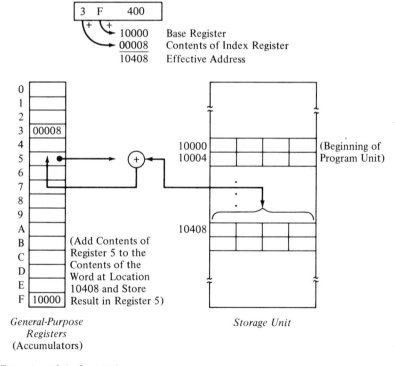

(c)   Execution of the Instruction

Figure 2.3   The structure and function of a typical computer instruction.

that program. This is a serious problem and most modern computers include storage protection mechanisms of one kind or another to prevent this from happening.

OPERATION AND ORGANIZATION

A computer operates under the control of the processing unit which contains several registers that are used by the control and arithmetic/logic units. A *register* is a high-speed storage mechanism, usually synthesized from expensive circuitry and components, and used to hold data or instructions temporarily for use by the processing unit. Some registers, such as general-purpose floating-point, or index registers, can be addressed (i.e., referenced) by a computer program. Other registers are designed into the functional structure of the processing unit and are not directly addressable. The control unit uses a *current address register* to keep track of the program address. When the control unit needs to "fetch" an instruction from the storage unit, it goes to the current address register to find its address. During the execution of an instruction, the storage address in the current address register is incremented by the length of the instruction (in bytes or words). Thus, when the control unit goes to the current address register to find the address of the next instruction to be executed, it is directed to the next instruction in sequence.

The execution of an instruction takes place in (or involves) two cycles: the instruction cycle and the execution cycle. The instruction cycle involves the control unit and the execution cycle usually involves the arithmetic/logic unit. During the *instruction cycle*, the control unit fetches an instruction from the storage unit and places it in an *instruction register*, where it is decoded. The control unit also computes an effective address so that the instruction operands can be fetched from the storage unit. During the *execution cycle*, the operand(s) is fetched from the storage unit and control signals are sent to the arithmetic/logic unit to have a specific instruction executed.

Execution of the processing unit then continues with another instruction cycle. Normally, the current address register is updated between the instruction and execution cycles. Also some instructions do not use the arithmetic/logic unit. The branch instruction, for example, is executed by simply placing the target address in the current address register. Many instructions use accumulator-type registers for performing arithmetic operations. Some computers employ both a single accumulator for additive operations and an extension to it (often called the multiplier or multiplier-quotient register) for multiplicative operations. Other computers employ separate fixed- and floating-point registers for fixed- and floating-point operations, respectively. In general, arithmetic registers reflect the design philosophy of the computer and are not particularly significant from the standpoint of data management or data base technology.

The processing unit also controls or initiates input and output operations. Normally, input and output is initiated when an instruction is executed commanding the computer to start an input/output operation; the unit on which input or output is to be performed is usually supplied with the instruction. Also supplied at this time is the location of a list of input/output commands, held in the storage unit, that specify the specific input/output operations that should take place. After input or output is initiated, the processing unit continues with the execution of the next instruction and input/output is performed asynchronously under the control of an "input/output data channel." An *input/output* data channel is a hardware component that operates like a small hardwired computer. The address in the storage unit of a list of input/output commands is passed to the input/output data channel by the processing unit. The input/output data channel then decodes these commands and performs the required operations. A typical input/output command format is given as Figure 2.4, and

Input/Output Operation Code	Data Address	Flags	Count

Figure 2.4   Typical input/output command format.

a typical command might be: "read 80 bytes into main storage beginning with byte location 40132." Some input/output functions require several commands. They are placed consecutively in the storage unit and executed sequentially by the input/output data channel. A typical input/output interface is depicted in Figure 2.5. For output operations, the input/output data channel moves infor-

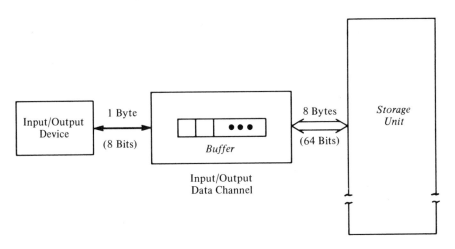

Figure 2.5   Typical input/output interface.

mation from the storage unit to the specified input/output device. For input operations, the process is reversed. The input/output data channel also initiates control operations, such as the rewind of a tape or the positioning of a disk mechanism. In most operating environments, each user does not perform his own input/output; rather input/output is performed for each user by a data management subsytem that operates on a system-wide basis.

Several components in a computer system have been introduced without relating them to the total system concept. Figure 2.6 depicts a typical computer system configuration. As mentioned, the processing unit controls the execution of the system under program control. The storage unit is used to hold programs and data for "active" programs currently being executed. Input/output data channels are used to control input/output operations and transmit information between the storage unit and input/output devices. An *input/output control unit* controls the operation of one or more input/output devices. An *input/output device* acts as a slave to its input/output control unit and performs an elementary input/output operation—read, write, seek, etc. An *input/output medium* represents the physical medium on which information is recorded. Typical input/output media are: a punched card for the card reader and card punch device; a magnetic tape reel for a magnetic tape device; and a disk pack for a magnetic disk drive.

PROCESSING UNIT

The processing unit controls the operation of the entire computer system. All storage references, data manipulation, and input/output operations either are performed by the processing unit or are initiated by it. Although specific knowledge of these functions is not required for a study of data managment and data base technology, a conceptual understanding is assumed.

Operating control of the computer is reflected in a computer word termed the *status word*. The status word together with the machine registers reflect the current state of the processing unit at any point in time. The contents of a typical status word is given as Figure 2.7. Changing the contents of the status word is tantamount to changing the status of the computer since the processing unit uses it to determine how instructions and conditions that arise should be processed. The status word contains the following kinds of information:

1. The location of the storage unit of the instruction currently being executed (i.e., the current address register).
2. The storage protection key (covered later).
3. Codes that determine which interruptions (also covered later) can occur and specify conditions that currently exist.
4. State indicators that govern the operational state of the processing unit.

The status word is used in four ways: (1) to hold information that tells what *has*

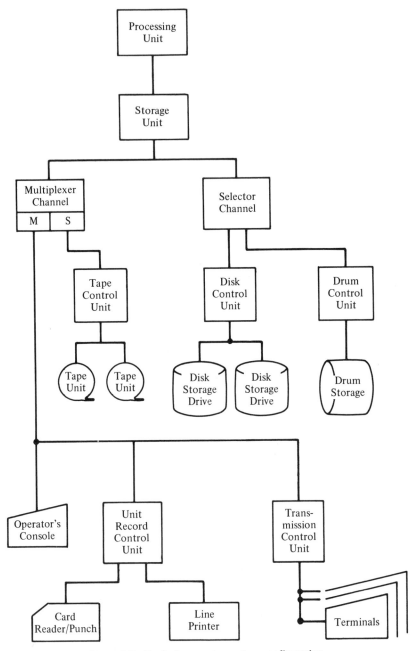

Figure 2.6 Typical computer system configuration.

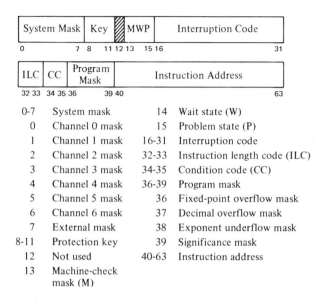

System Mask	Key	MWP	Interruption Code
0 7 8 11 12 13 15 16			31

ILC	CC	Program Mask	Instruction Address
32 33 34 35 36 39 40			63

0-7	System mask	14	Wait state (W)
0	Channel 0 mask	15	Problem state (P)
1	Channel 1 mask	16-31	Interruption code
2	Channel 2 mask	32-33	Instruction length code (ILC)
3	Channel 3 mask	34-35	Condition code (CC)
4	Channel 4 mask	36-39	Program mask
5	Channel 5 mask	36	Fixed-point overflow mask
6	Channel 6 mask	37	Decimal overflow mask
7	External mask	38	Exponent underflow mask
8-11	Protection key	39	Significance mask
12	Not used	40-63	Instruction address
13	Machine-check mask (M)		

Figure 2.7 Typical status word.

happened in the processing unit, (2) to hold information that denotes what is currently happening in the processing unit, (3) to hold information that governs what operations can or cannot be performed by the processing unit, and (4) to hold information denoting what can or cannot happen in the future. Thus, the status word is composed of mask fields, state bits, codes, lengths, and addresses. The significance of the status word is amplified in subsequent paragraphs.

Modern computers are designed to accommodate several active users in the storage unit simultaneously—an operational technique known as *multiprogramming*. This technique requires that the operating system* manage the resources of the computer system dynamically (including the processing unit, storage unit, and input/output facility) and that the users be protected from one another. It is not difficult to imagine the confusion and inefficiency that would result from several users in a multiprogramming environment, attempting to perform their own input/output, and utilizing external storage as well. For this reason, most modern computers limit the functions that can be performed by an application program. In general, two states of the processing unit are defined: the supervisor state and the problem state. A program operating in the *supervisor state* has access to the facilities of the entire computer system. This is achieved through privileged and nonprivileged instructions. *Privileged instructions* are used to

*An *operating system* is a set of control programs used to manage the resources of a computer system.

initiate input/output operations, load the status word, manipulate storage keys, and perform other critical functions. *Nonprivileged instructions* are used to perform ordinary data processing functions—those functions that cannot affect or access the program of another user. It follows that a program operating in the supervisor state can use both privileged and nonprivileged instructions. The *problem state* is a state of the processing unit that permits only nonprivileged instructions to be executed and is intended for application programs (often called processing programs).

Routines of the operating system that are involved with the overall management of the computer system normally operate in the supervisor state. When a program operating in the problem state requires the services of a routine that operates in the supervisor state, two functions must be performed:

1. Program control must be passed to the required routine.
2. The state of the processing unit must be changed to the supervisor state.

The manner in which these two functions are implemented is discussed in the next section, entitled "Interruptions."

The supervisor/problem state is perhaps the most obvious state that the processing unit can be in since it determines the kinds of instructions that can be executed by an operating program. Other states that affect the operation of the processing unit are:

1. The Stopped/Operating state.
2. The Wait/Running state.
3. The Masked/Interruptable state.

When the processing unit is in the *stopped state*, instructions cannot be executed and interruptions cannot be taken. (In other words, the computer is not operating.) If the processing unit is in the operating state, then it is either waiting or running. If it is in the *running state*, then instructions are being processed and interruptions can be taken. In the *wait state*, instructions are not executed but interruptions can take place. Normally, the operating system will put the processing unit into the wait state when it has no more work to do. The processing unit is subsequently taken out of the wait state by an interruption that denotes an external event, a condition, or a request that must be attended to by the operating system. When the processing unit can be interrupted for a given event, that interruption is said to be *enabled* and a mask bit in the status word (or auxiliary control register) is set. When the mask bit is not set, the interruption is said to be *masked off* or *disabled* and that particular interruption is not recognized. In general, a masked/interruptable state exists for each type of interruption; however, some interruptions are of prime importance and can never be masked off.

The processing unit is put into a particular state by loading a status word with appropriate bits set. In general, a new status word is loaded with a "load status word" instruction that can be issued by a program executing in the supervisor state or as the result of an interruption that causes a new status word to be loaded.

INTERRUPTIONS

The processing unit is designed to execute instructions sequentially, as mentioned previously in this chapter. The address of the current instruction (often called a location counter or the current address register) is maintained by the processing unit. Execution proceeds as follows:

1. The control unit of the processing unit fetches the instruction located at the storage address specified in the current address register.
2. The instruction is decoded by the control unit.
3. The current address register is incremented by the length attribute of the instruction fetched.
4. The specified computer operation is performed by the execution unit of the processing unit.

The process cycles back to step 1 and, in that way, instructions located in the storage unit are executed sequentially until one of two conditions arises:

1. An instruction is executed that alters the sequential order.
2. An independent event interrupts normal computer processing.

An independent event that interrupts normal computer processing is called an *interruption* and can occur for one of several reasons:

1. The computer detects an erroneous or unusual condition in a program currently in execution.
2. A device external to the processing unit needs attention.
3. The error detection circuitry of the computer detects a hardware malfunction.
4. A program executing in the problem state requires the services of a routine that executes in the supervisor state and issues an instruction that causes an interruption.

For each type of interruption recognized by the processing unit* there are two fixed locations in the storage unit—each of which can hold a replica of the status word. The first location is referred to as the *old status word* and the second is referred to as the *new status word*. When an interruption occurs, the *current status word* at the moment of interruption is stored in the old status word location and the status word located at the new status word location replaces

---

*The interruption scheme used with the 360/370 computers is described here.

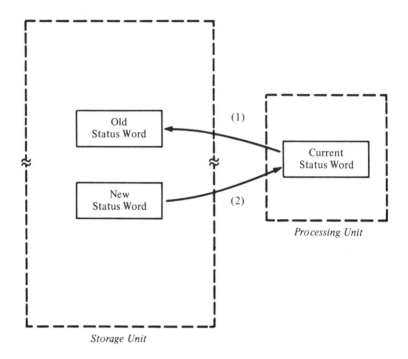

Figure 2.8 Switching of the status word after an interruption.

the current status word for the processing unit. The current address field of the new status word contains the storage location of a routine developed to process that type of interruption and the other bits of the status word are set appropriately. The switching of status words is performed automatically by the processing unit when an interruption occurs for a condition that has been enabled. (See Figure 2.8.) A disabled interruption may be ignored or left pending, depending upon the type of condition and the design of the processing unit.

Interruption systems are designed differently in different computers. Some computers permit interruptions to occur at different priority levels for a large number of independent events. Other computers permit only a small number of interruptions. Regardless of the design philosophy, additional information on the independent event causing the interruption is required; that information is stored as an interruption code in the old status word or elsewhere in the storage unit. The interruption code may specify the condition and/or the physical component associated with the interruption. A basic set of interruptions is required for descriptive purposes. They are listed and described as follows:

1. *Input/output interruption*—signals the processing unit that an input/output channel is free, that the activity of a specific channel or control unit has

been completed, or that a special condition has arisen. The interruption code usually specifies the channel and control unit address of the associated input/output device.

2. *Program interruption*—caused by an improper specification of computer hardware facilities, or an illegal use of a computer instruction or data. The condition causing the interruption is stored as the interruption code.

3. *Supervisor call interruption*—requests a change to the supervisor state from the problem state. Usually this type of interruption is issued when a function permitted only by a program executing in the supervisor state must be performed.

4. *External interruption*—caused by a signal from a device external to the processing unit or by an alarm from a timing device. System timers and inter-computer communication features frequently use this facility.

5. *Machine check interruption*—results from a computer system malfunction. This type of interruption is dependent upon a particular model of computer.

Although each type of interruption serves an important function, two specific types are particularly significant from the point of view of data management and data base technology: the input/output interruption, used to control input/output operations: and the supervisor call interruption, used to put the computer in the supervisor state so that actual input/output can be performed.

STORAGE UNIT

The storage unit serves a well-defined function in the structure and operation of a computer system. Two related concepts are used to extend the capacity and insure the integrity of the computer system: large capacity storage and storage protection.

Large-capacity storage is a bulk storage facility that is directly addressable by the processing unit. Addresses in large-capacity storage are regarded as an extension of the storage unit; however, the time required to address large-capacity storage is greater than that of the storage unit. Also, programs that operate out of large-capacity storage or use data that are stored there operate in a degraded state, as compared to cases where the same information was held in the storage unit. The combination of conventional storage and large-capacity storage constitutes a *storage hierarchy*. For some applications, it is efficient to transfer instructions and data from large-capacity storage to the storage unit before processing. In other cases, the overhead involved is not justified and information is used directly from large-capacity storage. For many applications, such as an on-line data base, the use of large-capacity storage as a bulk storage device is superior to using a mass storage input/output device, such as magnetic disk, because access to it is more rapid. However, the use of data management routines provides facilities for insuring data integrity that are not possible with directly-addressable large-capacity storage. Most modern computer systems, therefore, include a storage protection feature of some kind.

One of the characteristics of most modern computer operating environments is that distinct programs and data can reside concurrently in directly-addressable storage. A hardware storage protection feature is available with many computer systems that prevents a program from making storage accesses to an area in storage occupied by another program. Storage protection is implemented by dividing the storage units into fixed-size blocks and by associating a *storage key* with each block. (The IBM 360/370 computers, for example, use a 2048-byte block for storage protection.) Each active program has a *protection key* that is usually maintained as a part of the status word. A store operation into an area of storage is permitted only if the keys match or the protection key is zero.

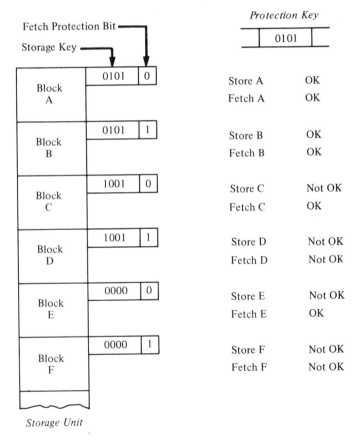

Figure 2.9   Example of storage protection.

Keys are assigned by the operating system so that each block of storage assigned to the same program has the same storage key, and the protection key assigned to that program matches the storage key. The zero protection key, taken generally to be the *master key*, is used by the operating system and is never assigned to a user's program. Two levels of protection exist: store protection and fetch protection. *Store protection* guards against data being stored in a given block of storage. *Fetch protection* guards against data being fetched from a given block of storage. A fetch protection bit is frequently implemented along with the storage key. If the *fetch* protection bit is zero, then protection applies only to a store operation. If the protection bit is one, then protection also applies to a fetch operation as well as to a store operation into that block of storage. Figure 2.9 gives some examples of storage protection.

Storage protection applies to input and output operations as well as to storage accesses by the processing unit. When an instruction is executed that initiates an input/output operation, that instruction specifies either explicitly or implicitly depending upon the computer, at least three items:

1. An input/output device address.
2. An address in storage of the first command in a list of input/output commands.
3. A protection key.

Figure 2.10 depicts a channel address word used in the System 360/370 computers to specify items 2 and 3. The *protection key* is used by the input/output

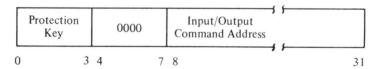

Protection Key	0000	Input/Output Command Address

0   3 4   7 8   31

Figure 2.10   The channel address word used in the System 360/370 computers to specify the storage protection key and the input/output command address.

data channel when storage is accessed for either a store or a fetch operation. Storage protection in the input/output data channel operates in the same manner as when under processing unit control.

VIRTUAL STORAGE CONCEPTS

Virtual storage, as suggested by Figure 2.11, allows extended storage addresses that are mapped into a combination of real storage and auxiliary storage. The basic element of a virtual storage system is a *page*—a fixed-size unit of storage, such as 2048 or 4096 bytes. Virtual storage, real storage, and auxiliary storage are logically divided into pages. Although instructions and data must be located

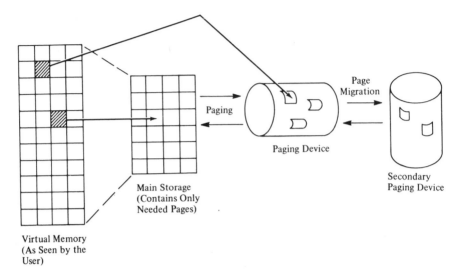

Figure 2.11 The operation of virtual storage.

in the storage unit before they can be used by the processing unit, the complete program need not be in the storage unit when only a part of it is needed for execution to continue. This is the main concept behind virtual storage; that is, only needed pages are brought into the storage unit. Thus, the storage unit can be "overcommitted" since only needed pages are brought in at any one time. The processing of moving pages between main storage and auxiliary storage, as needed, is referred to as "paging."

The design philosophy behind virtual storage as a storage management technique is that a storage address serves two purposes: (1) it represents the name of a data item, and (2) it represents the location of the data item. By considering the two items separately, the name can be used in a table lookup operation to determine the location of the data item. The process of mapping between a storage space is depicted in Figure 2.12. The process is essentially the same as applying a function $(f : N \rightarrow S)$ to each address in the name space (virtual storage) to arrive at a location in the storage space (real storage). When used as a storage management technique, some data items are not in the storage unit so that the function is undefined for some arguments.

Virtual storage is usually *segmented*, which means that storage is regarded as a collection of "blocks or segments." Within a segment, information is stored linearly. Segments are named symbolically or linearly. Those that are named linearly have a segment number so that segments can be arranged consecutively in much the same way that information within a segment is arranged linearly.

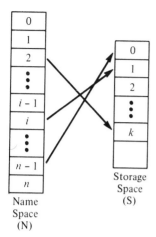

Figure 2.12 Mapping between a name space and a storage space.

One method of implementing virtual memory is to organize a linearly segmented name space and the address space into page-size units, such that addresses within a page need not be translated. Page locations are translated using a table lookup procedure. Figure 2.13 depicts the use of a single-level page table. Single-level page tables have distinct disadvantages; the most important is that the page table becomes excessively long and it must be in the main storage unit when the program to which it corresponds is in the state of execution. This disadvantage led to the development of what is known as two-level page tables. With two-level page tables, each user's virtual storage is divided into segments such that a page table exists for each segment and only the page tables required for the executing

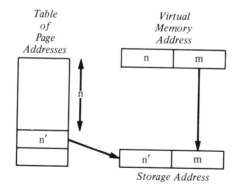

Figure 2.13 Address translation using a single-level page table.

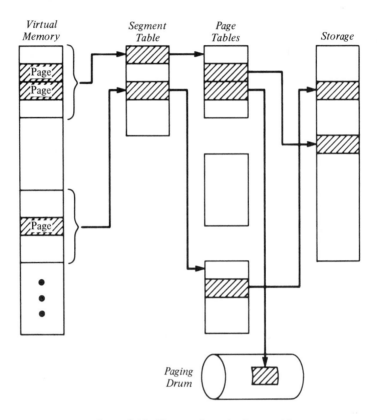

Figure 2.14 The use of two-level page tables.

program need be located in the storage unit. The use of two-level page tables is depicted in Figure 2.14.

DYNAMIC ADDRESS TRANSLATION

Virtual storage operates with a hardware feature known as *dynamic address translation*. Each effective address formed by the processing unit is translated to a real main storage address prior to each storage reference when operating in the "relocate" mode. Computers that permit the use of virtual storage include several hardware features not found in computers without virtual storage capability. The features include:

1. An extended status word that permits a "normal" mode and a "relocate" mode. When operating in the normal mode, the computer operates as any computer. When in the relocate mode, dynamic address translation is performed.

2. A set of special registers that are used during dynamic address translation. In particular, one of these registers (called the *segment table register*) points to the segment table.

3. A DAT box (DAT is an acronym for Dynamic Address Translation). The DAT box physically performs the address translation and generates a program interruption if the referenced page is not in the storage unit or the virtual storage page has not been allocated (i.e., a page table entry does not exist for it).

4. A small high-speed associative memory. The dynamic translation of addresses requires two storage references to access the segment and page tables. The real storage locations of the most recently referenced pages are stored in this associative memory. When an address is to be translated, the segment-page fields of the virtual storage address are compared in parrallel with the virtual storage addresses in the associative memory. If a match is found, the corresponding address in the storage unit is taken directly from the associative memory and no storage accesses are required for the segment and page tables.

When operating in a virtual storage environment, the processing unit computes an effective address for storage references in the usual fashion. This fact is important and means that a program contains virtual storage addresses and not real storage addresses. If the processing unit is operating in the "normal" mode, then the effective address becomes the real storage address. When operating in the relocate mode, dynamic address translation takes place as described in the following paragraphs.

A virtual storage address is divided into three parts: segment number, page number, and the byte number as depicted in Figure 2.15. Ordinarily, pages within a segment are allocated consecutively. However, segments are used for different purposes so that the ith segment need not be completely allocated before a page allocation is made to the $(i + 1)^{st}$ segment. Each program requires

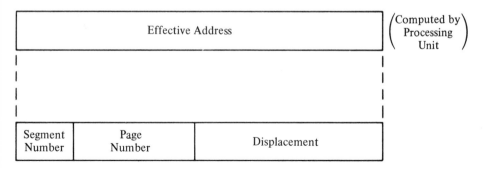

Figure 2.15 Virtual storage effective address.

the following for execution:

1. A special register that gives the segment table origin.
2. A segment table that gives the origin of the page tables.
3. A page table for each segment.

Each page table entry gives the real main storage address of the corresponding page. These tables are created by the operating system for each program; the tables are updated as the system operates and pages are moved between the main storage and auxiliary storage units. The page table entry requires the following information:

1. Real storage address in the storage unit.
2. A flag denoting whether the storage address is valid or invalid.
3. An external page address giving the device address and relative page number within the device.

A conceptual page table entry is given in Figure 2.16. If the real storage address is invalid, then the external page address tells where the page can be found so

Storage Address (A)	Flags (F)	External Page Address (E)

Figure 2.16   Conceptual page table entry.

that it can be brought into storage by the operating system on a demand basis. When a program is given control of the processing unit, its segment table and/or page tables are brought into the storage unit. If each program has its own segment and page tables, then a program is protected against access from other programs since its page addresses are only in its own page tables. If programs share a single segment table, then segment table entries for programs other than the active program are marked as unavailable so that the pages of a particular program are protected against reference by other users. It should be noted here that virtual storage and the use of segment and page tables automatically provides both "store" and "fetch" protection. The process of dynamically translating effective addresses from virtual storage references to real storage references (called *dynamic address translation*) is summarized as follows: it is performed for each storage reference:

1. The special control register is used to locate the segment table.
2. A segment table entry is used to locate the page table for a virtual storage segment.
3. During dynamic address translation, the segment field (number) of the virtual storage address (being translated) is added to the segment table origin to select a segment table entry.

4. Next, the page field (number) of the virtual storage address (being translated) is added to the page table origin selected in step (3). This gives the
physical address of the required page in real storage or denotes that it is
located on an auxiliary mass storage device.

5. If the requested page is available in the storage unit, then the page address
in the page table becomes the high-order portion of the storage address.
(Byte positions within a page are unchanged by dynamic address translation.) If the page is currently unavailable, then an appropriate interruption
is generated to signal that a page should be brought in by the operating
system.

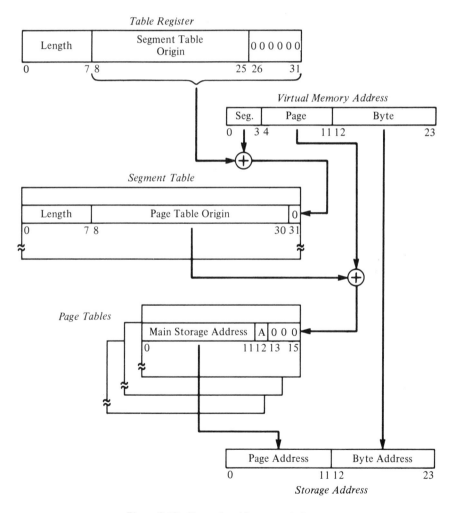

Figure 2.17 Dynamic address translation.

The process of dynamic address translation is depicted in Figure 2.17. Although the translation is performed by the hardware (the tables are built by software), each translation requires two storage references to reference the segment table and the page table. When the processing unit is operating in the virtual storage mode, each storage reference would require three storage accesses instead of the customary one, resulting in a performance degradation. Therefore, in most computers that provide virtual storage capability, dynamic address translation is augmented with a small associative memory (see Figure 2.18). The associative memory is located in the processing unit and contains the virtual storage and real storage address of the most recent storage references. When a virtual storage address is to be translated, the segment and page numbers are compared with the first position of all associative registers in parallel. If an equal match is found, the second portion of the matched associative register becomes the page address directly and the storage accesses for the segment and page tables need not be made. Thus, the use of a small associative memory effectively speeds up the dynamic address translation process. Dynamic address translation utilizing an associative memory is depicted in Figure 2.19. During dynamic address translation, the associative compare and the search through segment and page tables are initiated together. If an equal comparison is made in the associa-

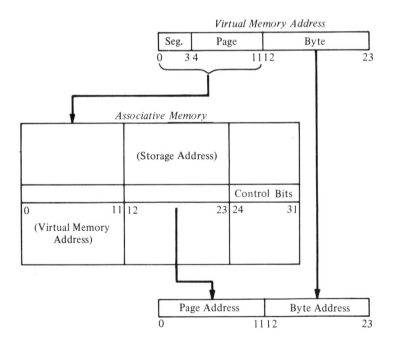

Figure 2.18 Use of an associative memory during dynamic address translation.

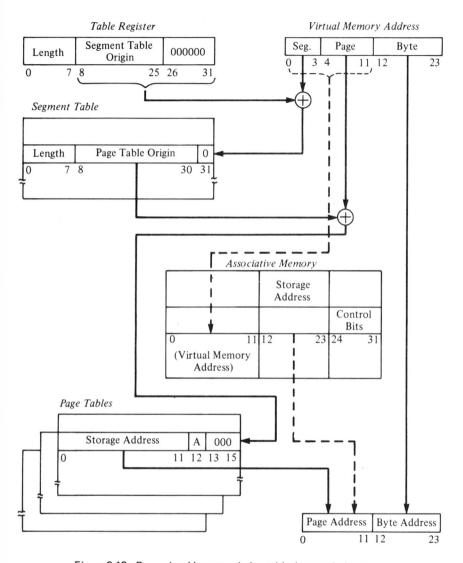

Figure 2.19   Dynamic address translation with the associative memory.

tive registers, relocation is performed from the associative registers and the table search is terminated.   If no equal comparison is made the real storage page address from the page table entry is used during relocation and that page address is put into the associative memory for subsequent use during dynamic address translation.   The virtual memory and main storage page addresses displace the least recently used associative register.   The process of bringing pages in and out of main storage, called "paging," is a software function. It is discussed in the next chapter on computer software.

INPUT AND OUTPUT ORGANIZATION

In early computers, all data entering and leaving the computer passed through the processing unit, forcing it to operate at input/output speeds in many cases. This obstacle to good performance was alleviated in the 1950s with the widespread use of the input and output data channel (referred to as an IO channel). An IO channel is essentially a small hardwired or microprogrammed computer, as mentioned earlier in this chapter, that controls the operation of an input/output device or a group of input/output devices. An IO channel has access to the storage unit independently of the processing unit; in fact, the processing unit and IO channels are designed to operate concurrently. The structure of a sample input/output subsystem is given in Figure 2.20. The IO channel is the key link

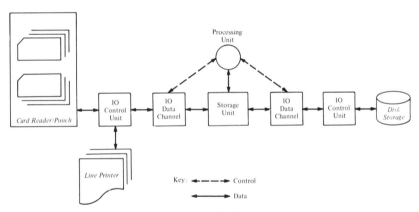

Figure 2.20   Structure of a sample input/output subsystem.

in an effective input/output subsystem. An input/output device is attached to an IO channel via an input/output control unit. (In general, peripheral devices external to the computer are referred to as input/output devices regardless if they are used for input or output or for mass storage.)

The manner in which an input/output subsystem operates is directly related to its functional organization. The following hierarchy of operation is established:

1. The processing unit controls the operation of the IO channels.
2. An IO channel controls the operation of input/output control units attached to it.
3. An input/output control unit controls the operation of input/output devices attached to it.

An *input/output channel* directs and controls the flow of data between the storage unit and input/output devices and allows the processing unit to operate concurrently with input/output operations. An input/output channel interfaces with the storage and input/output control units and operates as a hardware data buffer for the following reasons:

1. The large difference in data rates between the storage units and input/output devices.
2. The difference in access width between the main storage units and the input/output channel and between the input/output channel and the input/output control units.
3. The fact that several input/output channels and the processing unit are competing for access to main storage, and once an input/output channel gains that access, it is a good idea to transmit enough data to make the effort worthwhile.

As a result, the input/output channel requires storage facilities and logical circuitry to manage the control of input/output facilities, and the storage and transmission of data. Channel facilities required by a single input/output operation are referred to as a *subchannel*. A subchannel requires, minimally, storage areas for the following kinds of information: a count, a storage address used for data transmission, the storage address of the input/output command, control and status data, and a buffer storage area. Thus, a considerable amount of physical componentry is required to sustain a single input/output operation. When the data rate of an input/output device is high (e.g., 3 megabytes per second), then the use of a single input/output channel for a single input/output operation is certainly justified. However, when the data rate of an input/output device is low (e.g., 10 bytes per second), then an input/output channel must be shared to justify its existence. An input/output data channel is classified on the basis of the number of subchannels that it can sustain concurrently. In general, subchannels of a given input/output channel share logical circuitry while storage facilities are not shared. Three types of input/output channels are recognized: selector channel, byte-multiplexer channel, and block-multiplexer channel.

A *selector channel* is designed for use with high-speed input/output devices, such as disk or drum storage. A selector channel includes a single subchannel and can sustain one input/output operation at a time. Once a connection between a selector channel and an input/output device is established, that connection is maintained until the input/output operation is complete. In other words, the input/output channel is "busy" for the duration of the input/output operation. Several input/output devices can use the same selector channel; however, only one device can be active at any one time.

A *byte-multiplexer channel* is designed for use with several low-speed input/output devices and includes multiple subchannels. A byte-multiplexer channel can sustain an input/output operation on each of its subchannels concurrently.

A byte-multiplexer subchannel remains connected to an input/output device for the duration of an input/output operation; however, it utilizes channel facilities only for the transmission of a single unit of data, usually defined as a byte. (Hence, the name byte-multiplexer channel.) As a result, many low-speed devices share the channel, justifying its existence on a system-wide basis. Most byte-multiplexer channels also operate in a *burst* mode for short periods of time allowing medium-speed devices, such as magnetic tape, to be connected to the computer without requiring a selector channel.

The third type of input/output channel is a *block-multiplexer channel* that combines the speed of a selector channel with the interleaved operation of a byte-multiplexer channel. The block-multiplexer channel is shared by multiple high-speed devices in the same way that the byte-multiplexer channel is shared by multiple low-speed devices. Instead of multiplexing bytes like the byte-multiplexer channel, the block-multiplexer channel multiplexes blocks, which correspond to physical data records. The design philosophy underlying the block-multiplexer channel is that it is freed during non-data transfer operations (such as disk seek) so that it can be used by another subchannel.

An *input/output control unit* controls the operation of one or more input/output devcies that fall in its domain. For example, there are disk control units for disk storage devices, magnetic tape control units for magnetic tape devices, and unit record control units for devices such as a line printers or a card reader/punche. A control unit manages the data flow to and from an input/output device and performs other non-data transfer operations such as tape rewind or a disk seek. A single control unit frequently controls several devices.

An *input/output device* is the component that physically interfaces with the physical storage medium. It is important to distinguish between an input/output device and an input/output volume. An input/output volume is the physical medium on which data are recorded. (For example, a magnetic tape or a disk pack is a volume.) In any computer system, the number of devices is limited. There are n tape units, m disk units, etc. If a volume is removable, such as a magnetic tape or disk pack, then the amount of data that can be stored on that medium is theoretically unlimited. However, only a subset of the total amount of data is available to the computer at one time. Some devices, such as magnetic drum, have volumes that are not removable. Devices of this type are usually used for storing data on an intermediate basis, or when frequent access to a large volume of data (such as in a stock quotation or an airline system) is needed in a real-time system. Input/output devices are used for input/output or for mass storage. Unit record devices, such as card readers and line printers, are usually used for input/output. Devices with removable volumes are used for either input/output or mass storage.

In a general sense, data management is concerned with the effective utilization of all peripheral devices—regardless if they are used for input/output or for mass storage. Data base technology primarily involves the use of direct-access storage because it is a high-volume medium that it usually shared among users. Direct-access storage is normally allocated and accessed through data management routines.

DIRECT-ACCESS STORAGE

Much of modern computer technology involves the use of direct access storage. Routines of the operating and data management systems are usually stored on a direct-access volume and most complicated input/output procedures involve the use of direct-access storage. This section is limited to a discussion of disk storage. Other devices fall into the category of direct-access devices but disk is the most frequently used. The major objective of this section is to establish terminology since most readers are already familiar with the basic concepts.

Disk storage is a recording medium similar in concept to that of a phonograph record except that the tracks are concentric instead of spiral. A disk volume has several recording disks, each coated on both sides with a magnetic material such as ferrous oxide, and mounted on a rotating shaft.

Data are recorded in tracks on the disk surfaces and are read or written as the disks rotate. A disk storage unit has three major components: the recording surfaces, the access arms and read-write heads, and the disk mechanism. (See Figure 2.21.) Collectively, these components are referred to as a *disk module*. Some disk drives (i.e., disk input/output devices) include a single module and others include as many as nine modules. The disk mechanism causes the disks to rotate and the access arms to move in and out as directed by the disk control unit. The stack of disks is referred to as a *disk volume*; if the volume is removable, it is referred to as a *disk pack*.

Data are recorded on both surfaces of a disk (except possibly the top of the first disk in a stack and the bottom surface of the last disk) and a single access arm controls two read-write heads: one for the upper surface and one for the lower surface. The access arms form a comb-type assembly and usually move in and out together. (Notable exceptions exist where the arms move independently in some disk mechanisms, and are stationary in other disk systems; however, the benefit of the comb-type approach is that it is useful for introducing the cylinder concept.) Thus, a single read-write head is used to access an entire surface.

Data are recorded serially by bit on a track, as implied in Figure 2.22, so that a byte occupies eight bit positions. The concentric tracks are designed so that each track holds the same amount of information. Since all read-write heads are always positioned in the same vertical position, several tracks (one corresponding to each recording surface) can be read or written without moving the access mechanism. The positioning of the read-write heads at any track location provides access to a *cylinder* of information. There are as many cylinders per volume as there are tracks per surface. The cylinder concept is utilized by the

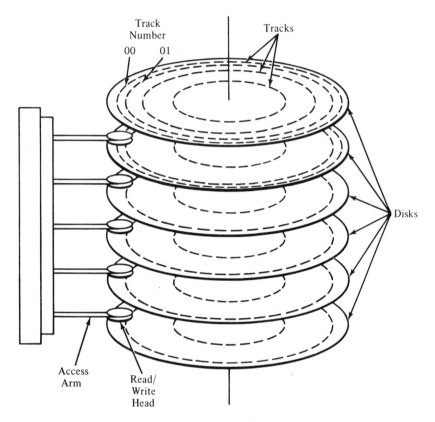

Figure 2.21   Disk storage module.

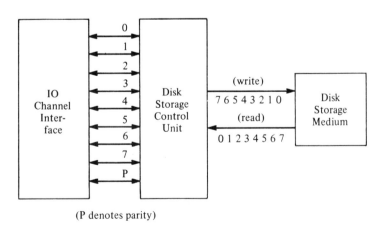

(P denotes parity)

Figure 2.22   Data transfer between disk storage and the input/output channel.

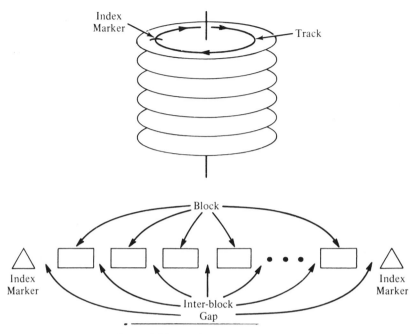

Figure 2.23   Track format for disk storage.

data management facilities of an operating system to reduce the access time necessary to store or retrieve data.

Considering the above discussion, a specific track is located by read-write head number and by track number. (Another means of locating the same track would be by cylinder and head number.) It seems reasonable to assume that most records written on a track would be either less than a track in length or greater than a track in length. Therefore, a track must be formatted using a combination of hardware and software facilities to enable it to be used effectively. Each track, as depicted in Figure 2.23, is closed such that a single index marker denotes both the beginning and the end of the track. The index marker is a property of the disk volume itself and not of a specific track. Data are recorded on a track as a series of consecutive bytes called a *block*. Blocks are separated by special gaps that are used for orientation and control. A single physical data record is recorded as a series of three blocks, as depicted in Figure 2.24. The *count block* denotes the beginning of a data record and contains flags, control information, the key length, the data length, and a record number. The *record number* is used to locate a specific record on a track. A typical count block is given as Figure 2.25. The *key block*, which may be elided, contains a data field that can be used to locate a particular record in a file. The *data block*, which can never be elided, contains the data portion of a data record.

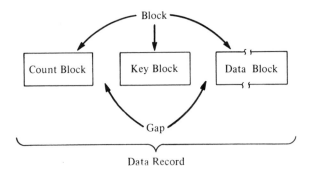

Figure 2.24 Block format of a disk data record.

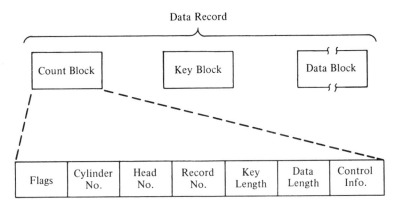

Figure 2.25 Detailed information in the count block of a disk data record.

As far as storing information on disk is concerned, several data records are stored on the same track provided that each has a unique record number. When the data length of a record exceeds track length, it is usually stored as a record that is continued on the next track of the same cylinder. The latter method can be used only if the disk storage mechanism has an automatic track overflow facility. Detailed programming operational procedures for disk storage are necessarily dependent upon a specific unit.

REFERENCES

Blaauw, G. A., and I. P. Brooks, Jr., "The structure of System/360: Part I. Outline of the logical structure," *IBM Systems Journal*, Volume 3, Nos. 2 and 3 (1964), pp. 119–135.

Denning, P. J., "Third generation computer systems," *Computing Surveys*, Volume 3, No. 4 (December 1971), pp. 175–216.

IBM System/370, *Principles of Operation*, White Plains, N.Y., IBM Corporation, Form GA22-7000.

Katzan, H., *Computer Organization and the System/370*, New York, Van Nostrand Reinhold Company, 1971.

Katzan, H., *Operating Systems: A Pragmatic Approach*, New York, Van Nostrand Reinhold Company, 1973.

3 | SOFTWARE CONCEPTS

INTRODUCTION

The purpose of this chapter is to provide an overview of programs, program execution, and computer software. A *program* is a well-defined sequence of machine instructions that control the operation of the computer. *Computer software* is the name used to denote a collection of programs that allow the user to interface with the computer and to control its operation. Most programs written by users of the computer are referred to as *application programs*.

When a programmer writes a program, he expresses the procedure he wants the computer to follow in a computer language. A computer language* is not directly executable by the computer; it must first be translated into complex operation codes, modifiers, and storage addresses that can be interpreted by the computer. The translation process is complicated and for this reason, it is performed by the computer under the control of a program known as a *language translator*.

A program, as written by the programmer, is referred to as a *source program;* it is usually punched into cards or keyed in at a computer terminal. It is translated to the machine language of the computer by a language translator (see Figure 3.1). The translated version of the source program is referred to as an *object program*. A program cannot be executed on the computer until it has been translated from source program form to object program form.

---

*Sample computer languages are assembler language, FORTRAN, and COBOL.

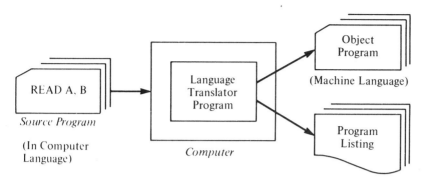

Figure 3.1   Translation of a source program to an object program (machine language).

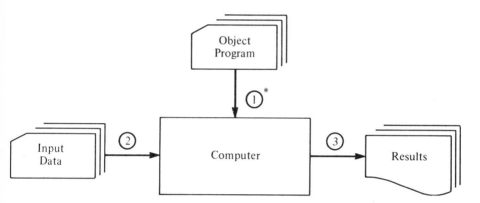

Figure 3.2   The loading and execution of an object program.   (*Performed by loader program.)

The execution of an object program is depicted in Figure 3.2. A "loader program" is used to load an object program into computer storage and initiate its execution.   The object program, as designed and written, reads input data and produces results.

Normally, the computer processes jobs continuously without human operator intervention through the use of another set of programs called an "operating system."   An *operating system* manages the resources* of the system so as to maximize the utilization of the system or to provide a given level of service to the user.

Routines designed to manage input/output operations and to provide access to information on mass-storage devices are referred to as "data management

*System resources are usually taken to be processing time, main storage, input/output devices, and space on mass-storage volumes.

routines." *Data management routines* are usually provided by the operating system and shared (or used) by users on a system-wide basis.

COMPUTER LANGUAGES

Languages used for computer programming are divided into two major classes: assembler language and programming languages. This section provides an introduction to languages that fall into these categories.

Assembler language closely resembles the internal language of the computer (i.e., machine language) except that (1) the operations and operands, used to form instructions, are specified as mnemonic symbols and (2) locations are given symbolic names so that the corresponding machine addresses need not be used. The obvious benefits are that programs are easier to write (than in machine language) and that instructions do not reference machine addresses. Thus, instructions can be inserted or deleted without disrupting an entire program. Figure 3.3 depicts a simple example of the use of assembler language. Because assembler language is closely related to machine language, it tends to differ among the various kinds of computers. However, one defining characteristic exists: for each assembler language instruction written, one machine language instruction is generated by another program designed to translate programs from assembler language to machine language. It is termed an "assembler program" and is covered later in this chapter. Assembler instructions that can cause more than one machine language instruction to be generated are either special instructions or are macro instructions.

A *macro* is a well-defined sequence of assembler language statements that is given a name. When a user desires to use a macro in an assembler language program, he supplies the name of the macro along with argument(s), if any. Figure 3.4 defines a simple macro that computes an expression of the form $ax + b$ and shows how that macro might be used. Obviously, a macro must be defined before it can be used and is ordinarily supplied to the assembler program in one of two ways: by the system or by the user. User-defined macros are supplied by the user with his source program. System macros are stored by the operating system for use during the assembly process. A *system macro* is used to utilize services that are provided by the operating system and to perform operations outside of the scope of an application program. Privileged input/output operations, for example, which can only be executed in the supervisor state, are usually initiated in an assembler language program through the use of macros. Macros are usually used for convenience, efficiency, and standardization.

A *programming language* is a form of computer language that permits the user to avoid the details of assembler language programming. When using a programming language, the user specifies a series of statements to be executed in performing a particular task on the computer. In this respect, a programming language is much like assembler language. The key difference is that a statement from a programming language denotes an operational function that is equivalent

Location	Operation	Operand
	START	
	.	
	.	
	.	
ITER	L	6,A
	A	6,B
	A	6,C
	L	5,ZERO
	D	5,THREE
	ST	6,AVER
	.	
	.	
	.	
	B	ITER
	.	
	.	
	.	
ZERO	DC	F'0'
THREE	DC	F'3'
A	DS	F
B	DS	F
C	DS	F
AVER	DS	F
	.	
	.	
	.	
	END	

Key to operation codes:

L—specifies "load"
A—specifies "add"
D—specifies "divide"
ST—specifies "store"
B—specifies "branch"
DC—specifies "define constant"
DS—specifies "define storage"

Figure 3.3 Assembler language program to compute the average of the values A, B, and C. (Registers 5 and 6, in this case, are used as a double register for division.)

to several machine language operations. It is also convenient to design a programming language around a particular class of applications so that familiar notation and technology can be employed. The following examples from FORTRAN (for scientific computing) and COBOL (for data processing), respectively, serve to illustrate the latter point:

SUM=SUM+A (I) ** 2   (FORTRAN)
MOVE NAME TO REPORT-FIELD.   (COBOL)

Location	Operation	Operand
	MACRO	
	AXPLUSB	&A,&X,&B,&R
	L	6,&A
	M	5,&X
	A	6,&B
	ST	6,&R
	MEND	
	.	
	.	
	.	
	AXPLUSB	DIG,FOX,W,ANS
+	L	6,DIG
+	M	5,FOX
+	A	6,W
+	ST	6,ANS

Figure 3.4 Definition and use of a macro. The symbol MACRO initiates a macro definition and MEND terminates it. AXPLUSB is the name of the macro. + denotes an instruction generated when the macro is used.

There are a multiplicity of programming languages in widespread use; BASIC (an easy-to-learn language for the problem solver) and PL/I (a multipurpose programming language) are two other names that are frequently encountered. Collectively, programming languages have reduced the time and costs necessary for preparing programs and have enabled the nonprofessional programmer to utilize the computer effectively. The different kinds of statements from programming languages can be conveniently grouped into five classes: data manipulation, program control, input and output, declarative, and subprogram.

1. *Data manipulation* statements perform the calculations, data movement, list processing, or string editing required by a particular application. As a result of data manipulation, computation is performed and/or the value of a data variable is replaced.

2. *Program control* statements provide a facility for altering the sequential flow of execution in a program. Control statements are divided into four categories: (1) unconditional branches, (2) conditional branches and condi-

tional statement execution, (3) looping, and (4) execution control. *Unconditional branches* alter sequential execution and denote the statement to be executed next. *Conditional statements* allow the user to change the sequence of execution or to execute a given statement on a conditional basis. *Looping statements* allow a computer program to execute the same operations repetitively. During the execution of a loop, the statements comprising the body of the loop are executed using one or more of the following modes of control: (1) the loop is executed a specified number of times; (2) the loop is executed until a given condition is met; and (3) the loop is executed as a control variable assumes a given set of values. *Execution control statements* are used to halt or terminate the execution of a program.

3. *Input and output statements* are used to transmit information between an external storage medium and the computer. Two forms of input and output (IO) are usually available: formatted IO and unformatted IO. During formatted IO, data are converted from an external form to an internal form during input under the control of format statements. The process is reversed during output. During unformatted IO, information is transferred between an external medium and main storage without "software" conversion, even though hardware conversion may be required depending upon the physical IO device used.

4. *Declaration statements* provide information on the manner in which data are to be stored and can be used to specify file types, establish storage requirements, and denote action to be taken when certain execution-time conditions arise.

5. *Subprogram statements* allow a program to be structured into a main program and one or more subprograms. Subprogram statements are used, *in a subprogram*, to specify the name attributes, and parameters of the subprogram and to cause programs to return to the calling program when the processing of the subprogram is complete. A statement of the former type known as a *subprogram header*. Various forms of the RETURN statement are used to pass program control from the subprogram back to the calling program. In a *calling program*, a function subprogram is invoked by using the function name with appropriate arguments as a term in an expression, and a subroutine subprogram is usually invoked with the CALL statement.

Obviously, a variety of other statement types exist in programming languages. They cover facilities that range from dynamic storage allocation and the processing of interrupt conditions to block structure and macro facilities.

Because a computer language is the key interface between man and the machine, there continues to be widespread interest in this area and new developments are currently being made. Another area of computer languages involves the capability of defining a problem—rather than writing a program—and letting a computer program called a *generator* translate the "statement of the problem" into a program. The *report program generator* (RPG) language and several proprietary languages fall into this category.

LANGUAGE PROCESSORS

Language processors are programs that execute in the computer much like an ordinary application program. However, language processors serve as an aid in using the computer and are generally classed as computer software. Four basic types of language processor are identified: assemblers, compilers, generators and interpreters, and linkage editors. The first three types are presented in this section. The linkage editor is discussed in the next section on "program execution."

Before language processors can be introduced two minor topics need to be mentioned. First, an object program is more than a sequence of machine language instructions. Control information is needed so that the instructions can be loaded into the computer and effectively combined with other object programs. For example, when the programmer uses statements such as:

$$B = SQRT(X)$$

and

$$CALL\ BAKER(X,Y/3,25)$$

the subprograms SORT and BAKER must be loaded into the computer and combined with the object program that contains these statements. An object program along with its control information is termed an *object module*. Later in the book, two programs, a loader program and a linkage editor program, are introduced that operate on object modules and are capable of combining two or more object modules into a single object module. Finally, the output of a language processor usually consists of an object module and a program listing. The *program listing* gives a copy of the source program, diagnostics (if any), and a list of the machine language instructions that are generated during the translation process.

An *assembler program*, or more simply an *assembler*, is a computer program that translates a program written in assembler language to an equivalent program in machine language. The translation is frequently referred to as *assembly* or the *assembly process*. Assembly is usually accomplished in two passes over the source program. In the first pass, addresses are assigned to symbols in the location field and macros are identified (i.e., located in the user's source input deck or retrieved from the macro library) and expanded. In the second pass over the source program, symbolic operation codes and operands are replaced by internal codes and addresses, respectively, and the object module and a program listing are produced. Error checking is performed and erroneous conditions are identified, appropriately, in the program listing. Assembly is essentially a straightforward replacement process and the user has a great amount of flexibility in how he can use the assembler language. In general, the logical flow of a program written in assembler language is not analyzed so that the user can apply the features of the given computer to his particular problem.

The process of translating a program written in a programming language to machine language is termed *compilation*; it is performed with a *compiler program*. Functionally, the use of a programming language subordinates the details of programming to the compiler program. For each statement in a programming language, several machine-language instructions are usually generated by the compiler. (This is in contrast to assembler language, characterized by the fact that one machine language instruction is usually generated for each assembler language statement by the assembler program.)

Compilers are necessarily dependent upon the language being processed; however, the following steps are usually involved:

1. The source program is read and analyzed on a statement-by-statement basis.
2. A *lexical analysis* routine scans each source statement and identifies reserved words, variables, operator symbols, constants, etc.
3. A *syntactical analysis* routine identifies the type of statements and verifies that the structure of that statement is admissible.
4. Tables and lists of symbols, expressions, and statements are maintained so that an interstatement analysis can be made.
5. Analysis is made of logical flow of the source program and a global error analysis is made.
6. Machine language instructions, in an intermediate symbolic form internal to the compiler, are generated and optimization is performed as required.
7. An object module is generated from the intermediate language and a program listing is produced.

Like an assembler program, the compiler is simply another program to the computer system. The compiler has nothing to do with the execution of a source program. It performs a translation of a source program to an object program and produces its result in the form of an object module, and as with an assembler, the compiler also produces a program listing with diagnostic information.

Much like its counterparts, the assembler and the compiler, the *program generator* accepts a problem definition as input and produces an object module that can be loaded into the computer and executed. The sequence of translating a source program into a machine language form, combining that program with required subprograms, loading it into the computer, and then causing execution to begin, is a time-consuming process; and in many cases, the amount of work performed by the computer is not justified by the results obtained. This is particularly the case with very small "one-shot" jobs or in cases when "exploratory" work is being performed. A language processor that avoids the sequence of steps mentioned above is known as an interpreter. An *interpreter* is a language processor that interprets and executes a source program without producing an object program. It operates as follows:

1. The source program is processed on a statement-by-statement basis.
2. Each statement is scanned, analyzed, and interpreted to determine what operations should be performed.
3. The operations are executed by the interpreter and the intermediate results are saved.
4. The next statement to be executed is obtained and step 2 is repeated.

The technique of using an interpreter has several important characteristics:

1. The entire source program is *not* completely analyzed and is not translated to an object program before execution is initiated.
2. The next statement to be interpreted is dependent upon the results of the previous statement, such as with a GO TO statement.
3. Only intermediate results are saved and no object program is produced. (It should be noted that some interpreters convert a source program into an internal language to avoid reinterpreting a statement because of a loop or similar construct.)

Simple, easy-to-use languages are frequently implemented by using an interpretive technique.

PROGRAM STRUCTURE

Programs are frequently structured into a main program and one or more subprograms for convenience, for efficiency, or simply to make use of subprogram libraries. A subprogram* is characterized in three ways:

1. It is a function or subroutine.
2. It is open or closed.
3. It is external or internal.

As mentioned previously, a *function* returns an explicit result and can be used as a term in an expression. A *subroutine* does not return an explicit result and is usually invoked with a special statement of the language, such as the CALL statement. Figure 3.5 depicts examples of open and closed subprograms. In any program, only one copy of a given *closed* subprogram exists. Each time that subprogram is used, linkage is established so that program control can be returned to the "point of call." However, in many cases, the overhead instructions necessary for using a closed subprogram are not justified by the size of the subprogram. In these cases, a copy of the subprogram is inserted by the compiler into the machine language program directly and no linkage is necessary. A subpro-

---

*The term subprogram is frequently referred to as a routine. Unfortunately, the term "routine" is not a precise term and means different things to different people.

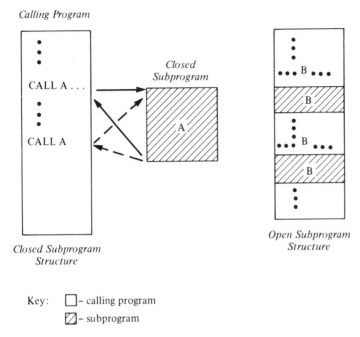

Figure 3.5 Closed and open subprogram structure.

gram of this type is termed an *open* subprogram, since program control flows through it without executing additional linkage instructions.

The computer instructions necessary to call a subprogram and later return to the calling program are termed *linkage instructions* and the process of actually executing those instructions is termed *linkage*. It is important to note that both the calling program and the subprogram participate in the linkage process. The calling program must supply arguments, establish a save area so that the subprogram can store the contents of machine registers, designate a return address, and branch to the subprogram. When it is activated, a subprogram saves machine registers in the designated save area and sets up parameters for execution. After the execution of a subprogram is complete, the return linkage instructions establish the explicit result (in the case of a function subprogram), restore machine registers and branch to the return address supplied by the calling program. An overview of subroutine linkage is suggested by Figure 3.6. Subroutine linkage is necessarily machine-dependent; however, the concepts apply in general.

PROGRAM EXECUTION

The output of a language processor is an *object module* that cannot be executed directly by the computer and must be prepared for execution by either of two

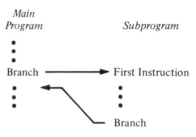

Figure 3.6   Overview of subprogram linkage.

service programs: a "linkage editor" or a "loader." Assume that a particular program is composed of a main program and one or more subprograms. Prior to execution, the main program and the subprograms exist as object modules. Before the program can be executed, the object modules of which the program is composed must be linked together so that program control can pass between modules directly. The information necessary to combine object programs is generated by the language processors and exists along with other control information as a part of the object modules. An object module consists of three entities: an external symbol dictionary, a relocation dictionary, and the text. The external symbol dictionary contains an entry for each external symbol defined or referred to within the object program. An external symbol dictionary entry includes the name of the external symbol (which is the symbol itself), the type of reference it is, and its location in the program. The relocation dictionary contains an entry for each relocatable address constant that must be adjusted before a module is executed. A relocation dictionary specifies an address constant by indicating its location in the program. The text contains the instructions and data of the object program.

The linking of object modules prior to execution is termed *linkage editing* and is performed by a service program termed the *linkage editor*. As depicted in Figure 3.7, input to the linkage editor can take four forms:

1. Object modules and linkage editor control information supplied by the user.
2. Object modules from a user-supplied program library.
3. Object modules from the system's "automatic call library."
4. Load modules.

Output from the linkage editor is a *load* module that can be loaded into storage for execution by a routine of the operating system. Each input module processed by the linkage editor possesses a program origin that was assigned during assembly, compilation, or during a previous execution of the linkage editor. When producing an executable load module, the linkage editor assigns an origin

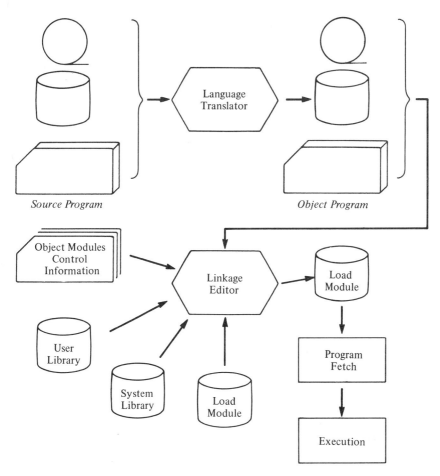

Figure 3.7   Preparing a load module for execution.

to the text for the first module and adjusts address constants accordingly. The text for other modules, as well as address constants, is assigned addresses relative to that origin so that the combined text for all modules occupies consecutive addresses in the load module. External references between modules are resolved by matching the referenced symbols to defined symbols. The load module is in a relocatable format, as are the object modules, but the text represents executable machine code. It is placed in an executable program library for subsequent loading by a "program fetch" routine of the operating system. When the user requests that his program be executed, the program fetch routine retrieves it from the library and relocates it in main storage using the composite relocation dictionary. It is then ready for execution.

During its processing, the linkage editor attempts to resolve external references from the object modules supplied by the user. Symbols that are still undefined after all input modules have been processed cause the linkage editor to search a hierarchy of program libraries for the unresolved reference. User-defined libraries are searched first, followed by a search of the system library. (A familiar example of this situation is the typical application program that uses the square root [SQRT] routine that is almost always retrieved from a library of subroutines maintained as part of the operating system.)

Some operating systems do not utilize the concept of a linkage editor and employ a *loader program* that effectively combines the linkage edit and program fetch phases. Other operating systems contain both a linkage editor and a loader program. A loader program is used when there is no need to product distinct load modules for program libraries. The loader combines object modules produced by the language processors and loads them directly into main storage for execution. An example of the operation of a loader program is depicted in Figure 3.8. Most loader programs are designed to search user-defined libraries and/or system libraries for resolving symbol references.

Several phases in the preparation and the execution of a program have been introduced: the concept of programming languages, language processors, linkage editing, and loading. A program is executed by combining these phases in a useful manner. A *job* is the execution of a series of related processing programs that comprise a total processing application. The execution of a single processing program is termed a *job step*. (A simple sequence of job steps might be: [1] compilation, [2] assembly, [3] link edit, and [4] execution of load module produced in the link edit step.) When a user submits a unit of work to the computer system, he submits a job that consists of control cards, programs, and data. Control cards must always be used since they direct the operating system to perform the desired functions. Programs or data may alternately be stored in li-

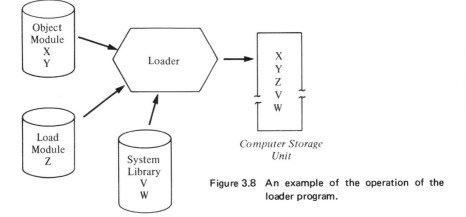

Figure 3.8 An example of the operation of the loader program.

braries or data files, respectively, for retrieval by the system. Information is placed on control cards using a *job control language*. Most job control languages consist of a few major statements plus a variety of miscellaneous statements. Three major statements are:

1. The *job statement* (JOB) marks the beginning of a job, identifies the user, contains accounting information, and specifies general conditions that govern how the job is to be executed.
2. The *execute statement* (EXEC) marks the beginning of a job step and specifies the name of the load module to be executed.
3. The *data definition statement* (DD) is used to describe a data file and to request the allocation of input/output resources. The DD statement is also used to specify the disposition of that data file after the job step is completed. One or more DD statements is used with each job step.

The input deck setup for a typical job is given in Figure 3.9.

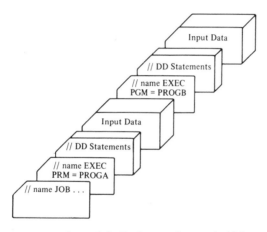

Figure 3.9   Deck setup for a typical job.

Usually a computer system is employed to service a multitude of users. Thus, input to the operating system takes the form of several jobs, arranged in a sequence called the *input job stream*, as depicted in Figure 3.10. As input to the computer, the job stream is normally read from punched cards, magnetic tape, or a direct-access device. In actual practice, however, the jobs may not be executed in the sequence that they are found in the job stream. The nature of the operating system, the priorities of the respective jobs, and the available input and output devices generally determine how the resources of the computer system are utilized.

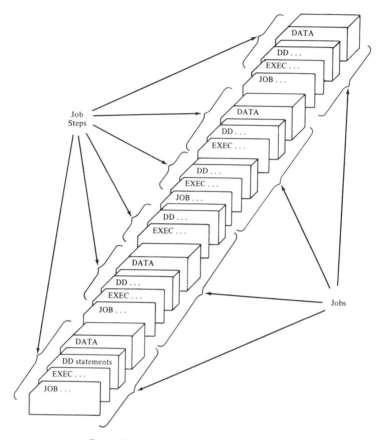

Figure 3.10   The form of an input job stream.

OPERATING SYSTEM CONCEPTS

An *operating system* is an organized collection of programs and data that are specifically designed to manage the resources of a computer system and to facilitate the creation of computer programs and control their execution in that system. The functions performed by an operating system can be covered from the viewpoint of a distinct job and from the viewpoint of the system as a whole. From the viewpoint of a distinct job, the operating system performs the following functions: (1) it reads control cards, i.e., job control language statements; (2) it allocates input/output devices, data sets, and mass storage space to the job; (3) it loads processing programs into storage and initiates their execution in the processing unit; (4) it handles requests for service from processing programs— typical requests are for dynamic storage allocation, input/output processing, and program loading; and (5) it terminates job processing.

From the viewpoint of the system as a whole, the operating system performs the following functions: (1) it assigns the processing unit to a ready program, (2) it assigns storage to processing programs, (3) it readies programs for execution, (4) it allocates input/output devices to programs, (5) it allocates mass storage space to programs, and (6) it performs input/output operations as a service function. In general, the operating system operates so as to maximize the utilization of the various resources and to provide a given level of service to the users.

Modern operating systems utilize an operational technique known as *multiprogramming* that allows several jobs to share the resources of the computer system. Usually, the various jobs co-reside in "main" storage and overflow to an auxiliary storage device, when necessary. Each job is given control of the processing unit according to a scheduling algorithm and executes in the processing unit until one of two events occurs:

1. The program comes to a natural wait condition, such as for an input operation.
2. The program has exceeded the time allocated to it.

Control of the processing unit is then given to another job and the process continues. In the latter case, termed *time slicing*, each user is given a short "burst" of time on a periodic basis. A typical multiprogramming system is depicted in Figure 3.11. Input jobs are read by a *reader program* that places them on direct-access storage as an "input queue" of jobs. Jobs are read into the system ahead of the time when they are to be executed. Similarly, program output is placed in an "output queue." Output is processed after a job is complete by a *writer program*. The input reader and output writer programs are referred to as "spooling routines."* Whenever there is space in storage for another job, it is read from the input work queue by the job initiator and prepared for execution. When a job finishes execution, it is deleted from main storage and its output is processed.

The major objectives of a multiprogramming system are twofold: (1) increased throughput, and (2) lowered response time. *Throughput* is increased by using the "wait" time of the processing unit to run other programs. *Response time* is lowered by recognizing the priority of a job as it enters the system and by processing jobs on a priority basis. In this context, response time is used synonymously with "turn-around time." The spooling operation, mentioned earlier, is a normal function in a multiprogramming system. The *reader* and *writer* routines of the spooling package are simply assigned a high priority such that they are given processing time on a demand basis. This operational philosophy allows low-speed input/output devices to be operated at close to maximum speed.

---

*The term "spooling" is derived from the acronym SPOOL that stands for Simultaneous Peripheral Operations On-Line—an operational technique used with early computers.

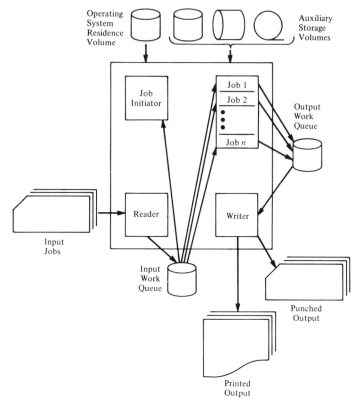

Figure 3.11   Simplified description of a typical multiprogramming system.

STRUCTURE AND OPERATION OF AN OPERATING SYSTEM

A multiprogramming operating system is composed of two types of programs: control programs and processing programs. *Control programs* are concerned with the operation of the computer and the operation of a job. *Processing programs* operate under control of the control programs and exist as a unit of work to the system. Processing programs do not require privileged facilities and they operate in the problem state. In general, the execution of one processing program cannot affect the execution of another processing program or control program. Processing programs are conveniently divided into three categories: *language translators* (such as a FORTRAN compiler), *service programs* (such as the linkage editor), and *user programs* (such as a payroll program).

The heart of an operating system is the control programs designed to manage the resources of the computer system. These routines are conveniently grouped into three classes: task management, job management, and data management.

Task management provides a logical interface between the hardware and the remainder of the software system, and is responsible for the allocation of the processing unit and main storage. Task management routines, which operate in the supervisor state and are primarily core-resident, are frequently referred to as the *supervisor* of the operating system. The supervisor performs the following functions: (1) interruption handling and processing, (2) scheduling and execution supervision, (3) main storage allocation, (4) dynamic storage management, (5) clocks and time supervision, and (6) management of actual input/output operations.

Job management provides a logical interface between task management and a job or between task management and the system operator. Functions performed by job management are: (1) analyzing the input job stream, (2) preparing a job for execution, (3) processing job terminations, (4) analyzing and processing operator commands, and (5) transmitting messages from an operating program to the system operator. Job management routines are frequently regarded as ordinary "units of work" to the operating system and are multiprogrammed along with user jobs.

Data management provides a software interface between processing programs and auxiliary storage. Functions performed by data management are: (1) assigning space on direct-access volumes, (2) maintaining a catalog of file names, (3) performing support processing for IO operations (i.e., *open, close*, etc.), and (4) initiating input/output operations and performing buffering and blocking/ deblocking. Data management is covered as a separate topic in a later chapter.

A multiprogramming system is characterized by the manner in which it operates in response to requests for service. A job becomes a unit of work to the operating system when its JOB control card is read from the system input device by an operating system routine designed for that purpose. An initial program structure is created for the job and a *control block* is built to hold control information (i.e., registers, location counter, pointers to other control blocks, etc.) that is maintained dynamically for that job. After a job is initiated as a unit of work, input/output devices are assigned, and the load module for the first job step of that job is loaded. The job is then ready for execution and is subsequently given control of the processing unit by a scheduler routine of the operating system. At any given time in an operating system, there are usually several jobs in various stages of execution—some beginning, some part-way through execution, and others finishing. However, only one program can be actively executing in the processing unit. A job is also assigned an internal priority, computed as a function of external priority and arrival sequence.

When the supervisor routine of the operating system has no more "supervisory" work to do, program control is given to a scheduler routine to dispatch the processing unit to a processing program. The scheduler selects the job with the highest internal priority that is in the "ready" state to be executed. The job operates until an interruption occurs, which means that the supervisor program of the operating system has more work to do. The interruption may be caused by input/output completion for another job, a machine check interruption, or a program, supervisor call, or timer interruption for the active job. Each type of interruption is processed appropriately by a supervisor routine designed to process that type of interruption. Interruptions can take place anytime—that is, when a processing program is executing or when a supervisor routine is executing. If a processing program is executing when an interruption occurs, the registers, location counter, and other control information for that job are stored in its control block. When that program is activated again, execution is resumed from where it left off, if the "state" of the program has not changed as a result of the previous interruption.

Note here that priority and scheduling take care of themselves. A high-priority job that loses control of the processing unit because of an event independent of it, eventually gains control of the processing unit again when the supervisor is finished with its work. If a higher priority job becomes ready for execution as a result of the interruption, then it gains control of the processing unit next time around. If an interruption occurs when the computer is executing in the supervisor state, then that interruption is "queued up" and the supervisor resumes execution from its point of interruption. In this manner, the supervisor can complete its work in an orderly manner. An operating system that operates in a manner similar to that described above is said to be *interrupt-driven* in the sense that a program continues to execute until it is interrupted. Interruptions take place automatically when a need arises; in a sense, therefore, the computing system is designed to monitor itself.

STORAGE MANAGEMENT AND PAGING

One of the prime objectives with multiprogramming is to have several programs concurrently occupy the user area of storage. This is achieved in one of two ways: (1) by using storage partitions, and (2) by allocating storage dynamically in regions in which the user is constrained to operate. Using the *partition method*, storage is partitioned into fixed-size areas, as depicted in Figure 3.12. User jobs are assigned to a particular partition depending upon their priority class and storage requirements. Once a job is assigned to a partition, it is required to operate in the storage partition to which it is assigned. Using the dynamic *region method*, each job either specifies its storage requirements or is assigned a default value, as it is selected for processing by the operating system on a priority basis. In general, as many jobs are loaded into the user area as possible, provided sufficient contiguous storage space exists. If insufficient storage space is available for a job selected for execution, the job must wait. Regioned storage organization is depicted in Figure 3.13. When a job terminates, using this method of storage allocation, the storage space assigned to it is freed for as-

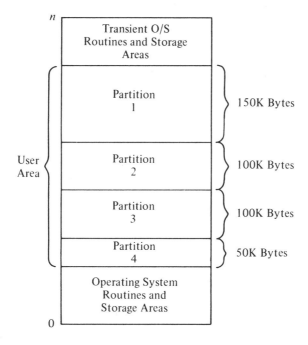

Figure 3.12 Partitioned storage organization in a multiprogramming operating system.

signment to other jobs. In general, storage utilization is more efficient with region allocation than with partitioned allocation since the case of a partially used
partition never takes place. Using either partitioned or region storage management techniques, the number of active jobs is limited, as mentioned above, by
the number of different possible storage keys.

Another method of storage management involves virtual storage. The virtual
storage for each processing program is mapped into a combination of "main"
storage and an auxiliary storage volume, such as magnetic drum or disk. Recall
here that "main" storage as well as virtual storage and the auxiliary storage volume (frequently referred to as the "paging device") are managed on a page basis.

When a program references a page in its virtual storage, the dynamic address
translation hardware checks to see if it is in main storage. If it is, address translation is performed and execution continues. If the needed page is not in main
storage, then an interruption is generated. A routine of the operating system
processes the interruption and brings the needed page into main storage so that
it can be used. Frequently a page in main storage must be moved to the paging
device to make room for the needed page. The process of moving pages between
main storage and the paging device is termed *paging*; it is the basis of a virtual
storage system. Paging operates as a high-priority input/output operation so that

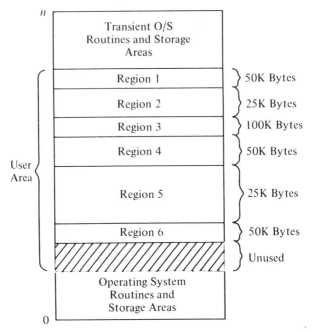

Figure 3.13 Dynamic region storage organization in a multi-programming operating system.

needed pages are brought into main storage as quickly as possible. When a program needs a page and that page must be brought into main storage, the processing unit does not wait but goes on to another program. The program needing the page is put into "page wait." When the needed page is finally brought into main storage, then the waiting program is made "active," and it continues with its processing the next time it is given control of the processing unit.

The control block that is built for a job when it is initiated for execution is also used to hold a job's page tables in a virtual storage environment. When a job is given control of the processing unit, the page tables are made available for use during dynamic address translation. Other pages are brought in on a "demand" basis. In other words, only the "needed" pages are "paged in." If the dynamic address translation hardware encounters a page marked as unavailable,* the resultant interruption causes the required page to be "paged in" by the paging routine of the operating system. The location on auxiliary storage of the required page is determined from the page table entry. When a page is "paged

*One of the flags in a page table entry is used for this purpose.

out," its page table entry is modified accordingly. The process of moving out the pages of a program is governed by the following conventions:

1. If a page has been changed, then it is marked to be paged out; if it previously occupied space on auxiliary storage, then that space is released for reuse.
2. If a page has not been changed and a copy exists on auxiliary storage, then the main storage occupied by that space is released for reuse.

The paging process is depicted in Figure 2.11 (Chapter 2). As the system operates, pages are constantly being moved between main storage and a direct-access storage device. The paging device is formatted to handle pages in an efficient manner; however, this device has limited capacity, so infrequently-used pages are migrated from a higher-speed device to a lower-speed device (such as from drum to disk).

TERMINAL-ORIENTED SYSTEMS

Terminal-oriented systems permit a computer system to be used at a remote location using telecommunications facilities. They are used for two basic reasons: (1) to make the computational and data processing facilities of a computer system more appropriate to the needs of the user, and (2) to provide an operational capability that is usually not available with traditional processing systems. Remote batch processing, conversational remote job entry, and time sharing fall into the first category. They are the subject matter of this section. Applications such as data acquisition, message switching, and data base/data communications (DB/DC) fall into the second category. They are usually implemented as a high-priority job that uses telecommunications facilities while running in a multiprogramming environment.

Batch processing systems are designed to utilize the components of a computer system in the most efficient manner and, as such, are more system oriented than user oriented. Work is normally "queued up" for each resource in the system to minimize delays caused by heterogeneous requests for service. For example, there exists in most systems, an input job queue, a queue of programs ready for execution, and an output queue. Turnaround time can range from two hours to several days. Moreover, processing time is only a small part of turnaround time. Other times include delivery time to the computer, setup time, and delivery time to the user. In addition, several passes through the batch loop are usually required to eliminate program errors. Thus, the elapsed time for problem solution is lengthy and frustrating. Many jobs that need to be done are not done because results are needed before they can be obtained.

Remote batch processing—frequently called *remote job entry* (RJE) or *remote job output* (RJO)—permits a user with a terminal-oriented work station to enter his job into the input work queue and receive his output directly from the output queue. Turnaround time is reduced by eliminating delivery and wait times. However, the user cannot interact with his job once it is in the work queue; and the normal operational delays, inherent in batch processing, still exist.

An alternate approach to the submission of jobs in a batch processing mode is *conversational remote job entry* (CRJE). The user, at a low-speed keyboard-type terminal, creates a data file that can be entered into the input work queue as a job—including control cards, programs, and data. The data set is saved on-line for subsequent editing and reprocessing. CRJE is not time sharing but frequently approaches that mode of operation by providing diagnostic and control information to the user. Output from a system providing CRJE support returned to the user via the normal batch delivery service. Low-speed printed output is, however, sometimes available at the remote location with the keyboard-type terminal.

Through years of development, batch processing systems have evolved to a high level of sophistication. The knowledgeable user is provided with a tremendous computational capability. On the other hand, a considerable amount of knowledge is required to run a simple job; this fact has contributed to the characteristic delays of batch processing mentioned previously.

Time sharing is a user-oriented means of utilizing a computer system. When *time sharing*, multiple users concurrently engage in a series of interactions with the system via remote terminal devices. The user is able to respond immediately to system responses, and similarly, the system can respond immediately to requests for service by the user. Actually, the time sharing control program is designed to service many users on a "round-robin" basis; each user is given a "time slice" of processing time. Users' thinking and reaction times are used to perform other work in the processing unit. Thus, a user has the operational advantage of having a machine to himself; in reality, the system is time sharing. When a program error is detected by the system, the user is informed immediately. At that point, the user can correct his error and continue. Response time is measured in seconds and turnaround time is rarely considered. Processing unit time is required to provide this sort of time sharing service: thus, a trade off is made between efficient computer utilization and effective user service.

Not all jobs lend themselves to time sharing. A long-running file processing job, for example, is perhaps more effectively run in a batch processing mode of operation. A short one-shot FORTRAN program is perhaps best developed in a time sharing mode of operation.

Time sharing systems differ in capability and in complexity; they are conveniently divided into two categories: closed and open. In a *closed* system, the user is limited to a single programming language, such as BASIC or APL. Closed time sharing systems are frequently designed to operate as a single high-priority job in a multiprogramming environment. When implemented in this fashion, the time sharing system usually performs its own scheduling and storage allocation for the users in its domain. Another method of implementing a closed system is to dedicate a complete computer system to that service (called a *dedicated system*).

In an *open* time sharing system, the user is provided with access to all of the capability of the system—assembler language, programming languages, data management, utilities, etc. The primary difference between open time sharing and batch processing is that in open time sharing the user can access the system with a terminal device and that the system permits an interactive mode of operation. Most open time sharing systems permit two modes of operation: the conversational mode and the batch mode. The facilities of the system are essentially the same in both modes except that the ability to interact with the system in order to enter programs and data, to perform debugging, and to enter modifications is not available in the batch mode. Moreover, the ability to initiate a batch job from a terminal and to start a job in the conversational mode and complete it in the batch mode is usually provided.

AN IMPORTANT NOTE

Many users of a computer system utilize a programming system that obscures many of the "messy" details ordinarily involved with using the computer. Thus, the interface between man and the computer is software. Whether it is obvious or not, all modern computer systems utilize software.

One aspect of computer software has not been mentioned because it is the subject of this book: data management and data base systems. Data management and data base systems provide a means of storing information on an external device in an efficient manner and in a form so that it can be retrieved by a control program or a processing program. Thus, the emphasis is not only on storing and retrieving data but organizing it as well. Both the user and the software programs view data logically; but this data must be stored physically. Data management and data base systems provide an interface between the two concepts.

REFERENCES

Denning, P. J., "Virtual memory," *Computing Surveys*, Volume 2, No. 3 (1970), pp. 153–189.

IBM System/360 Operating System, *Concepts and Facilities*, White Plains, N.Y., IBM Corporation, Form GC28-6535.

Katzan, H., *Advanced Programming: Programming and Operating Systems*, New York, Van Nostrand Reinhold Company, 1970.

Katzan, H., *Operating Systems: A Pragmatic Approach*, New York, Van Nostrand Reinhold Company, 1973.

Mealy, G. H., "The functional structure of OS/360: Part I. Introductory survey," *IBM Systems Journal*, Volume 5, No. 1 (1966), pp. 3–11.

Rosin, R. F., "Supervisory and monitor systems," *Computing Surveys*, Volume 1, No. 1 (1969), pp. 37–54.

4 | DATA AND STORAGE CONCEPTS

INTRODUCTION

The development of computer programs requires a conceptualization of data called a *data structure;* common examples are ordinary data values, lists, and tables. Programs are designed to operate on these structures and produce computed results. One of the advantages of computer software is that it permits the user and his programs to address data using well-defined conventions that are logical and consistent, and at the same time, independent of a particular computer and a specific operating environment. *Storage structures* are the actual symbols that represent the data structures in the storage units of the computer, and this chapter is primarily concerned with the techniques used to represent data structures as storage structures.

DATA STRUCTURES

A single item of data, such as a numerical value, a string of characters, or a truth value, is known as a *scalar*. A scalar value has a single component and can be used to represent such diverse items of information as a person's age, the name of a commodity, or the result of a comparison operation.

A set of homogeneous data items is known as an array;* normally in programming, only the entire array is assigned a name, and elements of the array are

---

*An array is conveniently regarded as a family of related data items. Each element of an array has the same data attributes.

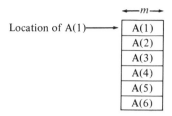

(a) Linear array.

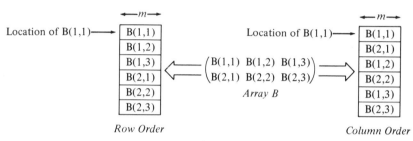

(b) Two-dimensional array.

Figure 4.1 Array data.

selected by subscripts. For example, the subscripted variable A(I) selects the Ith element of array A. The subscripts vary during the execution of a program so that the location of an element must be computed.* Figure 4.1 depicts a simple linear array A. The size of each element is m storage units—usually taken to be words or bytes—and the location of the beginning of the array [i.e., A(1)] is known. Thus, the location of the Ith element is computed as follows:

$$location[A(I)] = location[A(1)] + (I-1)*m$$

Figure 4.1 also depicts a two-dimensional array B where the size of each element is again m storage units. Arrays with dimensions greater than one are stored in row order or column order. Consider an array with M rows and N columns. The location of the (I,J)th element of an array B stored in row order is computed as follows:

$$location[B(I,J)] = location[B(1,1)] + m*[(I-1)*N+J-1]$$

Similarly, the location of the (I,J)th element of an array B stored in column order is computed as:

$$location[B(I,J)] = location[B(1,1)] + m*[(J-1)*M+I-1]$$

*Computer instructions to compute the location of an element of an array are generated by the compiler when a program is compiled.

The concepts are extended systematically to arrays of higher dimension. Arrays are conveniently characterized in four ways:

1. Number of dimensions.
2. The beginning and ending index for each dimension—called the *bounds* of that dimension. (In the preceding examples, the lower bound for each dimension was implied as 1.)
3. The number of elements in each dimension—referred to as *extent*.
4. How the array is stored—i.e., row order or column order.

A structure is a data aggregate in which individual data items are permitted to possess different data attributes, as demonstrated in the following examples from the PL/I language:

<pre>
DECLARE 1 PAYREC,
           2 EMPLOYNO FIXED DECIMAL (6),
           2 NAME CHAR (25),
           2 PAYRATE FIXED BINARY (6,2),
           2 DEP FIXED BINARY (2);
</pre>

or from the COBOL language:

<pre>
o1 PAYREC.
    02 EMPLOYNO PICTURE 9(6).
    02 NAME PICTURE X(25).
    02 PAYRATE PICTURE 9999V99
       USAGE IS COMPUTATIONAL.
    02 DEP PICTURE 9(2) USAGE IS COMPUTATIONAL.
</pre>

The components of a structure may be either scalar values or arrays, as shown in the PL/I structure:

<pre>
DECLARE 1 A...,
          2 B...,
          2 C(3)...,
          2 D...,
            3 E...,
            3 F...,
</pre>

that is depicted as follows:

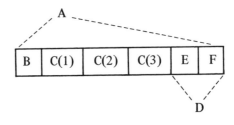

A structure with a dimension attribute is known as an *array of structures* (or a repeated group) as shown in the COBOL structure:

02 H OCCURS 3 TIMES.
    03 I PICTURE . . . .
    03 J PICTURE . . . .

that is depicted as:

I(1)	J(1)	H(1)
I(2)	J(2)	H(2)
I(3)	J(3)	H(3)

A structure frequently corresponds with the familiar data record used in data processing.

A *list* is a one-dimensional structure of data elements that has the following properties: (1) the elements are ordered—either by physical arrangement or by a key value. and (2) each element has the same data attributes. (In fact, a linear array is an example of a list.) Three types of lists are well-known: stacks, queues, and deques (pronounced "decks").

A *stack* is a list maintained on a last-in-first-out (LIFO) basis. A *queue* is a list maintained on a first-in-first-out (FIFO) basis. A *deque* is a list in which insertions and deletions are made at both ends. Actually, stacks and queues are special cases of a deque. A deque that is input and output restricted at one end, is a stack; a deque that is input restricted at one end and output restricted at the other, is a queue.

A *table* is a list of symbol value pairs of the form ⟨*s,v*⟩; each entry is a structure and the value pair (*v*) may include several data elements. The symbol field (*s*) is used for insertion, retrieval, and deletion. Essentially, a table is an array of structures that may be sorted on the symbol field or left unsorted. A table is normally accessed linearly by simply searching down through the table, or directly by performing a mathematical operation on the symbol field to determine the location in storage of the desired entry. The latter technique is known as *hashing* for which a collection of methods have been developed.

The manner in which data structures are represented in storage is known as "storage structures."

STORAGE STRUCTURES

A data structure is represented by arranging units of storage in a characteristic manner. This is *storage structure*. The basic concepts of storage structure are independent of the physical storage medium used; however, the terminology differs so that it is necessary to distinguish between units of the various storage devices. A unit of the "main" storage unit is usually a byte or a word, so that storage is measured or allocated accordingly.

A fixed unit of storage, such as the *page*, is defined in some systems so that storage management can be handled on a page basis. A typical page size is 4096 bytes. A unit of auxiliary storage is dependent upon the medium involved. A serial medium, such as magnetic tape, is frequently measured by the number of feet (of that medium) used or by the number of data records stored. A direct-access medium, such as magnetic disk storage, is usually measured by the number of tracks or cylinders used. Unit record storage storage is measured in columns and cards for punched card technology and in lines printed for printer technology.

The page concept is also used with auxiliary storage—especially when main storage also utilizes the technique. The correspondence between a physical page and the number of tracks or cylinders needed to store that much information is usually determined by the data management system. Regardless of the storage technology used for recording information, a storage structure is characterized by three properties: storage class, storage organization, and storage access.

The attribute of a storage structure that determines when that storage is allocated is called *storage class*. Storage can be allocated statically or dynamically. *Static storage* is allocated before the program that uses it begins execution. *Dynamic storage* is allocated during execution on an "as needed" basis. The concept applies to both programs and data in the storage unit of the computer, and to data files on auxiliary storage media. In the computer storage unit, an allocation of contiguous storage is called an area. A *static storage area* is established when a program is loaded for execution; a *dynamic storage area* is requested by a program and is allocated by the operating system on a dynamic basis. On an auxiliary storage device, (usually taken to be direct-access storage) an allocation of contiguous storage (i.e., bytes, tracks, or cylinders) is called an *extent*. Before a program is executed, the user requests a *primary allocation* and a *secondary allocation* for a "new" data file.* The primary allocation is assigned to the job statically before execution. If additional space is needed, it is assigned dynamically in units of storage specified as the secondary allocation. Thus, the user is protected against running out of allocated storage space and thereby causing an abnormal termination of his job.

The manner in which storage is organized to represent a data structure is called *storage organization*. The concepts apply to the entire data structure— i.e., the array, list, etc. and not elements of that structure—and include four basic methods: consecutive, linked, keyed, and regional. *Consecutive organization* denotes an allocation of storage occupying contiguous storage locations, as shown in Figure 4.2. An array held in computer storage and a file on magnetic tape are familiar examples of consecutive organization; however, storage can also be organized consecutively on a direct-access medium by assigning contiguous tracks or cylinders. Lists and tables are frequently stored using consecutive organization.

*A "new" data file is one that is created during the execution of a program.

A(1,1)
A(1,2)
A(2,1)
A(2,2)
A(3,1)
A(3,2)

An array in computer storage.

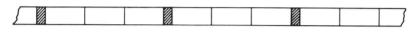

A data file on magnetic tape.

Figure 4.2 Consecutive organization.

Linked organization utilizes small allocations of contiguous storage—called *nodes*—that are chained together to represent a data structure, as shown in Figure 4.3. In computer storage, a linked structure is known as a *linked list* that represents an array, a list, or a table. On auxiliary storage, the records that comprise a data file are linked through "pointer" fields in the records that contain cylinder/head information.

Keyed organization specifies a form of storage organization in which data is located by means of a data key that is part of a data record (or node) or is maintained as a separate field, as in the block in a direct-access data record. As illustrated in Figure 4.4, keyed organization incorporates an index of keys that is used to access information that is stored in a consecutively organized storage area or extent. With this type of storage organization, data can be accessed sequentially, by "tracing down" the index of keys, or directly, by locating a particular key in the index. A variation to keyed organization allows data to be located by applying a mathematical function to the key—called *hashing* or *randomizing*—to locate a desired data element in the storage area or extent. This technique is presented later in the discussion of data management.

With *regional organization*, a region of a storage area or extent is located by name, index, or key—as with keyed organization. After a region is located, however, it is treated as though it were organized consecutively, as depicted in Figure 4.5. In most cases, regional organization simply defines partitions of a storage space that is otherwise organized consecutively.

The manner in which storage is referenced is known as *storage access*. Two methods of storage access are usually defined: sequential and direct. *Sequential access* indicates that an element of a data/storage structure is referenced in an order dependent upon the sequence in which the elements are physically stored. Punched cards, tape, and simple lists in computer storage are normally accessed

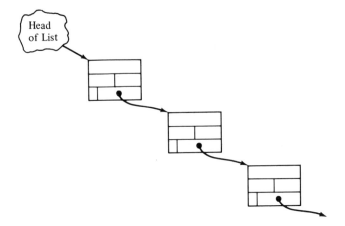

Linked list in computer storage.

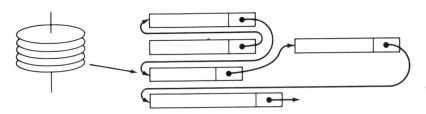

Chained records on direct-access storage.

Figure 4.3   Linked organization.

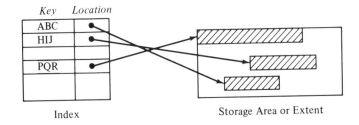

Key   Location

Index   Storage Area or Extent

Figure 4.4   Keyed organization.

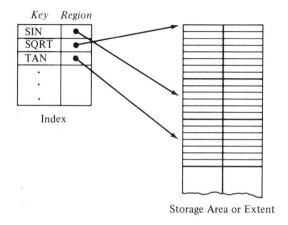

Figure 4.5   Regional organization.

sequentially. However, a linked list or a keyed data file can also be accessed sequentially by following the pointers and by referencing the keys in the order they are found in the index. *Direct access* indicates that an element of a data/ storage structure is referencing without passing over or referencing preceding information in that structure. Several forms of direct access are given as follows:

(1) A data element in computer storage or a record on direct-access storage is referenced by knowing its physical location on that medium.
(2) A key is matched against an index to determine the physical location of the data.
(3) A mathematical transformation is performed on the key to give the relative position of a data element in a storage area or extent.
(4) An element of an array is located by indexing—as described earlier in this chapter.

Clearly, storage class, storage organization, and storage access are related but are also distinct in the sense that the use of a particular attribute does not implicitly require that another attribute must be used. For example, keyed organization does not necessarily require that direct access be used. The effective use of storage structures is an important aspect of data management systems and data base technology.

MANIPULATION OF LINKED LISTS

A linked list uses linked organization to tie together the elements of a data structure. A data element in a linked list is a structure (as introduced earlier) and at least one field in a node is a pointer value that is used to point to other nodes. A variable termed the *head-of-the-list* is used to point to the first element of a linked list and serves to anchor the storage structure within the storage area. In general, a node can include any number of pointer fields.

A *singly-linked list* is a data/storage structure in which elements are chained in one direction. Similarly, a *doubly-linked list* is a data/storage structure in which elements are chained in both directions. Both cases are illustrated in Figure 4.6. A given node can be an element of any number of linked lists.

Two basic operations are performed on linked lists: deletion and insertion. To delete an element from a singly-linked list, two items of information are needed:

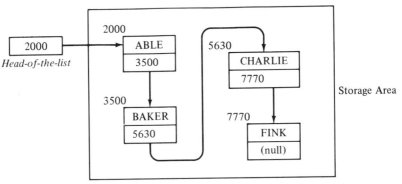

Singly-linked list

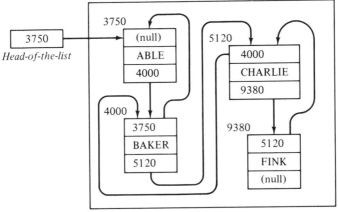

Doubly-linked list

Figure 4.6 Conceptual view of singly- and doubly-linked lists. (The arrows serve only as a visual convenience.)

(1) the address of the node to be deleted (α), and (2) the address of the preceding node in the linked list (β). If *link* denotes the address (or pointer) field in a node, then the deletion process for a singly-linked list is given symbolically as:

$$link(\beta) \leftarrow link(\alpha)$$

The deletion of a node from a doubly-linked list requires only one item of information, the address of the node to be deleted (α). If *blink* denotes the backward pointing address field in a node and *flink* denotes the forward pointing address field of a node, then the deletion process for a doubly-linked list is given symbolically as:

$$flink(blink(\alpha)) \leftarrow flink(\alpha)$$
$$blink(flink(\alpha)) \leftarrow blink(\alpha)$$

To insert an element in a singly-linked list, two items of information are needed (as in the deletion process): (1) the address of the node to be inserted (α), and (2) the address of the node after which the new node should be added (β). If *link* has the same meaning as given above, then the insertion process for a singly-linked list is given symbolically as:

$$link(\alpha) \leftarrow link(\beta)$$
$$link(\beta) \leftarrow \alpha$$

The insertion of a node on a doubly-linked list requires the same two items of information. If *blink* and *flink* have the same meaning as previously given, then the insertion process for a doubly-linked list is given symbolically as:

$$flink(\alpha) \leftarrow flink(\beta)$$
$$blink(\alpha) \leftarrow \beta$$
$$blink(flink(\beta)) \leftarrow \alpha$$
$$flink(\beta) \leftarrow \alpha$$

Insertion and deletion are representative list processing operations. Dealing with list elements at the beginning and the end of a linked list frequently requires special attention because of the absence of "preceding" and "following" elements. In addition, some uses of linked list technology, such as table structures, require that elements be maintained in a sorted order. Also, searching through a linked list by following the pointers is a list operation that is frequently encountered.

Another area of concern involves the creation and elimination of list elements. A list element is created when an executing program requests the required number of units of storage from the operating system through a language statement such as ALLOCATE. The storage is assigned to the requesting program by the operating system and its address is made available for subsequent use. The program creating the list element can then supply data needed for various fields in the node, and then perform the addition or insertion operation to the linked list, as required. When a list element is eliminated, the element is removed from the list through a deletion operation and the storage that is released through the delete operation is returned to the operating system through a language statement such as FREE.

The inclusion of pointer values with list elements requires additional storage—a disadvantage that is nullified by two significant advantages: (1) processing time for list operations is reduced because most operations can be performed by simply adjusting pointer values rather than actually moving data from one place to another, and (2) the storage for lists and tables can be assigned dynamically allowing flexibility in list and table size that is not available with consecutive storage that is allocated statically. Linked list structures are used in data base technology to minimize redundant information by chaining together related data on a system-wide basis.

DATA COMMUNICATIONS CONCEPTS

The term *data communications* refers to the use of teleprocessing facilities for the transmission of data. Facilities of this type are used for three major reasons:

(1) To provide computational facilities to a user at a remote location.
(2) To allow information to be entered or retrieved from a data base system on a dynamic basis.
(3) To transfer data between locations at a high rate of speed.

Obviously, other reasons for using data communications facilities exist. However, these three reasons have given rise to the more "popular" applications, such as time sharing, computer networks, message transmission and switching, and information-base systems. A communications system is defined as having five components: (1) a message source, (2) an encoder, (3) a signal channel, (4) a decoder, and (5) a message destination. The model of a communications system is depicted in Figure 4.7.

The purpose of the *channel* is to transport data from one location to another. The services used to transmit data are telegraph, telephone, microwave, and broadband telephone. Telegraph and telephone facilities usually exist as open

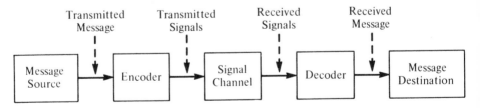

Figure 4.7   Model of a communications system. (Hall, p. 381)

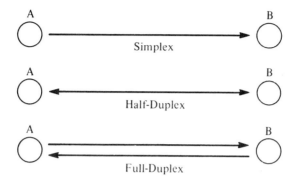

Figure 4.8   Classes of communications lines.

wires, co-axial cable circuits, and microwave systems. Communications lines are classed as implex, half-duplex, and full-duplex, as shown in Figure 4.8. *Simplex lines* transmit in one direction only. *Half-duplex lines* can transmit in either direction but not simultaneously. *Full-duplex lines* can transmit in both directions at the same time. Public telephone lines operate in the half-duplex mode, and full-duplex service is available at an increased rate. Simplex lines are not used in data communications because control signals must be sent back to the transmitter. Most data communications systems are half-duplex lines so that a two-way dialogue is possible.

For data transmission, data is normally represented as a train of bits, as depicted in Figure 4.9. Successive bits denote a specific character according to a predetermined method of coding. The number of bits necessary to represent a character generally range from 5 to 8 plus a vertical parity bit. A longitudinal redundancy check (i.e., a longitudinal parity bit) and cyclic check codes are also frequently used to aid in error detection.

Data is transmitted in one of three modes: asynchronous start-stop, synchronous, and parallel. With *asynchronous transmission,* one character is transmitted at a time and start and stop codes are used to achieve calibration between transmitter and receiver. The *start code* is a zero bit with a one bit-unit time duration.

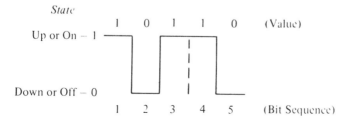

Figure 4.9   Representation of data as a bit train.

The *stop code* is a one bit with a time duration of 1.42 bit units. With *synchronous transmission*, a block of characters is sent at one time without start and stop codes. The block is accumulated in a buffer prior to transmission and the synchronization of transmitter is controlled by oscillators. Synchronous transmission is more efficient since there are no start and stop bits and no pauses. Block length varies and is usually dependent upon the physical characteristics of the hardware. *Parallel transmission* uses several communications channels to transmit a character. Usually, a channel exists for each bit in the code structure.

Communications lines are classified according to the data rate that they can sustain. Data rates are measured in bits per second. Three classifications are usually used: subvoice grade, voice grade, and wide band. *Subvoice-grade lines* transmit at rates that range from 45 to 180 bits per second; lines in this category are customarily used for teletype service. *Voice-grade lines* can sustain data rates from 600 to 1200 bits per second; public telephone lines fall into this category. *Wide band lines* (also called *broadband lines*) are used to transmit data at line speeds of 19,200, 40,800, and 50,000 bits per second; broadband facilities operate in the duplex mode and are supplied by common carriers such as Western Union and The Bell System.

The different types of lines used for data transmission vary widely in the amount of information that can be transmitted over them in a fixed unit of time. This capacity is frequently referred to as *bandwidth*. Bandwidth is measured in cycles per second (or Hertz as it is usually called). A significant characteristic of communication lines is whether they are switched or private. Telex, TWX, and public telephone lines are switched through public exchanges—even though they may be used to transmit data. Private or leased lines avoid the public switching network. The advantage of switched lines is the fact that they are located practically everywhere. Leased lines can be less expensive than switched lines depending upon volume and distance. Leased lines can also be "conditioned" to reduce transmission errors.

Data can be transmitted in a digital form or an analog form. With a digital form of transmission, a sequence of on/off pulses are transmitted in much the same manner that data is moved in the computer (a digital device). Figure 4.10(a) depicts a digital signal that contains two voltage levels—representing 0 and 1. The original telegraph system used digital transmission. One of the disadvantages of digital transmission is that the pulses become distorted, as in Figure 4.10(b), when they have to travel long distances and at a high rate of speed over communications lines. Regenerative repeaters are used to reconstruct the bits and pass them on.

With an analog signal, a continuous range of frequencies is transmitted, as depicted in the oversimplified example in Figure 4.10(c). Analog signals can be distorted through attenuation, delay characteristics of the signal, and noise on the communications line. Amplifiers are used to increase the signal strength of

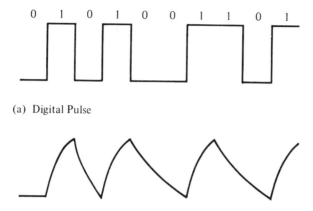

(a) Digital Pulse

(b) Digital Pulses Distorted at the Receiver

(c) Analog Signal

Figure 4.10   Analog and digital transmission signals.

analog signals. Most communications lines that can be used for data transmission are designed to carry analog signals, and the computer is a digital device. The process of converting digital data to analog form is called *modulation*. The reverse process of converting analog signals to digital data is called *demodulation*. A small hardware device that performs modulation/demodulation is called a *modem*. Two types of modems are used: a dataset* and an acoustical coupler.

A *dataset* is supplied by the telephone company and is connected to the telephone and the data source—either a terminal device, a high speed transmission unit, or a transmission control unit of a computer. A dataset establishes a fixed connection between one terminal and one telephone line. When a user desires to make a data communications connection to the computer using a dataset, he pushes the TALK button and dials the number of the computer. After the telephone rings, it is answered by the computer and a high-pitched sound is heard. Next, the DATA button is pushed and the receiver is cradled. A line connection is made.

*This dataset should be distinguished from the data management data set.

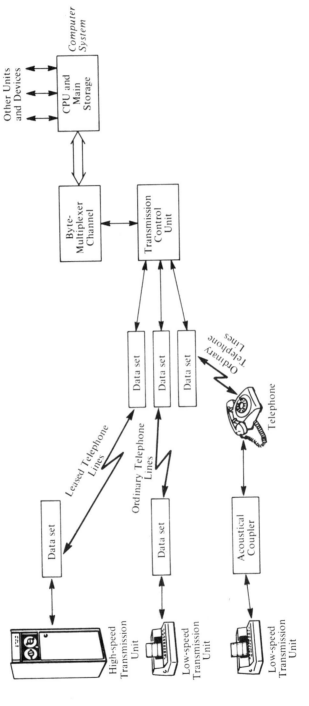

Figure 4.11   Sample data communications system.

An *acoustical coupler* is a device that converts digital signals to audible tones. The acoustical coupler must be attached to the transmitting device but not to a telephone line. Thus, the terminal can be portable. When a user desires to make a data communications connection to the computer using an acoustical coupler, he simply dials the computer over an ordinary telephone. After the computer answers the telephone and produces a high-pitched sound, the receiver of the telephone is clamped in to the coupler mechanism and a line connection is made.

A sample data communications system is depicted in Figure 4.11. Several concepts are depicted: leased lines, datasets, acoustical coupler, transmission control unit, and the computer system. Computer programs that utilize data communications facilities are similar to conventional programs. Generally speaking, a data communications line is treated as an input/output device and telecommunications access methods, similar to data management access methods, are used to handle input and output operations.

REFERENCES

Chapin, N., *Computers: A Systems Approach*, New York, Van Nostrand Reinhold Company, 1971.

Data Communications Primer, White Plains, N.Y., IBM Corporation, Form C20-1668.

Hall, A. D., *A Methodology for Systems Engineering*, New York, Van Nostrand Reinhold Company, 1962.

Katzan, H., *Computer Data Security*, New York, Van Nostrand Reinhold Company 1973.

Katzan, H., *Operating Systems: A Pragmatic Approach,* New York, Van Nostrand Reinhold Company, 1973.

Martin, J., *Introduction to Teleprocessing*, Englewood Cliffs, N.J., Prentice-Hall, Inc., 1972.

PART **II** # DATA MANAGEMENT CONCEPTS

5 | DATA MANAGEMENT: CONCEPTS AND FACILITIES

INTRODUCTION

The manner in which data is managed in a computer system and in a computer installation determines the degree to which user needs can be satisfied and governs the efficiency of an information system. Input/output and external storage devices* are the limiting factor on the efficiency of most information-based systems, even though devices such as the channel, and operational techniques such as multiprogramming, are commonly used to increase overall system performance. Therefore, the manner in which input and output are performed, the methods used for data storage and organization, and the techniques employed to access data are of prime importance to most computer users. In the previous chapter we have been talking about *data management* that characteristically incorporates several data-related concepts, including input and output processing, data storage and organization, access methods, and related systems concepts.

Data management facilities are normally provided through the services of a computer operating system. Operating systems technology and data management go together like "bread and butter;" one good reason for this is that input and output operations are the biggest problem in the design of an operating system that effectively manages the use of system resources. Another good reason, albeit related, is that the execution of actual input and output instructions are

---

*Input/output and external storage devices are collectively referred to as IO devices—obviously referring to computer input and output. The distinction between the two is generally well known.

privileged in the sense that problems and data must be protected in a multiprogramming environment; they *must* be managed by the operating system on a system-wide basis.

Other related reasons exist. Modern direct-access storage devices can store millions of bytes of information and it is convenient and efficient for operating system routines to allocate space on them. Also, users prefer to reference data files by name so that file names and attributes must be stored within the system. File names, attributes, and storage requirements are specified with control cards* that are read and processed by job management routines.** Thus, data management is usually considered to be part of an operating system. In this and subsequent chapters data management concepts are taken out of an operating systems environment and presented as a separate topic, even though operating system facilities will be referred to occasionally.

BASIC CONSIDERATIONS

In data management, a distinction is usually made between units of data and units of storage. Scalars, arrays, structures, lists, queues, stacks, deques, and tables are commonly regarded as elements of data structure. For input and output operations,† these elements are grouped to form *data records*—also called *logical records*—and a set of related data records is referred to as a *file*. A familiar example of these concepts is a single employee's record in a payroll file. Most data processing and information management applications are programmed to deal with data records and files, and as a result, can be regarded as being "data structure" oriented. This is desirable because a program can be developed independently of how the data is organized and on what type of media it is stored. Thus, every time the organization or media changes, the program does not have to be modified.

Another way of looking at the situation is that a special copy of the program does not have to exist for each form of data organization and each type of storage media. What happens is that when the program is run, the data organization and device type are specified with control cards. Then, facilities of the data management system and the operating system make whatever adjustments are necessary. This technique is referred to as *late binding*, obviously referring to the process of binding a program to its data.

The computer system, on the other hand, deals with storage structures. A group of bytes or words comprise a *field*, which is the smallest unit of storage. If a field were broken down further, it would lose its meaning. For example, the characters "PRATT INSTITUTE" on a punched card refer to an entity that

---

*Control cards are also referred to as *Job Control Language*.

**File names, attributes, and storage requirements can be built into a program. However, this necessarily limits the range of data for which the program can be used.

†Again, the terms *input* and *output* refer to the computer. Clearly, these operations may involve "mass storage" devices.

actually exists. The characters taken individually are simply letters of the alphabet. Actually, a field is commonly regarded both as an element of data structure and an element of storage structure, because a data record is also said to be comprised of fields. In this case, the concept of a field is more important than the distinction as to where it should be classified.

The unit of interchange between a main storage and an external storage medium is a block that is composed of either bytes or bits. When the computer system performs a read operation, a whole block is read by the input device, even though the input operation may involve only a part of the block. When reading punched cards for example, the whole card must be read to obtain the first n columns, where $n \leqslant 80$. A similar methodology holds true for output operations. Each time the computer system executes a write operation, a block is written by the output device. This is a simplification of the input and output processes because the computer does not "zap out" hundreds or thousands of bytes all at once. From the viewpoint of a computer program and the data management routines, however, input and output operations involve blocks and the details of data transfer are subordinated to the hardware input/output system.

The term block is often used interchangeably with the term *physical record*, commonly associated with magnetic tape. On tape, consecutive blocks are separated by interblock gaps and control information. On direct-access devices, as introduced previously, a data block is recorded as either two or three blocks* (also referred to as *subblocks*) separated by interblock gaps and control information. A file does not necessarily occupy consecutive tracks on direct-access storage. The reason is obvious. As a file grows, secondary allocations of direct-access storage space probably do not occupy contiguous tracks to previous allocations. A set of consecutive tracks on direct-access storage is referred to as an *extent*, and a file on a direct-access storage medium is composed of one or more extents.

RECORD STRUCTURES

Records and files exist for purposes of performing input and output operations so that a correspondence must be made between data records and blocks.** The manner in which data records correspond to blocks is referred to as *record structure* (or *data record format*). Three options exist:

1. A block corresponds to one data record.
2. A block is composed of two or more data records.
3. A block contains a segment of a data record.

---

*A data block is stored as two subblocks when the key block is not used and as three subblocks when the key is used.
**The terms "logical record" and "physical record" are not used, in favor of "data record" and "block," respectively.

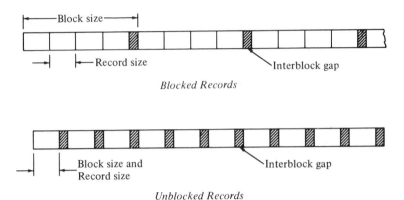

Blocked Records

Unblocked Records

Figure 5.1   Fixed-length record structure.

When one data record is stored in a block (option 1), the record is known as an *unblocked record*. When several data records are stored in a block, the records are known as *blocked records*. When a data record is stored in two or more blocks, the record is referred to as a *spanned record*.

Data records are grouped (frequently denoted as "blocked") according to one of three formats: fixed-length records, variable-length records, or undefined-length records. The size of a *fixed-length record* is constant for all data records in a block; the size of the block is also fixed, as depicted in Figure 5.1. Fixed-length records may be blocked or unblocked.

With *variable-length records*, the size of a data record is variable length, and the size of the block is variable also. Normally, a maximum must be stated so that input/output buffer space can be allocated. Variable-length records are depicted in Figure 5.2; the *block length* (L) is included in the block, preceding the data, so that the data management system can manipulate the data correctly. The record size (*l*) is included with each data record and precedes the actual data part. The length (L) of a variable-length block is referred to as a *block descriptor word*; similarly, the length (*l*) of a variable-length record is referred to as a *record descriptor word*. Even though block and record descriptor words require storage space, the objective of variable-length records is to conserve storage space.

The basic idea is that with variable-length records the need is eliminated to carry along unused fields, as would be the case with fixed-length records. Fixed and variable-length records can be blocked or unblocked, depending upon the needs of a particular application. Blocked records require less storage space on the external medium because some interblock gaps are eliminated; moreover, fewer input/output operations are required since the execution of a single operation essentially involves the transfer of several data records. On the other hand, the use of blocked records involves increased buffer space and requires additional data manipulation functions.

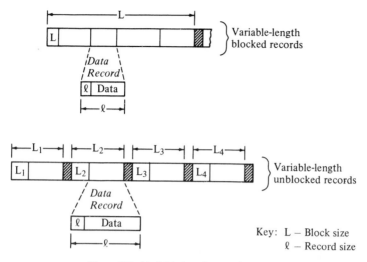

Figure 5.2   Variable-length record structure.

Undefined-length records, depicted in Figure 5.3, are permitted in many operating environments to permit the reading and writing of records that do not satisfy the specifications of fixed and variable-length processing.   When undefined-records are used, the user is responsible for performing the housekeeping tasks associated with data management.

Figure 5.3   Conceptual   view   of   undefined-length
records.

A *spanned record* is a record format and a blocking technique. Spanned records are used when the length of a block is fixed for some reason. Typical cases result from limited buffer space, and the need to store a record on direct-access storage that exceeds the length of a track (and an overflow feature is not available). A spanned record, named B, is depicted in Figure 5.4. The record is composed of segments that occupy three consecutive blocks. The data contained in each segment is preceded by a "segment length" field and a "control code" that allows the record to be processed by data management routines.

BASIC DATA MANAGEMENT FUNCTIONS

Apart from input and output that can be considered as basic system operations, data management routines perform two basic functions: blocking/deblocking and buffering. The process of grouping data records to form a block is referred

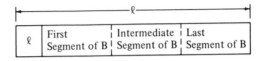

Data Record B

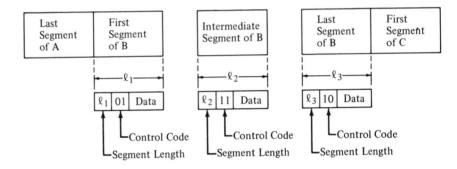

Physical Storage

Control Codes:

00 — Complete data record
01 — First segment of a multi-segment record
10 — Last segment of a multi-segment record
11 — Intermediate segment of a multi-segment record

Figure 5.4   Spanned record.

to as *blocking* and the reverse process is known as *deblocking*. Normally, blocking and deblocking are performed by data management routines that are invoked by assembler language macro instructions or statements in a programming language that cause the same basic functions to be performed.

Data management routines enable the user to perceive his file as a series of data records, and the blocking and deblocking processes are transparent to him. Blocked input is a good example. When the first logical record in a block is referenced by an application program, the entire block is read from external storage and the first data record of the block is passed to the program. When the following records in that block are referenced, data management does not have to perform a read operation, and simply returns to the requesting program the next sequential data record in that block. For output, a block is not written until it is filled with data records.

The process of reading and writing blocks is made more efficient by buffering.

A *buffer* is a storage area used to compensate for a difference in operating speeds of two devices. An *input buffer* is an area of storage used to hold input blocks prior to processing. Blocks are read ahead of time so that when a data management routine needs a block, it is already in storage. An *output buffer* is an area of storage used to hold blocks prior to an output operation. Data management routines initiate the filling of a new block as soon as the preceding one has been filled and without waiting for the associated write operation to be completed. When using buffering, the processing unit can effectively utilize the input–output–compute overlap capability provided with an input/output data channel.

FILE ORGANIZATION AND ACCESS

Data files are organized according to the manner in which they are used. Four methods of file organization are usually identified:

1. Sequential.
2. Direct.
3. Indexed sequential.
4. Partitioned.

Sequential organization denotes that the data records must be referenced in a manner dependent upon the sequence in which the data records are physically stored.* Card decks and magnetic tape files are always organized sequentially and files on direct-access storage divices are frequently, but not necessarily, organized in this manner. *Direct organization* denotes that a data record may be referenced without "passing over" or referencing preceding information. Data records are located by their physical position on the direct-access storage volume.

Indexed sequential organization permits data records in a file to be referenced sequentially or directly. The defining characteristic of an indexed sequential file is that data records are logically arranged by collating sequence, according to a *key field* contained in each record. Indexes of keys are maintained to provide direct or sequential access. When an indexed sequential file is referenced sequentially, the keys in an index are processed in order; associated with each key is the physical location on a direct-access storage volume of the corresponding data record. When an indexed sequential file is referenced directly, the key is looked up in the index (analogous to a table) to determine the physical location of the desired record. Data files with indexed sequential organization must reside on a direct-access volume.

Partitioned organization denotes a data file that is divided into sequentially organized members. Each member is composed of data records. Logically, a partitioned data file is a file of files. Each file is assigned a name (such as the name of a program) and each name is stored in a directory, along with the physi-

---

*Clearly, sequential file organization can utilize two of the "general" methods given in chapter four: consecutive and linked.

cal location of the beginning of the member. The directory is stored along with the file. After a member is located, the data records are referenced as though that member were organized sequentially. Partitioned files are usually used to store programs.*

Two different techniques are normally available to the user for transferring data between storage and an external storage medium. These techniques are referred to as access methods and are implemented as access routines supplied by the data management subsystem of the operating system. The access routines are available through macro instructions recognized by the assembler system. The access techniques are classified by their treatment of buffering and input/ output synchronization with processing. The two techniques are named queued access and basic access. The *queued access* technique provides automatic blocking and deblocking on data transfers between main storage and input/output devices. Queued access also provides look-ahead buffering and automatic synchronization of input/output operation and processing. The access method routine controls the use of buffers such that sufficient input blocks are in storage at one time, preventing the delay of processing unit operation. When using queued access, the user need not test for input/output completion, errors, or exceptional conditions. After the completion of an input or output macro instruction control is not returned to the processing program until the operation is logically complete.

The *basic access* technique does not provide automatic blocking and deblocking; neither does it provide anticipatory buffering or automatic event synchronization. Basic access is used when the sequence in which records are processed cannot be predicted in advance. With the basic access technique, the user must perform his own blocking and deblocking. Moreover, input and output macro instructions only initiate input/output processing; both operations must be checked for completion with an appropriate macro instruction. In other words, automatic event synchronization is not provided.

STRUCTURAL ASPECTS OF FILE UTILIZATION

The primary objective of a modern data management system is to facilitate input/output processing, and the storage and retrieval of large amounts of data. A data management system of this type necessarily provides four basic facilities:

1. Device independence.
2. Allocation of space on direct-access devices.
3. Late binding of programs to data files; thus, specifications such as buffer size, blocking factors, device identification, and device type need not be specified until execution time for a particular job step.
4. Automatic location of data files by name.

*The indexed sequential and partitioned organizations are forms of the keyed and regional organizations, respectively, that were given in chapter four.

These facilities are provided through a system of data sets, volumes, libraries, and catalogs.

The concept of a data file is generalized to a data set. Whereas a data file usually refers to a group of data records related in some form to a data processing function, a data set refers to one of several categories of information, such as a source program, an object program, a numeric table, a payroll file, or a collection of subroutines. Thus, a *data set* is a collection of related data items, together with a "data set label," stored along with the data set. Common examples of a data set are an ordinary data file, a library of object programs, and a source program stored as a set of source data records. The *data set label* includes the name of the data set, its physical attributes, and its boundaries on a storage medium; and should be distinguished from a tape label or a file label used for identification purposes in data processing. A data set name along with the location of the data set can be stored in a catalog, so that a data set can be used without knowing its volume identification or physical attributes. The name of the data set is specified with a control card and the information necessary for processing is retrieved from the data set label. With direct-access devices, the data set label is termed a *data set control block*; it is stored on the direct-access volume containing the data set. With magnetic tape, the data set label is part of the data set header label, and includes a data set sequence number. A data set sequence number on magnetic tape is used for checking and positioning when more than one data set is stored on the same magnetic tape reel.

A standard unit of auxiliary storage is termed a *volume*, such as a magnetic tape reel, a disk pack, or a drum. Several data sets can reside on a single volume, which is usually the case; or a single data set may span two or more volumes. Each volume has a volume label that identifies the volume; it is used by the data management system to ensure that the correct volume is mounted. Magnetic tape volumes can be labeled or unlabeled. A labeled volume includes the following:

1. Volume label (one per volume).
2. Data set header label (including data set sequence number) for each data set.
3. Data set trailer label for each data set.
4. User labels as required.

The identity of labeled tapes are verified by the operating system.

Each direct-access storage device volume is labeled in a standard location (usually the first track—corresponding to read/write head 0—of cylinder 0). Each direct-access volume label minimally includes the following:

1. Volume serial number.
2. Volume security information.
3. VTOC pointer.

The *volume table of contents* (VTOC) is important since it includes the "data set control block" of all data sets stored on the volume. More specifically, the VTOC contains:

1. A data set control block for the VTOC itself.
2. A data set control block for each data set on the volume.
3. A data set control block for all tracks on the volume that are available for allocation.

The volume label and a skeletal VTOC are placed on a direct-access volume when it is initialized by a utility program. When a data set is to be stored on a direct-access volume, the attributes and space requirements of that data set must be supplied to the data management system. These specifications are used by direct-access space allocation routines in maintaining the VTOC for a given volume. Direct-access organization is suggested in Figure 5.5.

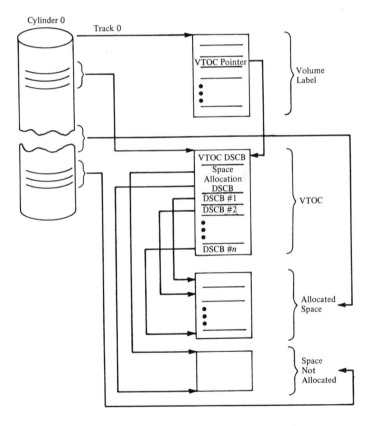

Figure 5.5   Direct-access storage device organization.

In utilizing the concepts that have been presented thus far, the data management system needs the following information to retrieve a data set: data set name, the device type, a volume identification, and possibly a data set sequence number. Specification of this information can be cumbersome to the user, especially when several users are working cooperatively. A *catalog* allows data sets to be referenced by name alone. A *data set name* is usually a simple name (e.g., 1-8 alphanumeric characters the first of which must be alphabetic) or a series of simple names separated by periods, such as DIV15.YORK.ABC. The catalog is a tree-organized set of indexes held in direct-access storage. The master index is a basic structural entity in the catalog; the level of subsequent indexes is determined by the users of the system. Figure 5.6 depicts the catalog structure

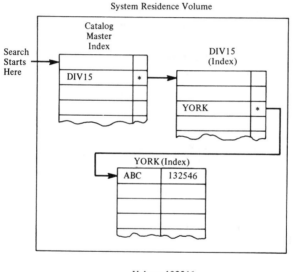

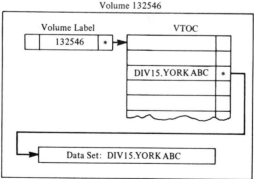

Figure 5.6 Catalog and search procedure. (The catalog is searched for a data set named DIV15.YORK.ABC.)

and search procedure. When the user specifies an "already existing" data set by name alone, the system can determine its attributes by performing a catalog search and retrieving the file characteristics from the data set control block of the data set. Not all data sets need be cataloged depending upon the needs of a particular user and upon the operating practices of an installation. Most operating systems have a catalog that resides on the system residence volume. When it is desired to conserve space on the system residence volume or when a data set is used infrequently, its name is not cataloged. A data set name is usually cataloged upon request only.

A *partitioned data set* is a data file that is divided into sequentially organized members.* Each member is composed of records. Data sets of this type are most frequently used to store object programs—each member corresponds to a single object program. This partitioned data set as a whole is referred to as a *library*. Operating system libraries and user libraries are stored in this fashion. Figure 5.7 depicts a typical partitioned data set. An ordinary data set is referred to by name. For example, data sets MFILE and RIVER.JOHNS would be specified in job control language as:

DSNAME=MFILE

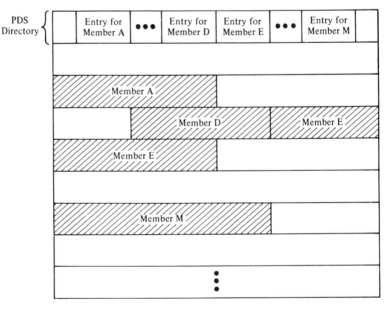

Figure 5.7 Partitioned data set. (Each member is composed of one or more blocks.)

*See regional organization discussed earlier.

or

DSNAME=RIVER.JOHNS

where DSNAME is the keyword for the data set name parameter. When a member of a partitioned data set is specified, the member name is enclosed in parentheses following the partitioned data set name. For example, member APROG of partitioned data set BIGLIB is specified as:

DSNAME=BIGLIB(APROG)

Data set libraries are used to store routines of the operating system and data management system, user programs, and system-supplied subroutines.

DATA MANAGEMENT SYSTEM ORGANIZATION

An operating system normally contains four types of routines to support a comprehensive data management system. Although routines of this type vary between systems, the following descriptions should supply an "idea" of the manner in which the various "pieces" fit together:

1. *Direct-access device space management routines.* These routines are used primarily during job initiation and control the allocation of space on a direct-access volume through the volume table of contents.
2. *Catalog management routines.* These routines are used during the initiation and termination of a job to catalog or uncatalog data sets used.
3. *Input/output support processing routines.* These routines perform open processing, close processing, and end-of-volume processing. As part of their normal function, input/output support processing routines insure proper volume mounting, construct tables and control blocks, and cause access method routines to be loaded.
4. *Input/output processing routines.* Input/output processing operations are performed in two parts: (1) problem state routines (i.e., access methods) that prepare control information required by the input/output supervisor to start an input/output operation, and (2) supervisor state routines (i.e., the input/output supervisor) that initiate and control input/output operations.

A description of each type of routine is not given; however, the functions performed by these routines are reflected in the next chapter, which is concerned with data management operations.

REFERENCES

Chapin, N., *Computers: A Systems Approach*, New York, Van Nostrand Reinhold Company, 1971.

Dodd, G. G., "Elements of data management systems," *Computing Surveys*, Volume 1, No. 2 (June 1969), pp. 117–133.

IBM System/360 Operating System, *Supervisor and Data Management Services*, White Plains, N.Y., IBM Corporation, Form GC28-6646.

Katzan, H., *Operating Systems: A Pragmatic Approach*, New York, Van Nostrand Reinhold Company, 1973.

6 | INPUT AND OUTPUT OPERATIONS IN A DATA MANAGEMENT ENVIRONMENT

INTRODUCTION

In a data management environment, input and output processing takes place at two levels: the user level and the system level. This chapter is concerned with the user level and the next chapter covers the system level. The two levels are not as distinct as one might imagine since the system uses descriptive information that the user provides, and the user must utilize the system and supply information to it on the basis of how it operates.

A user provides information to the data management system in three ways:

1. Through control cards (i.e., job control language).
2. Through descriptive information built into a computer program.
3. By the sequence of data management requests that are made by an executing application program.

The data management system also obtains information on the physical attributes of a data set from its data set control block.

The concepts presented here are relatively standard among the various data management systems. The terminology reflects that used with IBM's well-known OS/MFT/MVT/VSI/VS2 operating systems, which has become a *de facto standard* for terminology in the industry.

DATA CONTROL BLOCK

The primary method of communication between an application program and the Data Management System is a storage block in the application program called a *data control block* (DCB). A DCB is required for each data set used by a program. In assembler language a data control block is created with the DCB macro. When using a programming language, the DCB is generated by the compiler.

The purpose of the DCB is to describe the characteristics of the data set. Information for the DCB is supplied in three ways:

1. Preassembled into the DCB.
2. From the DD statement for that data set*;
3. From the data set label for that data set (the data set control block—in the case of direct-access storage).

Since the DCB is a storage area in a program, the various fields in it can be modified dynamically during program execution. (In fact, the execution of the OPEN macro causes the DCB to be completed dynamically.)

One of the most significant advantages of using the DCB concept is that it allows data set independence. This is the case since data set description information can be supplied to the DCB at run time with the DD statement.

DATA DEFINITION STATEMENT

The data definition (DD) statement describes a data set to be used with a job step, and may specify input/output facilities required for using that data set. A DD statement must be present for each data set used in a job step. The DD cards for a job step follow the EXEC card, as described in chapter three. The format of the DD statement is:

//ddname DD operands comments

For example,

//ABL DD DSNAME=MFILE,UNIT=2314,
DISP=(NEW,KEEP),SPACE=(CYL,(10,2))

The "ddname" logically connects the DD statement with the DCB of an application program. The DCB contains the "internal" name of a file. For example, the ddname field in the DCB corresponds to the FD name in COBOL or the FILE name in PL/I. The DSNAME parameter specifies the name of a data set. The DD statement establishes the correspondence between the two so that the program can use the named data set. Thus, the data set that an application pro-

---

*The *data definition* (DD) statement is introduced in chapter three, "Software Concepts." The form of the DD statement is given in this chapter.

gram processes can be changed by replacing the DSNAME parameter of the DD statement.

Parameters of the DD statement are coded in the "operand" field and serve to complete the DCB, specify device requirements, and supply control information. One of four positional parameters and a variety of keyword parameters can be used. DD statement parameters are summarized in Table 6.1.

From an operational point of view, the most significant parameter of the DD statement is the DCB parameter. The DCB parameter is used to complete the DCB and exists as an alternate means of specifying data set characteristics. Parameters that do not vary between "runs" of a program are placed in the DCB during assembly. Parameters that vary between "runs" and are established at run time are supplied via the DCB parameter. The DCB subparameters are listed in the next section. Any of the DCB fields can be assigned values with the DD statement. The general form of the DCB parameter is:

$$DCB=(list\ of\ attributes)$$

or

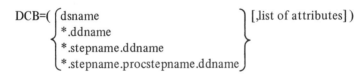

where:

[ ] denotes optical material;

{ } denotes selection;

dsname specifies that DCB information should be copied
   from the data set label of the cataloged data set
   named "dsname;"

*.ddname specifies that DCB information should be copied from an
   earlier DD statement in the job step;

*.stepname.ddname specifies that DCB information should be copied
   from an earlier DD statement in the named job step; and

*.stepname.procstepname.ddname specifies that DCB information should
   be copied from a job step in a cataloged procedure.

The most important concept to be gained here is that one DD statement can reference another DD statement—using one of the above forms (as in the third DD statement given below). Sample DD statements depicting the DCB parameters are listed as follows:

```
//ONE DD DSNAME=JOE,DISP=(NEW,CATLG),
          DCB=(RECFM=FB,LRECL=140,BLKSIZE=840),
          UNIT=2400
```

TABLE 6.1   DD STATEMENT PARAMETERS

Parameter	Positional or Keyword	Function
Input data	*	Specifies that data following this statement are to be entered in the input stream.
	or	
Special input data	DATA	Specifies that the input data following this statement may have // in columns 1 and 2.
Dummy data set	DUMMY	Creates a dummy data set (EOD returned when accessed).
	or	
	DYNAM	Specifies the dynamic allocation of data sets (used with time sharing option).
Affinity (to another address)	AFF=	Causes channel separation relative to other data sets.
Data control block	DCB=	Completes the DCB.
Reference to other ddname	DDNAME=	Postpones data definition.
Data set disposition	DISP=	Gives disposition of data set after job step is complete.
Data set name	DSNAME=	Specifies the data set name.
	or	
	DSN	

Forms control buffer	FCB=	Specifies an image for the forms control buffer (3211 printer).
Data set label	LABEL=	Describes the data set label.
System output limit	OUTLIM=	Specifies a limit for the number of records on the system output data set.
Teleprocessing data	QNAME=	Defines data to be accessed by telecommunications methods.
Separation	SEP=	Specifies channel separation.
DASD space allocation	SPACE=	Requests space allocation on DASD.
DASD space allocation	SPLIT=	Allocates DASD space among several cylinders.
DASD space allocation	SUBALLOC=	Specifies that DASD space should be allocated from another data set.
System output data set	SYSOUT=	Assigns a data set to a system output writer.
Terminal IO	TERM=	Specifies a time sharing terminal as an input or output device.
Universal character set	UCS=	Specifies a set of print characters.
IO unit	UNIT=	Specifies or indicates device type or unit address.
Volume specifications	VOLUME= or VOL=	Identifies an IO volume and supplies its attributes.

```
//TWO DD DSNAME=MIKE,DISP=OLD,DCB=(RECFM=FB,LRECL=80,
     BLKSIZE=400)

//THREE DD DSNAME=PETE,DISP=(NEW,KEEP),UNIT=2400,
     LABEL=(,SL),DCB=*.TWO
```

In the last case, the parentheses for the DCB parameter can be elided if one sub-parameter is used.

Values used with DD statement parameters are coded values. For example, RECFM=FB above denotes a record format that is "fixed blocked." Coded values are not considered here since they represent nominal conventions established during system development.

DATA DESCRIPTION

Each data set used in an application program requires a DCB and a DD statement. Information for the DCB can be supplied from either source or the data set control block, if the data set existed previous to the job step. The correspondence between a DD statement and a DCB is made by using the DDNAME of the DD statement in the DCB macro instruction. For example, a DCB macro of the form:

location	*operation*	*operand*
SAMPDCB	DCB	DDNAME=MTAPE,DSORG=PS,. . .

is logically associated with a DD statement of the form:

```
//MTAPE DD DSNAME=MFILE,. . .
```

The following DCB parameters are typical of those needed to describe a data set:

Buffering technique (BFTEK)
Block size (BLKSIZE)
Buffer length (BUFLN)
Buffer number (BUFNO)
Cylinder overflow tracks (CYLO)
Data definition name (DDNAME)
Device type (DEVD)
Data set organization (DSORG)
End of data exit address (EODAD)
Error options for uncorrectable IO errors (EROPT)
Data set key length (KEYLEN)
Direct-access search limit in tracks (LIMCT)
Logical record length (LRECL)
Macro instruction and facilities (MACRF)
Master index location for indexed sequential (MSHI)

Number of READ or WRITE macro executions before CHECK (NCP)
Number of tracks in master index/cylinder (NTM)
Record format (RECFM)
Relative key position (RKP)
Error exit address (SYNAD)

Not all parameters must be specified by the user. In some cases, default values are assumed by the data management system when a parameter is not specified.

OPEN PROCESSING

The operations necessary for preparing a data set for processing are independent of the functions involved with preparing a program for execution. In many programs, several data sets are defined but only a few are used in any given computer run. Therefore, the convention of readying data sets for processing only when they are going to be used reduces the amount of system overhead and lessens the work load of the system operator.

A data set is readied for processing when it is opened. *Open* is a data management function executed by a routine of the operating system that performs the following functions:

1. Completes the data control block.
2. Loads the required access routines (if necessary) into the user's region (or partition).
3. Requests volume mounting.
4. Initiates data set processing by checking old labels or writing new labels and control information.
5. Constructs the system control blocks and buffers necessary for input/output processing and performs data set positioning.

Open is initiated by the execution of the OPEN macro instruction, which takes the form:

location	*operation*	*operand*
[symbol]	OPEN	(DCBaddress, . . .)

The key point is that the address of a data control block (DCB) is given which describes a data set to be opened. (The OPEN macro expands to a supervisor call instruction that invokes an OPEN routine.) This is where the DDNAME comes in. The OPEN routine searches a list of control information built by Job Management routines when the DD cards are processed to locate the corresponding data description. OPEN then performs the DCB merge suggested by Figure 6.1 to complete the DCB. After the DCB merge, the appropriate access routine is determined and loaded (if necessary). Input/output buffers are created and a channel program is created for the particular input/output operations to be used.

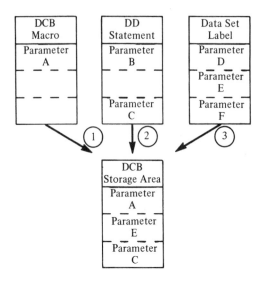

Figure 6.1 Conceptual view of the DCB merge.
(The DCB takes priority over the DD
statement which takes priority over the
data set label.)

The addresses of the access routine, the buffers, and the channel program are placed in the DCB for use during input/output processing, and in the case of queued access, an input buffer is also primed.

INPUT AND OUTPUT OPERATIONS

After a data set has been opened, it can be used in an application program. The importance of the open process cannot be over-emphasized; if a data set has not been opened, an access routine and a buffer do not exist for it, and there is no means of referencing it. Some programming languages* do not require that a data set be opened. This is misleading since the above requirements cannot be eliminated. All that happens is that the open process is performed by an input/output subroutine when the data set is accessed for the first time.

A conceptual view of program flow during an input/output operation is given in Figure 6.2. Input and output operations are processed somewhat as follows:

1. When queued access is used, the computer program includes statements, such as GET (for input) and PUT (for output). The execution of either GET or PUT causes program control to be passed to the access routine mentioned previously. The access routine initiates actual input/output

*Such as FORTRAN and PL/I.

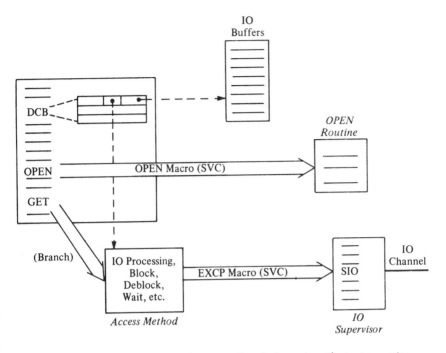

Figure 6.2 Conceptual view of program flow during an input/output operation.

processing and control is not returned to the computer program until the requested operation is logically complete.

2. When basic access is used, the computer program includes similar statements, such as READ (for input) and WRITE (for output). The execution of READ and WRITE also causes program control to be passed to an access routine. The access routine initiates input/output processing and control is returned to the computer program directly. Another statement, such as CHECK, is used to test whether the input/output operation is complete.

It should be remembered here that actual input/output instructions are privileged and can be executed only by operating system routines that execute in the supervisor state. Access routines, although they are supplied by the operating system, normally execute in the problem state. (There are several different access routines.) When an access routine needs to have an actual input or output operation performed, it causes computer control to be passed to the privileged input/output routine—usually called the "input/output supervisor."

CLOSE PROCESSING

When input/output processing is complete, a data set must be closed. The close operation (initiated with the CLOSE macro) empties input/output buffers, completes the data set label, and handles the disposition of the data set. CLOSE also restores the DCB to its original state so that it can be used again.

ACCESS METHODS

The characteristics of a data set as described in the DCB determine the access method that is assigned during open processing. An access method is the combination of data set organization and the technique used to access the data.

The *queued access* technique provides automatic blocking and deblocking on data transfers between storage and input/output devices. Queued access also provides look-ahead buffering and automatic synchronization of input/output operation and computer processing. The access method routine controls the use of buffers such that sufficient input blocks are in main storage at one time to prevent processing delay. The GET macro instruction is used for input and the PUT macro instruction is used for output. When using queued access, the user need not test for input/output completion, errors, or exceptional conditions. After the execution of a GET or PUT macro instruction, control is not returned to the application program until the operation is logically complete. Buffering techniques are discussed in the next section.

The *basic access* technique does not provide automatic blocking and deblocking; neither does it provide anticipatory buffering or automatic event synchronization. Basic access is used when the sequence in which records are processed cannot be predicted in advance. With the basic access technique the application program must perform its own blocking and deblocking. The READ macro instruction is used for input and the WRITE macro instruction is used for output. READ and WRITE macros only initiate input/output processing; both operations must be checked for completion with the CHECK macro. In other words, automatic event synchronization is not provided.

The access techniques are combined with data set organization to determine access methods. The basic access technique is used with all forms of data set organization; queued access is used only with sequential and indexed sequential organization. Six access methods are given in the following list and summarized in Table 6.2:

Basic Sequential Access Method (BSAM)
Basic Partitioned Access Method (BPAM)
Basic Index Sequential Access Method (BISAM)
Basic Direct Access Method (BDAM)
Queued Sequential Access Method (QSAM)
Queued Indexed Sequential Access Method (QISAM)

The processing of each of the above access methods is performed by a distinct access method routine; however, all users of the data management system use the same routines. Each routine uses the data set description in the DCB to determine the input/output processing that must be performed.

TABLE 6.2   ACCESS METHODS

Data Set Organization	Data Access Techniques	
	Basic	Queued
Sequential	BSAM	QSAM
Partitioned	BPAM	
Indexed sequential	BISAM	QISAM
Direct	BDAM	

BUFFERING

A *buffer* is a storage area used to compensate for a difference in operating speeds of two physical devices. In the case of data management in an operating system environment, an *input buffer* is an area of storage used to hold input blocks prior to processing. Similarly, an output buffer is an area of storage used to hold blocks prior to the output operation.

A collection of contiguous buffers is termed a *buffer pool*, which can be assigned to a single data set or to a group of data sets. A buffer pool is constructed in one of three ways:

1. By creating the necessary storage area in the processing program and by executing a macro instruction that effectively connects the buffer pool to the appropriate data set(s).
2. By executing a macro instruction that requests that the operating system create the buffer pool.
3. By letting the operating system create the buffer pool automatically when the data set is opened.

When *basic access* is used, buffers are controlled and used in two ways:

1. A buffer is obtained *directly* from a buffer pool with a macro instruction. That buffer is subsequently used with a READ or WRITE operation.
2. A buffer is obtained *dynamically* by requesting a buffer with the READ or WRITE macro instruction.

When *queued access* is used, buffering achieves its greatest utility. Two transmittal modes are covered:

1. *Move mode*—the record is moved to the application program's work area or from the work area to an output buffer.
2. *Locate mode*—the record is not moved but the address of the buffer holding the input record is placed in a general-purpose register (for input) or the address of the next output buffer is placed in a general-purpose register (for output).

The move and locate modes are referred to as *simple buffering,* because the buffers in a buffer pool are associated with a single data set. A channel command*
is associated with each buffer so that both input and output cannot be performed from the same buffer; thus, each data record must be moved from an
input buffer to an output buffer, etc. Processing can be performed in either
buffer or in a work area.   Four cases of simple buffering are identified:
GET(move)/PUT(move),   GET(locate)/PUT(locate),   GET(locate)/PUT(move),
GET(move)/PUT(locate).

   GET(move)/PUT(move) is depicted in Figure 6.3. The GET macro instruction
specifies the address of a work area into which the access method moves the
next record from the input buffer. The PUT macro specifies the address of a
work area from which the access method moves the output record into the next
output buffer.   *GET(locate)/PUT(move)* is depicted in Figure 6.4.   The GET

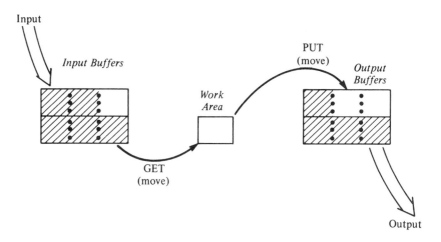

Figure 6.3   Simple buffering—GET(move)/PUT(move).

macro locates the next input record in the input buffer. (The address is passed
in a general-purpose register.) The PUT macro specifies the address of the output record (usually in an input buffer) from which the access method moves the
output record into the next output buffer. *GET(move)/PUT(locate)* is depicted
in Figure 6.5. The preceding PUT macro locates the address of the next available output buffer. (The address is passed in a general-purpose register.) The
GET macro specifies the address of the next output buffer into which the access
method moves the next record from the input buffer. *GET(locate)/PUT(locate)*
is depicted in Figure 6.6. The preceding PUT macro locates the address of the
next available output buffer. The GET macro locates the next input record in

*The channel command specifies an input/output operation, such as read or write.

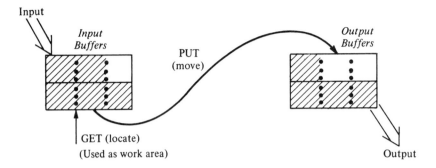

Figure 6.4   Simple buffering—GET(locate)/PUT(move).

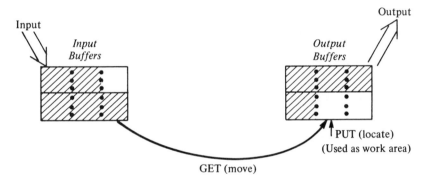

Figure 6.5   Simple buffering—GET(move)/PUT(locate).

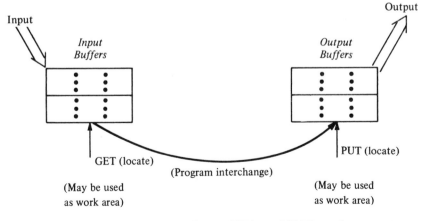

Figure 6.6   Simple buffering—GET(locate)/PUT(locate).

an input buffer. The processing program moves the data from the input buffer to the output buffer. Processing can be performed in either buffer.

Other buffering techniques exist. One of the most popular is *exchange buffering* in which buffers are not necessarily contiguous in storage and are not always assigned to the same data set. One of the primary advantages of exchange buffering is that the need to move a record for input or output, as required, is not necessary. The reader is directed to the references for detailed information on exchange buffering.

INDEXED SEQUENTIAL ACCESS METHOD

The indexed sequential method of data organization is of special concern since it allows the data set to be processed directly or sequentially. Records can be inserted or deleted, and basic or queued access can be used. The defining characteristic of an indexed sequential data set is that the records are arranged, by collating sequence, according to a *key field* contained in each record. Indexes of keys are maintained to provide direct or sequential access.

An indexed sequential data set must reside on a direct-access storage volume. Just like any other data set, it possesses a data set control block stored in the volume table of contents (VTOC) for that volume. Each indexed sequential data set can use three different storage areas:

1. The *prime area* contains data records and track indexes. The prime area is always used.
2. The *overflow area* contains overflow from the prime area when new records are added to the data set. Use of the overflow area is optional.
3. The *index area* contains master and cylinder indexes for the data set and is used when the data set occupies more than one cylinder.

The access to records is managed through indexes. When records are written in the prime area, the system keeps record of the highest key (i.e., the last record) for each track and forms a track index—one entry per track. There is a track index for each cylinder of the data set. If the data set occupies more than one cylinder, then a *cylinder index* exists for each cylinder; each entry in the cylinder index reflects the key of the last record in the cylinder. A *master index* is developed for groups of cylinders to increase the speed of searching the cylinder index. An indexed sequential data set is depicted conceptually in Figure 6.7.

The *track index* contains one entry for each track of a cylinder. Each track index entry includes a normal entry and an overflow entry. Initially, the normal and overflow entries are the same. When an overflow is associated with a track (due to an insert operation), the overflow entry contains the key to the highest overflow record and the address of the lowest overflow record associated with that track. A track index is generated automatically for each cylinder.

As each track index is generated, the data management system creates a

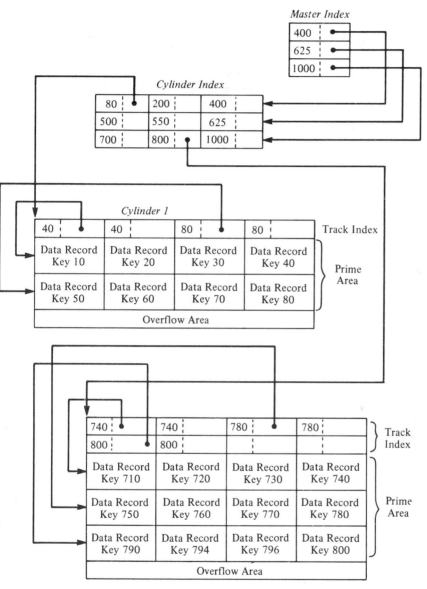

Figure 6.7   Conceptual view of indexed sequential data set organization.

cylinder index entry. If more than one cylinder index entry is created, then a *cylinder index* is formed. The *master index* is usually optional; the user can specify the number of tracks of the cylinder index that correspond to the master index entry.

As far as access is concerned, both queued and basic are defined. The queued index sequential access method (QISAM) is used to create an indexed sequential data set and add records to the end. The basic indexed sequential access method (BISAM) is used to insert new records, update old records, and access records directly. Both QISAM and BISAM are used to access the data set sequentially. QISAM is more efficient when large amounts of data are being read sequentially. Blocked records are permitted and the system automatically precedes each block with the key of the last record (i.e., with the highest key) in the block.

COMMENT

There is considerably more to input and output processing in a data management environment than the topics covered in this chapter. First, all possible options and facilities have not been presented. Second, special conditions, such as error processing, have not been mentioned. Lastly, the details of input/output processing have been subordinated to the routines of the data management system. Obviously, concepts are more important, at this stage, than details; however, the reader should be cautioned against thinking that data management is any less complicated than it is.

REFERENCES

IBM System/360 Operating System, *Supervisor and Data Management Services,* White Plains, N.Y., IBM Corporation, Form GC28–6646.

Katzan, H., Operating Systems: *A Pragmatic Approach*, New York, Van Nostrand Reinhold Company, 1973.

7 | INPUT AND OUTPUT SUPERVISION

INTRODUCTION

Thus far, the discussion of data management has centered around the user and the functions that the data management system performs for him. The user defines his data sets through the DD statement in the job control language and in the data control block (DCB) that is built into his program and serves as the communications link with the data management routines. The user performs input and output processing with macro instructions such as READ and WRITE or GET and PUT. Data management routines maintain the catalog, provide device assignment, allocate storage on direct-access storage volumes, and handle input and output operations. It does this in addition to a variety of other functions, such as input/output error processing. Input and output processing is handled by an access method routine of the data management system. The access method initiates physical input and output operations and performs blocking/deblocking and buffering as required. This chapter is concerned with the processing that takes place in the input/output supervisor in performing the physical input/output operations required by the access methods.

The methodology and terminology reflect that used with the OS/MVT* operating system. However, the presentation is sufficiently general so that it could apply to practically any general-purpose operating system that uses multiprogramming. The next section gives a brief description of an operating system—

*OS/MVT is an acronym for *Operating System/Multiprogramming with a Variable Number of Tasks.*

namely OS/MVT. The objective is to establish terminology that is used in subsequent sections.

OPERATING SYSTEM ENVIRONMENT

OS/MVT is a general-purpose operating system designed to support multiprogramming, data management facilities, teleprocessing, and multiprocessing over a wide range of operational environments. OS/MVT (usually referred to as simply OS) is composed of control programs and processing programs. Control programs are classed as Task Management, Job Management, and Data Management, all of which have been covered earlier. Processing programs include language processors, user programs, and utility programs.

OS uses the variable-sized "region" concept for storage allocation. Depending upon program size requirements and job priority, each job is assigned a region in storage in which it is constrained to operate. Each region is assigned a different storage protection key for protection, with the master key being assigned to the "Supervisor." Several jobs can occupy the storage unit of the computer at one time. The job steps that comprise a job are executed sequentially in the user's region.

To the user and to computer operations personnel, a unit of work is the job. To the Supervisor,* a unit of work is a task. More specifically, a *task* is an independent unit of work that can compete for the resources of the computer system. Usually, the program that constitutes a job step executes as a task. However, tasks can "spawn" subtasks and some functions of the operating system execute as system tasks. Associated with each task in the system is a *task control block* (TCB) that is an area of storage containing control information for that task. Typical task control information might be the old status word from when the task was last in execution, the general-purpose and floating point registers, task priority, and the address of the area of storage assigned to the task.

The TCBs are arranged by priority** on a *task queue* that is implemented as a linked list. Each task represented on the task queue is in one of the following states: in execution, ready for execution, or waiting for an event to occur.† When the Supervisor allocates control of the processing unit to a task, it chooses the first TCB on the task queue that is in the ready state.

An important consideration is event synchronization. In a multiprogramming system, events take place asynchronously and a task frequently has to wait for event completion in order that execution can continue. Synchronization is achieved through an *event control block* (ECB)‡ that is inspected by an appropriate macro instruction. As a result of an interruption, an ECB may be

---

*Task Management routines are referred to as the "Supervisor."
**Priority (or more precisely, internal priority) is a function of external priority and arrival sequence.
†Typical events might be input/output completion or the termination of an asynchronous task.
‡The event control block is simply a computer word in which selected bits are set.

set to "complete" by the Supervisor. Therefore, when the task inspecting that ECB is next given control of the processing unit, execution can continue past the point of synchronization.

SYSTEM ORGANIZATION

Control program and storage organization are closely related. Task Management routines* (the Supervisor) execute in the supervisor state and the most frequently used of these routines are resident in storage at all times. The other routines are loaded when needed. Job Management routines provide communication facilities between the user and the remainder of the operating system and operate as system tasks. Job Management routines execute in the problem state and operate out of a user's region or are shared among users of the system and reside in a specially designated area of storage (called the "link pack area"). Data Management routines, except for access methods, execute in the supervisor state and execute out of one of the following areas: "SVC transient area," "link pack area," or the user's region. Access method routines execute in the problem state and reside in the user's region or the "link pack area."**

During system initialization prior to execution (called IPL for *initial program load* four storage areas are established:

1. The *fixed area* contains the resident portion of the Supervisor called the *nucleus.* Two transient areas are embedded in the nucleus: the supervisor call (SVC) transient area and the IO Supervisor transient area. These transient areas are used by nonresident routines that process SVC instructions and nonresident IO error handling routines, respectively.
2. The *system queue area* supplies storage for queues and tables that are built by the Supervisor during operation of the system. The system queue area is a fixed-size area of storage adjacent to the fixed area.
3. The *link pack area* contains routines used by any task that requires them. The link pack area is located in upper storage and is loaded during initial program load.
4. The *dynamic area* is used for job steps and system tasks. The dynamic area extends from the system queue area to the link pack area and is allocated in blocks of 2048 bytes. As a task is accepted by the Supervisor as a unit of work, it is assigned a section of contiguous storage in the dynamic area called a *region.*

System organization is depicted in Figure 7.1.

---

*Recall here that Task Management performs the following functions on a system-wide basis: interruption handling, task supervision, storage allocation, contents supervision, timer management, input/output supervision, and the processing of exceptional and error conditions.
**The reader will have to bear with us here. It is impossible to present system organization without mentioning storage areas. They are covered next.

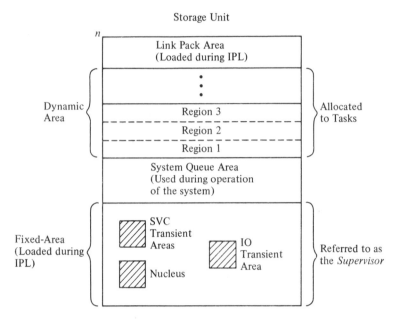

Figure 7.1   System organization.

SYSTEM OPERATION

It is difficult to separate the structure of the Supervisor from its method of operation. As mentioned previously, the system is interrupt driven. This means that all Supervisor processing begins with an interruption. (Recall here the five types of interruption: supervisor call, external, input/output, program, and machine check.) The overall flow of the Supervisor is as follows:

1. A task is executing.
2. An interruption occurs.
3. A new status word is loaded and a Supervisor routine is given control of the processing unit.
4. The interruption is analyzed.
5. The requested service or required action is performed.
6. The processing unit is dispatched to a task.

The general flow of system operation is depicted in Figure 7.2.

The Supervisor is organized according to the functions that it performs. When an interruption is accepted by the processing unit, it is initially processed by a First Level Interruption Handler (FLIH). The FLIH determines if the routine for processing that interruption is in storage; if so, control is passed directly to

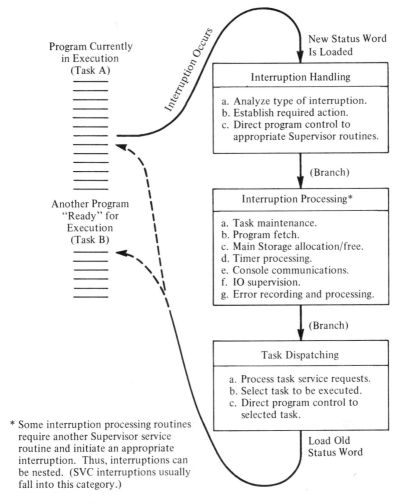

Figure 7.2 Flow of interruption processing.

that routine. This method of operation is suggested by Figure 7.3, which gives the modular flow of the Supervisor. If the routine for processing the interruption is not resident, then control is passed to a Second Level Interruption Handler (SLIH) to bring the needed routine into one of the transient areas. If the Supervisor must wait for the needed routine to be brought into storage, then control is frequently passed to the Dispatcher to give the processing unit a ready task until the needed routine can be read in. The general structure of the Supervisor is suggested by Figure 7.3.

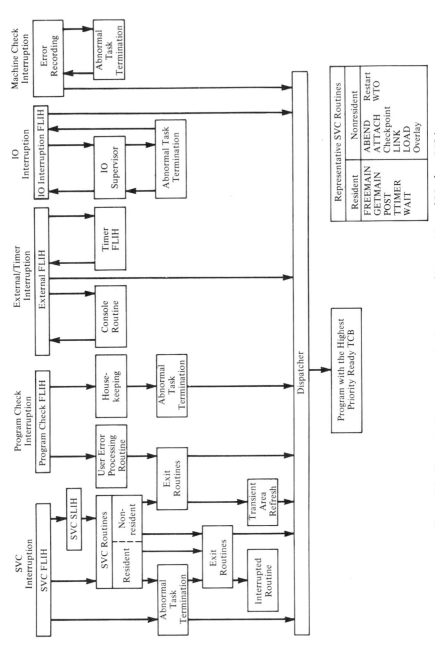

Figure 7.3 Operational structure of the Supervisor. (Adapted from [OSm], p. 348.)

INPUT AND OUTPUT PROCESSING

Input/output processing can be done with an access method or without an access method. When an access method is used, the user must supply a data control block (DCB), and he initiates input or output with a macro instruction such as READ and WRITE or GET and PUT. Execution of one of these macro instructions passes control to an access method routine that resides in the user's region or in the link pack area. The access method then handles the input/output processing for the processing program. A processing program is logically connected to an access method when a data set is opened. In addition to completing the data control block (DCB), the open routine also constructs a data extent block (DEB) for each DCB opened. The DEB is a logical extension to the DCB; it contains information on the volume location data set boundaries and access method, and points to the unit control block (UCB) for the associated input/ output device. (The UCB is introduced a little later.) The DEB is constructed in the system queue area and is chained to the TCB for the task. The access method provides an input/output "control" block (IOB—which is also introduced briefly), buffers, and a channel program to the Input/Output Supervisor and it initiates input/output requests with the EXCP macro instruction.

When an access method is not used in an application program, the user must create his own buffers, input/output "control" block, and channel program; however, an EXCP macro may be used in an application program in the same manner it is used in an access method.*

The execute channel program (EXCP) macro instruction is assembled as a supervisor call (SVC) instruction that specifies the address of the IOB for a particular input/output request. The resultant SVC interruption is handled by the SVC interruption handler that passes control to the Input/Output Supervisor.

When the Input/Output Supervisor receives control, it first verifies the correctness of the control blocks it has to use. The Input/Output Supervisor then constructs a "request element" that includes the addresses of the IOB, DEB, and the UCB, as well as control information about the channel program. The "request element" facilitates access to the control blocks since some effort is involved in determining their actual addresses. (More specifically, the Input/Output Supervisor locates the DCB from the IOB, locates the DEB from the DCB, and locates the UCB from the DEB.) If the channel or device (specified in the IOB) is busy, the request element is placed in a request element table and an exit is made to the processing program. If the channel and device are free, the Input/Output Supervisor initiates the requested input/output operation and control is returned to the processing program.

---

*Thus, to the Supervisor, it is immaterial where the EXCP is issued.

CONTROL BLOCKS AND TABLES

Because CPU processing and input/output processing operate asynchronously and because several input/output operations can be in progress concurrently, control information is stored in control blocks and tables. The control blocks and tables are used to initiate an input/output operation, to associate an interruption with a particular input/output operation, and to handle input/output error conditions.

Five control blocks are used during input/output processing: (1) input/output block (IOB), (2) data control block (DCB), (3) data extent block (DEB), (4) event control block (ECB), and (5) unit control block (UCB). The logical relationship between control blocks is given in Figure 7.4. The *input/output block* (IOB) is used for communication between the routine that issues the EXCP macro and the Input/Output Supervisor. (The address of the IOB is passed with the SVC instruction.) The IOB contains the address of the channel program, a storage area for a channel status word (provided by the Input/Output Supervisor upon input/output completion), the initial seek address for a direct-access storage device, the addresses of the DCB and ECB, and other control information. The *data control block* (DCB) contains data management information, the address of the DEB, and information on error procedures. The *data extent block* (DEB) supplements the DCB and contains information on the volume, data set, boundaries, and access method. The DEB points to the UCB. One DEB exists for each DCB. The *event control block* (ECB) is used by the Input/Output

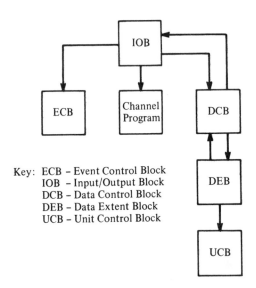

Figure 7.4 Relationship between input/output control blocks.

Supervisor to record the completion of an input/output operation. The ECB is pointed to by the IOB. The *unit control block* (UCB) describes an input/output channel and device. It contains the channel and device addresses, the device type, flag bits, and an area for sense information, table references, and a work area for error recovery. The UCB points to the request element for an input/output operation. One UCB exists per input/output device; it is built when the operating system is synthesized.

Seven tables are identified: (1) UCB lookup table, (2) channel table, (3) device table, (4) statistics table, (5) attention table, (6) request element table, and (7) logical channel word table. The *UCB lookup table* contains the addresses of the UCBs in the system. When an input/output interruption occurs or when an input/output operation is to be started, the supervisor determines the UCB that represents the input/output device from this table. The *channel table* is used to locate a channel search module for a given channel. A channel search module exists for each type of channel and is used to locate channel queues of request elements. The channel table is used to start input/output operations that are "queued up."

The *device table* is used to locate device-dependent routines which initiate input/output operations on a specific device. The *statistics table* is used to record input/output error statistics. The statistics table contains an entry for each device attached to the system. The *attention table* is used to locate routines that process "attention" conditions for input/output devices. This table is built when the operating system is synthesized. The *request element table* contains request elements that represent input/output operations. Each request element contains: UCB, DEB, IOB, and TCB addresses and the priority of the request.

The *logical channel word table* contains an entry for each logical channel queue in the system. (The set of all physical channel paths to a single device is called a *logical channel*. Through input/output switching, an input/output device can be connected to one of several physical channels.) Each logical channel word points to the first and last request element for each logical channel queue. Each logical channel possesses a *logical channel queue* that is used to represent input/output operations that are awaiting execution. A logical channel queue is composed of request elements.

In general, the Input/Output Supervisor calls upon routines to do its processing. Whenever a routine is needed for a special purpose, its address is determined from one of the above tables, depending upon the existing conditions. The control blocks and tables are also used to associate an input/output interruption with a particular input/output operation and to initiate input/output operations.

OPERATION OF THE INPUT/OUTPUT SUPERVISOR

The Input/Output Supervisor resides in the nucleus; its primary function is to manage input/output operations on a system-wide basis. The Input/Output

Supervisor executes in the supervisor state and issues privileged input/output instructions. The Input/Output Supervisor performs two major functions:

1. It handles input/output requests.
2. It handles input/output interruptions.

To perform these functions, the Input/Output Supervisor is divided into an "EXCP Supervisor" and an "Input/Output Supervisor." During their operation, these routines use the Input/Output Supervisor transient area and the SVC transient area for non-resident routines.

The *EXCP Supervisor* receives control from the SVC interruption handler (see Figure 7.3) and its primary function is to initiate execution of the channel program that performs the required input/output operations. The EXCP supervisor is comprised of three sections:

1. *Test channel* section that determines if a channel is available for the input/output device that is to be used with an input/output operation.
2. *Enqueue and dequeue* section that queues input/output requests that cannot be started. After an input/output operation is started, the request is removed from the queue.
3. *Start input/output* section that initiates an input/output operation on a given channel and device.

The EXCP Supervisor operates as follows:

1. A validity check routine checks the control blocks and performs initialization of the IOB.
2. A request element is constructed for the input/output operation.
3. The UCBs for the device are inspected to see if the device is available.
4. A test channel routine is entered to obtain a physical channel to the device. (The test channel routine is located via the logical channel word table.)
5. A start input/output module is selected for execution by means of the device table and control is passed to it.
6. Control is passed by means of the SVC exit routine to the dispatcher.
7. If the input/output operation cannot be started, then the request element is queued on the logical channel queue and control is passed to the dispatcher.

The *Input/Output Interruption Supervisor* receives control from the input/output interruption handler (see Figure 7.3). The objective of the Input/Output Interruption Supervisor is to analyze input/output interruptions, post input/output completions, initiate queued input/output requests, and process error conditions. The Input/Output Interruption Supervisor is composed of two sections:

1. *Channel search* section searches channel queues for the next input/output

request. Channel search is activated when one input/output operation is completed and another can be initiated.

2. *Trapcode* section provides information on an input/output operation and an input/output device after an input/output interruption associated with that device has been received.

The Input/Output Interruption Supervisor operates as follows:

1. The address of the UCB for the channel or device from which the interruption was received is determined by means of the UCB lookup table.
2. The status bits stored with the input/output interruption are analyzed to determine the processing required.
3. If the interruption is to record input/output completion, then the ECB for that IO request is posted.
4. The channel queues are searched for an input/output operation that can be started on the channel that is made available by the interruption.
5. If a request element if found for that channel, that input/output operation is started and an exit is made to the dispatcher, as described below.
6. If no request element for that channel is available, then the Input/Output Interruption Supervisor exits to the dispatcher.

The Input/Output Supervisor executes with all interruptions (except for machine check disabled. After an input/output interruption has been processed and before the Input/Output Interruption Supervisor exits to the dispatcher, two ckecks are made:

1. A channel search is made to see if a channel can be started for a stacked input/output operation. If so, a channel restart procedure is executed.
2. Input/output interruptions are enabled to test for input/output interruptions that may have been stacked during the input/output processing.

If no interruptions are pending, then input/output interruptions are again disabled and the Input/Output Supervisor returns to the dispatcher. Figure 7.5 depicts the overall flow of the Input/Output Supervisor and Figure 7.6 gives a simplified walkthrough of input and output processing.

Other conditions arise as input/output interruptions. When an attention condition is received for a particular device, the attention table is used to locate an attention routine for that device. After an appropriate attention routine has completed execution, it returns to the Input/Output Supervisor. The statistics table is used in a similar manner. This table contains an entry for each input/output device attached to the system. Each entry can contain a variety of counters to record occurrences such as read errors, write errors, and equipment checks. The statistics table is used by system error routines to maintain error records for later recall and analysis.

The EXCP Supervisor and the Input/Output Interruption Supervisor are con-

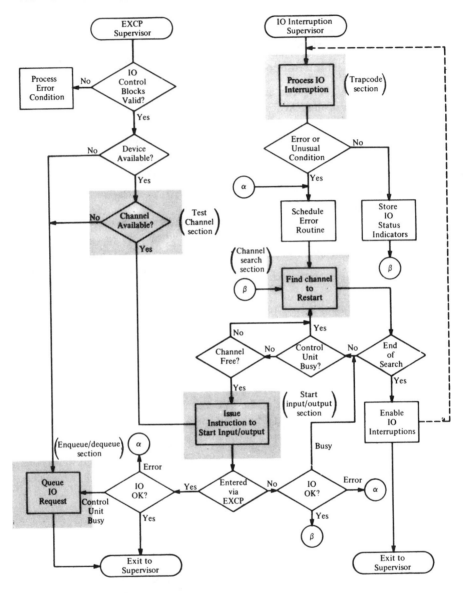

Figure 7.5 Overall flow of the Input/Output Supervisor.

siderably more complicated than described here. However, the overall flow of input/output operations is most important, and extensive detail, which certainly exists in the case of input and output, tends to obscure the concepts involved. In addition, a significant amount of input and output processing at the supervisor level is machine dependent, and as such, is not appropriate for general study.

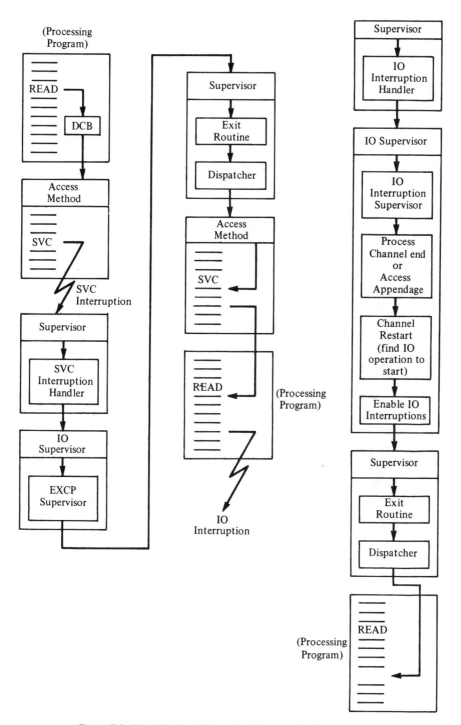

Figure 7.6 Simplified walkthrough of input and output processing.

REFERENCES

Clark, W. A., "The function structure of OS/360: Part III. Data Management," *IBM Systems Journal,* Volume 5, No. 1 (1966), pp. 30–51.

IBM System/360 Operating System, *Input/Output Supervisor Program Logic Manual,* White Plains, N.Y., IBM Corporation, Form GY28-6616.

Katzan, H., *Operating Systems: A Pragmatic Approach,* New York, Van Nostrand Reinhold Company, 1973.

Mealy, G. H., "The functional structure of OS/360: Part I. Introductory survey," *IBM Systems Journal,* Volume 5, No. 1 (1966), pp. 3–11.

8 | FILE ORGANIZATION CONCEPTS

FILE OPERATIONS AND ACCESSIBILITY

A *file* is a set of related records. The relationship between the records exists at two levels: the structural level and the content level. The structural characteristics of a file govern how the storage elements in the file are organized and how they can be accessed. The content of a file is determined by its user; although records can have different formats, the data records stored within a file are usually stored for a common purpose.

Collectively, the processes involved in utilizing a file are referred to as *file operations* that can be grouped as follows:

1. Operations that utilize the information content of the records that comprise the file—other than key fields.
2. Operations that are performed on the records of a file that do not involve the information content of the records—other than the key fields.

File operations in the first category are known as *file processes*. In a file process, two general operations are performed: (1) the file is transformed, or (2) the file is altered. *Transformation operations* generate new files, reports, special output such as bank checks, etc. *Alteration operations* change the information content of records that comprise the file.

The subset of records of a file upon which a file process is defined is referred to as the *domain* of the process. A domain is isolated by a file operation known as *searching*, which can be performed in a separate pass over the file or be integrated into the file processing operation. Searching is sometimes known as a *selection operation*—an operation that selects records that satisfy a given criteria. Clearly, selection does not use the information content of a record and falls into the second category given above. Other file operations that can be placed in this category are sorting, merging, collating, inserting, and deleting.

The objective of file organization is to permit file operation to be performed as efficiently as possible. One measure of efficiency is "accessibility," defined by C. T. Meadow.* *Accessibility* is a relative measure that can be used to compare file organization methods for a given application. An *accessibility index*, *a*, is defined as:

$$a = \frac{A}{A+R} = 1 - \frac{R}{A+R}$$

where A is the record access time and R is the record read time. The accessibility index ranges from zero to almost one. A sequential file processing operation using magnetic tape would have an accessibility index of zero—denoting that the access time is zero and there is no delay in reading. A random file operation on magnetic tape, on the other hand, might require a lengthy sequential file search and a negligible read time. Similar examples can be obtained for direct-access storage. When records are not accessed with equal probability, the "expected access time" (E) may be useful. The *expected access time* is the weighted average of the set of possible access times and is computed as follows:

$$E = \sum_{i=1}^{n} p_i A_i$$

where A_i is the access time for record i that is selected with probability p_i, and the number of records in the file is n. In this case, the accessibility index becomes:

$$a = \frac{E}{E+R} = 1 - \frac{R}{E+R}$$

Clearly, accessibility is a general measure used during the design phase of system development. The best method of evaluating the effectiveness of a file system is to collect and analyze actual performance data.

FILE SEQUENCE

The manner in which records are sequenced within a file determines the applications for which the file is appropriate and how efficiently these applications execute. Meadow** identifies four methods:

**C. T. Meadow, *The Analysis of Information Systems*, New York, John Wiley and Sons, Inc., 1967, p. 177.*
**Ibid., p. 185.

1. Random.
2. Sorted.
3. Relative random.
4. Partially ordered.

The methods are generally independent of the technique used for storage organization and we are concerned solely with the relative position of records with respect to each other.

Random sequence denotes that the records of a file have no sequential relationship to each other. If we have a file of payroll records in which an employee's name serves as the record identifier, locating Mr. Smith's record, for example, could involve a search of the complete file. If Mr. Smith's record were not contained in the file, determining that fact would necessarily involve an exhaustive search of all of the records that comprise the file.

Files are usually sequenced by an identifying field called a *sort key* (also referred to as a *retrieval key* or simply a *key*) and the file sequence is said to be *sorted*. The order in which records are sequenced by the sort key is referred to as *collating sequence*, which is governed to some extent by the bit patterns of the characters involved. For obvious reasons, a certain amount of standardization exists with regard to collating sequence. The use of sorted files is mandatory for most file operations. In particular, the sequential search operation can be aborted when a key higher in collating sequence than the one desired is encountered. The use of sorted files also permits sophisticated search techniques to be employed. Files are frequently ordered on the basis of two or more sort keys, wherein subordinate keys are used for relative positioning when the superordinate sequencing fields have the same values.

Frequently, it is necessary to search a sorted file on a field other than the sort key. An example might be the search of the telephone directory for subscribers that reside on Main Street. Clearly, the file is ordered but that ordering does not help with the search process. With regard to this type of file operation, the file is said to be in *relative random order*.

When a sorted file is searched on a subordinate sort key, the file is *partially ordered* with respect to that file operation. Consider, for example, an equipment file on a computer manufacturer that is sequenced by the following fields in the given order:

Customer name
Name of component
Model of component

Figure 8.1 depicts an instance of this equipment file. Assume the file is to be searched for all "CPU" records. The search would begin with each customer name (i.e., occurrence of the primary key), terminate temporarily with the first component name greater in collating sequence than "CPU," and resume again with the next customer name. Clearly, the search operation is not as inefficient

ABC Corp.	CPU	2085
ABC Corp.	Storage	3620
ABC Corp.	Disk	2311
ABC Corp.	Disk	2319
BEL Corp.	CPU	3135
BEL Corp.	CPU	3145
BEL Corp.	Storage	3160
BEL Corp.	Storage	3260
BEL Corp.	Tape	2460
CEK Corp.	Disk	3330
CEK Corp.	Tape	2460
CEK Corp.	Printer	3220
HLT Corp.	CPU	2085

Figure 8.1   An ordered file searched by a subordinate sort key (CPU). For this file operation, it is a partially ordered file.

as it would be if the file were in random or relative random order, and it is not as efficient as it would be if the file were sorted on the "name of equipment" field.

FILE ORGANIZATION METHODS

File organization methods are closely related to the methods of storage organization introduced in earlier chapters. Three methods are in general use:

1. Sequential organization.
2. Random organization.
3. List organization.

With *sequential organization*, the records in a file are sequenced by a key field and are stored using consecutive organization. Sequential organization is not the same as sequential access. A sequentially organized file must be accessed sequentially; however, a file need not be organized sequentially to be accessed sequentially. A case in point is the indexed sequential data set, mentioned previously, that can be accessed sequentially or directly. One of the major advantages of sequential organization is that the access mechanism is automatically positioned to access the next record. Operational difficulties are encountered with sequential organization when records must be altered, deleted, or inserted. When sequential media is used, the file must be copied to another volume with the modifications being made as required. With direct-access media, records can be altered provided that the altered record is not shorter or longer than the original. Performing update operations on files with blocked records is also a problem since the entire block must be rewritten.

With *random organization*, records are accessed through the physical location of the record or through a mathematical transformation on the key that produces the address of where the record is stored. Dodd* identifies three methods of accessing files with random organization:

1. Direct address.
2. Dictionary look-up.
3. Calculation.

Using the *direct address* technique, the physical location of the record on direct-access storage is known to the application program and it is supplied with a store or retrieve operation. With the *dictionary look-up* technique, keyed storage organization is employed, as in the indexed sequential access method, and the index (or dictionary, as it is frequently called) contains the key and the physical direct-access location of the corresponding record. The primary advantage of the dictionary look-up technique is that the file can be accessed directly or sequentially; however, the time spent in searching the index for a key value may offset some of the advantages of using random organization.

The *calculation* technique involves converting the key to a physical direct-access address that is not necessarily unique. The calculation technique is often referred to as a randomizing technique, and is discussed in detail in a subsequent section of this chapter. The direct-address and dictionary look-up methods always provide a unique record address, whereas the calculation method does not. What this means is that two or more keys can randomize to the same address so that a randomly organized file must always include the facility for pointer fields and overflow records. The "direct address" in a randomly organized file can be a physical cylinder-head address** or relative track number (relative to the beginning of the storage volume) that is translated by the data management system into a cylinder-head address. On the average, the accessibility of a "randomly selected" record† using random organization is relatively low compared to sequential organization, since preceding records in the file do not have to be "passed over."

A *list organized file* employs linked storage organization to chain together the records that comprise the file. The records do not necessarily reside in contiguous tracks; however, the tracks are located in extents assigned to the file. The chaining (or linking) of records is achieved through pointer fields that are contained in each record. Thus, the records that comprise a list organized file can be ordered on any field in the record; the only restriction, obviously, is that a pointer field must exist in each record for each logical ordering in which it

---

*G. G. Dodd, "Elements of data management systems," *Computing Surveys*, volume 1, No. 2 (June 1969), p. 120.

**The cylinder concept is in widespread use. An alternate means of referencing a location on direct-access storage is by track number and head number.

†That is, random or direct access.

participates as a member record. For example, consider a "part inventory" file in which each record contains the following fields:

> Part #
> Name of part
> Engineering drawing #
> Warehouse location
> Assembly in which the part is used

Figure 8.2 depicts a file in which three lists pass through each record: one list ordered by part #, another list ordered by part name, and the third list ordered by engineering drawing #. In the figure, the pointers are unidirectional for each list. Depending upon the needs of a particular application, they could also be bidirectional as described in chapter four. The advantages of list organization are significant: (1) a record updated as part of one list is automatically updated for all lists in which it participates as a member, (2) records

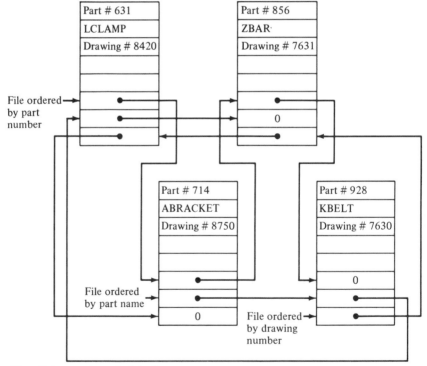

Key: 0 denotes the end of the list.

Figure 8.2 Parts inventory file using list organization, and ordered in three ways.

can be inserted and deleted with a minimum of processing, and (3) a record can be accessed directly if its direct address is known. The disadvantages of list organization are that the accessibility index is high and file operations, especially searching, are time consuming because of the separate accesses involved.

A list structure in the storage unit must be anchored and that location is known as the *head of the list*. The same function is performed in a list organized file by "master record" or by a "descriptor record"; clearly, a master record must exist for each ordering in which the records of the file participate as a member. A list structure that contains at least one element that is also a list is referred to as a *compound list*. For example, Figure 8.3 gives a compound list

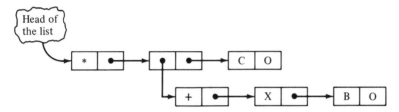

Figure 8.3 A compound list representing the expression (X+B)*C in prefix notation.

representing the expression (X+B)*C in prefix notation. A file organized in this manner is said to have a tree structure, as suggested by the file structure given in Figure 8.4, this is a method of organizing data based on its hierarchical structure.

RING STRUCTURES

A *ring structure* is a generalization of the list organization in which the last record in a chain points back to the first record or to the master record. The use of ring structures allows the records in a ring to be processed and to branch off and process logically-related records. Figure 8.5 depicts a policy file, implemented using list organization, in which claim records that belong to a particular policy are represented as a ring structure. Similarly, action records for a particular claim are also represented as a ring structure. Figure 8.5 additionally shows the flexibility of list organization with a distinct claim file composed of claim records.

With list organization and ring structures, the number of chain (or pointer) fields in a record are determined as follows:

1. One chain field for each list organized file in which the record participates, and two chain fields if the list is bidirectional.

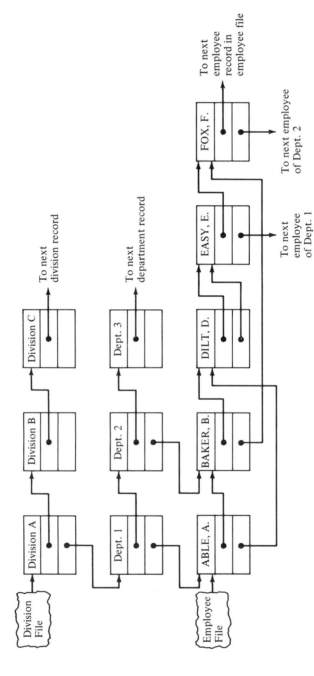

Figure 8.4   Tree structured file and its relationship to a sequential file.

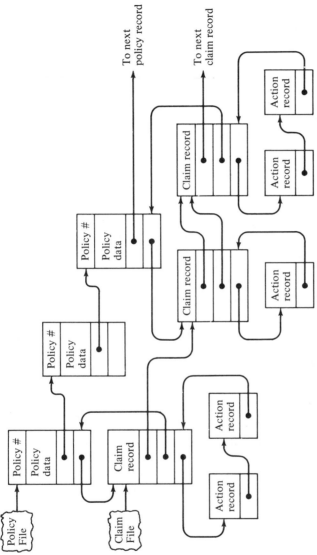

Figure 8.5   Policy and claim files using list organization with the use of ring structures to associate claim and action records with policy and claim records, respectively.

2. One chain field for each ring structure for which the record serves as a master record.

3. One chain field for each ring structure of which the record is a member.

Because ring structures are relatively short in terms of the number of records that participate, and because a ring can be traversed until the appropriate record is reached, record insertion at arbitrary points is less cumbersome without bidirectional pointers than "open ended" list structures.

RANDOMIZING TECHNIQUES

Randomizing techniques are used with random file organization where the address of a record is calculated. For files in which an actual record is expected to exist for each possible key value, the required storage for the file is simply the record size multiplied by the number of possible keys. Access to a record requires only a multiplication of the key value by the record size and the addition of a constant to obtain the record address. This method is known as the *direct multiplication transform*. For files in which the ratio of the number of actual records to the number of possible keys (known as the *loading factor*) is .5 or less, the direct multiplication transform is wasteful of storage space. Thus, randomizing techniques are generally regarded as methods for mapping large key spaces into smaller address spaces.

This section presents several alternate methods and related concepts. For an evaluation of the various techniques, the reader is directed to the research paper by Lum, Yuen, and Dodd.* The various transforms are given first and techniques for storage management follow. Numerical keys are assumed; however, alphanumeric keys are easily converted to numeric keys by using binary representation of the characters or by encoding the letters A to Z into the decimal numbers 11 to 36, etc. Lum, *et al.*, found no significant performance variations from treating alphanumeric keys in this manner.

A frequently used randomization technique is to divide the key by the largest prime number (N) less than the number of available addresses and use the remainder as the record address. This is known as the *division method*. If the storage space can hold 1000 records, then N would be equal to 997 and the transformation of the key 36741 would generate a record address of 849. (36741 divided by 997 gives a quotient of 36 and a remainder of 849) In actual practice, the addresses generated by the transformed keys normally range between numbers A and B, where A<B, usually taken to be relative record address locations. The divisor N is the largest prime number less than B–A.

*V. Y. Lum, P. S. T. Yuen, and M. Dodd, "Key-to-address transform techniques: A fundamental performance study on large existing formatted files," *Communications of the ACM*, Volume 14, No. 4 (April 1971), pp. 228–239.

The remainder R from the division operation is then added to A to generate the required record address.

Another method is based on a *digit analysis* of the set of possible keys. The distribution of digits in each position in the key is studied. The positions with the most skewed distribution of digits are eliminated from the key until the number of remaining digits is equal to the desired address length. Thus, if the key size is 6 digits, and there are 2000 keys, deleting 3 digits from the key would correspond to a loading factor of .5. For a given file, the same digits are deleted from each key. The criteria for eliminating digits usually involves deleting digit positions in which the distribution of digits has high peaks or has a high standard deviation. If A is the beginning address of an extent assigned to the file, and it is determined from a digit analysis that the 2nd, 3rd, and 6th digits of a six-digit key are to be eliminated, then the key 367415 would correspond to a record address of $A+341$.

In the *mid-square* method, the key is multiplied by itself and digits are truncated on both ends until an address of the desired size is obtained. For a storage space of 1000 records (addresses from 0 to 999), the key 367415 would correspond to a record address of $A+937$. Again, A is the beginning address of the extent assigned to the file and the intermediate calculations are:

$$367415 \times 367415 = 134993782225$$

The four leading digits (i.e., 1349) and the five trailing digits (i.e., 82225) are eliminated from the product.

In the *folding method*, the key is partitioned into fields the same length as the relative address length of the record storage area. Thus, the digits of the key are folded onto themselves and are added. Two variations to this method exist: "fold boundary" folds the key at the boundary of the parts as if folding paper; and "fold shifting" shifts over the parts to the further boundary before adding. Both variations are depicted in Figure 8.6. Thus, the key 29367415 is trans-

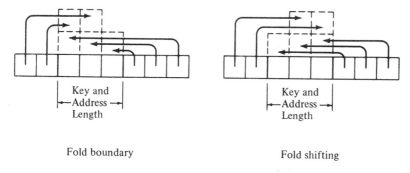

Fold boundary   Fold shifting

Figure 8.6   The folding randomization technique.

formed into a relative address of 791 for a storage area with 1000 record locations as follows:

$$
\begin{array}{r}
92 \\
514 \\
29 \boxed{367} 415 \\
\hline
791 \quad \textit{relative address}
\end{array}
$$

In this case, the "fold boundary" variation is used, and carries (from addition) are ignored.

The final method covered here is *algebraic coding* in which selected digits of the key are used as coefficients of a polynomial. Thus, a six-digit key of the form $k_1k_2k_3k_4k_5k_6$ might generate the following relative address for a storage area with 1000 records:

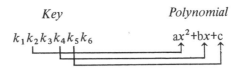

For example, a key of 367415 with a value of the independent variable x in the polynomial of 10 would generate the following relative address:

Key	Polynomial	Relative Address
3 6 7 4 1 5	$6 \times (10)^2 + 4 \times (10) + 1 =$	641

The respective digits in the key that are used as coefficients are fixed for all records in the file.

The use of randomizing techniques requires an embedded key—i.e., a key that exists as a field in the record. For insertion of a record in a file with random organization, a randomization technique is applied to a record key to obtain a record address in the file. If the computed record area is unoccupied, the record is inserted and the operation is complete. It is possible, however, that a previous record is stored in the record area since randomization techniques do not guarantee that unique addresses are generated. Records assigned to the same record area are called *synonyms*. The problem of synonyms can be handled in two ways: (1) an overflow area is used, and (2) the consecutive spill method is used. An *overflow area* is a portion of the file set aside for synonyms. When the first synonym record for a given record area occurs, that record is placed in the overflow area and a pointer to it is placed in the primary record area. Successive synonyms for the same record area are chained to previous synonyms in the overflow area. Therefore, when a synonym is generated for the insertion operation, the chain of previous synonyms is traversed to determine that the new record key is unique before it is placed in the overflow area and chained to previous synonyms. For retrieval, the search key must be matched with the record key for the record in the primary record area and for all synonyms in the overflow area.

With the *consecutive spill* method, the storage space is considered to be circular. When a synonym occurs, the insertion process successively searches for vacancies starting from the record's primary address, and places the record in the first vacancy found. If the search for a vacancy returns to the original address, then the storage space is full. For retrieval, a randomization technique generates a primary record address. If the search key and the key of the record in the primary record area agree, the record is retrieved and the operation is complete. Otherwise, the search key is compared with record keys from successive areas until a match is found—indicating success, or a vacancy is encountered—denoting failure.

A variation and a combination of the above techniques is known as the *bucket concept*. With this method, each calculated record address corresponds to a storage area that can hold several records. For a given record, a randomization technique supplies the address of an appropriate bucket. The consecutive spill method is used for records within the bucket and the overflow method is used when the bucket is full. Access time to successive records in a bucket should be shorter than the access time to the bucket itself. Therefore, a disk track is a convenient form for a bucket to take.

The use of randomization techniques requires a certain amount of sophistication in the sense that sequential organization is effectively used with the consecutive spill method and list organization is effectively used with overflow areas. However, randomization is an effective technique for what are known as "70-30 files," in which 70% of the activity concerns only 30% of the file.

INVERTED FILES

Selection operations on random, relative random, and partially ordered files are inefficient; and in many cases, an exhaustive search of all of the records in a file is required. One of the options obviously is to sort the file on the desired key, but then either a duplicate copy of the file is generated or the original ordering is lost. The use of an "inverted file" is a means of achieving the advantages of a sorted duplicate file without the processing and storage costs.

Meadow* uses the concept of "external referent" and "internal referent" files to introduce the notion of an inverted file. He further states, "Every meaningful record must contain information about something external to the record." The reason is obvious since a record that refers only to itself is of no value. A con-

*Meadow, p. 227.

Attribute

Employee Number	Name	S.S.#	City	Age	Job	Training	Marital Status	Home Status	Salary
1234	ROGERS, A. A.	639216034	NEW YORK	42	EXEC	BUS	M	O	37000.00
3198	ADAMS, J. C.	234169132	BOSTON	27	OPER	D.P.	S	R	9134.50
3201	KIRK, B. K.	639417734	NEW YORK	30	PROG	MATH	M	R	14500.00
4226	BART, B. B.	234774420	BOSTON	19	OPER	D.P.	M	R	7350.00
5784	KICK, W. F.	639011234	NEW YORK	54	EXEC	ENG.	M	O	74000.00
5814	FOX, F. C.	639144440	NEW YORK	47	EXEC	BUS	S	R	43500.00
6450	ABEL, Z. L.	513687290	NEWARK	25	PROG	D.P.	S	O	12680.00
7531	THOMS, F. K.	639382227	NEW YORK	28	SALES	BUS	M	R	31500.00

Figure 8.7   Entity/attribute matrix of a personnel information file.

ventional file is an *external referent* file since it records information about things or events external to the file itself. A file that records information about itself or a related file is an *internal referent* file. The distinction is useful but the concepts are not mutually exclusive. For example, a list organized file would probably be regarded as having features of both external and internal referent files.

Figure 8.7 gives an entity/attribute matrix for a personnel information file that could be stored sequentially, randomly, or in a form of list organization. The file is ordered by "employee number" that serves as the identifier field. Suppose that it is desired to select the records based, for example, on one or more of the following attributes:

> City
> Job
> Training
> Marital status
> Home status
> Salary

Clearly, with sequential organization or sequentially oriented lists, the entire file would have to be searched. With an *inverted file* structure, a list of the attributes on the basis of which a randomly organized file would be searched is predetermined and the identifier fields (or record addresses) of records that possess a particular attribute value are stored (along with that value) as an index file. The inverted file minimally contains attributes, attribute values, and internal references to records that possess the associated attributes. Thus, an inverted file can be classed as an internally referent file, and the original and inverted files are collectively referred to as a *file set*.

An inverted file structure for the personnel information file of Figure 8.7 is given as Figure 8.8. In this case, the file is inverted on all of the attributes and on all the attribute values. If the records of New York residents were needed, for example, the list of identifiers is retrieved by locating the attribute CITY and the attribute value **NEW YORK**, to obtain the following list of identifiers:

> **NEW YORK**
> 1234
> 3201
> 5784
> 5814
> 7531

The required records would then be accessed by either a direct access, dictionary look-up, or a randomizing technique. If retrieval is based on multiple attribute values, such as:

Attribute	Value	List of identifiers (or record addresses)
CITY	BOSTON	3198, 4226
CITY	NEWARK	6450
CITY	NEW YORK	1234, 3201, 5784, 5814, 7531
AGE	>30	1234, 5784, 5814
AGE	≤30	3198, 3201, 4226, 6450, 7531
JOB	EXEC	1234, 5784, 5814
JOB	OPER	3198, 4226
JOB	PROG	3201, 6450
JOB	SALES	7531
TRAINING	BUS	1234, 5814, 7531
TRAINING	D.P.	3198, 4226, 6450
TRAINING	ENG	5784
TRAINING	MATH	3201
MARITAL STATUS	M	1234, 3201, 4226, 5784, 7531
MARITAL STATUS	S	3198, 5814, 6450
HOME STATUS	R	3198, 3201, 4226, 5814, 7531
HOME STATUS	O	1234, 5784, 6450
SALARY	>50K	5784
SALARY	>25K and ≤50K	1234, 5814, 7531
SALARY	≤25K	3198, 3201, 4226, 6450

Figure 8.8   Inverted file structure for the personnel information file of Figure 8.7.

Resident of New York,
Single, and
Rents home

then a set operation (such as *intersection* in this case) would be used on the identifier lists as follows:

NEW YORK ∩ SINGLE ∩ RENT = Composite Condition

1234	3198	3198	5814
3201	5814	3201	
5784	6450	4226	
5814		5814	
7531		7531	

In this example, the record with identifier 5814 is the only one that satisfies each of the three conditions stated.

The disadvantage of an inverted file is that it must be updated each time the primary file is updated. Therefore, an alternate method is to use list organization and run a chain of pointers through records with a given attribute. This technique increases the number of pointer fields that must accompany each record, but exists as a viable alternative to the update problem.

REFERENCES

Burch, J. G., Jr., and F. R. Strater, Jr., *Information Systems: Theory and Practice*, Santa Barbara, California, Hamilton Publishing Company, 1974.

Dippel, G., and W. C. House, *Information Systems: Data Processing and Evaluation*, Glenview, Illinois, Scott, Foresman and Company, 1969.

Disk Forte User's Manual, Detroit, Michigan, Burroughs Corporation, Form 1044609.

Dodd, G. G., "Elements of data management systems," *Computing Surveys*, Volume 1, No. 2 (June 1969) pp. 117–133.

Lum, V. Y., Yuen, P. S. T., and M. Dodd, "Key-to-address transform techniques: A fundamental performance study on large existing formatted files," *Communications of the ACM*, Volume 14, No. 4 (April 1971), pp. 228–239.

Meadow, C. T., *The Analysis of Information Systems*, New York, John Wiley and Sons, Inc., 1967.

Senko, M. E., *Formatted File Organization Techniques*, Yorktown Heights, N.Y., IBM Corporation, May 16, 1967.

Senko, M. E., *Formatted File Techniques,* San Jose, California, IBM Corporation, March, 1970.

Senko, M. E., *et al., File Design Handbook,* San Jose, California, IBM Corporation, November, 1969.

9 | VIRTUAL STORAGE ACCESS METHODS—A BRIEF OVERVIEW

INTRODUCTION

Operating systems that employ virtual storage and paging as a storage management technique necessarily include the facilities for a powerful data management system. With virtual storage (or virtual memory as it is also called), storage is allocated and managed in page-sized blocks. Object programs are subdivided accordingly and the paging process moves pages between the storage unit and the paging device on a demand basis. The direct-access storage device that serves as a paging device* is also formatted to hold pages, and the paging input/output routine executes at a high priority in the system. What this means is that paging interruptions and paging input/output operations take precedence over all other Supervisor activity.

The basic concept behind virtual storage access methods is to use the paging input/output routines to perform conventional input and output operations. A standard block size that is equivalent to the system's page size is used, so that all data sets have the same physical attributes. The organization of the data blocks obviously differs according to the record format and access method used.

The manner in which actual input and output are performed is unique and the reader is alerted to this fact in preparation for the section entitled, "Input and Output Processing."

---

*Large capacity storage also has been used as a paging device on an experimental basis. However, direct-access storage is still used as a secondary device when large capacity storage space is exhausted.

The material presented here is intended to be conceptual in nature and does not necessarily represent an existing data management system.

PUBLIC AND PRIVATE STORAGE

One of the basic decisions in data management is whether on-line direct-access storage is for public use or for private use. The problem of direct-access storage management becomes more significant than ordinarily imagined when one recornizes that direct-access volumes can be used concurrently by more than one job. The extensive use of public storage and the system catalog frees the user of concern over the management of storage volumes. On the other hand, the use of private storage permits the user to control his storage volumes directly.

External storage is always managed on a volume basis and is divided into three classes: public storage, private storage, and system storage. *System storage* contains the libraries* that store the operating and data management system routines. System storage is used during system initiation to load permanently resident routines and during system operation to load transient routines and application-oriented subroutines.

Public storage is widely used with time sharing systems in which the number of concurrent users is expected to be much greater than the number of input/ output devices available for use as non-system storage. Public storage is also used in conventional operating systems for temporary data sets and in systems with virtual storage access method facilities. When an operating system is started up, a set of public devices is defined. When a user's task is created, that task automatically has access to all of the public volumes on the public devices via the data management system and the system catalog. Public storage is always allocated entirely by data management system routines, and access to it for input and output operations is provided by data management access method routines. Public storage is *on-line* in the sense that public volumes are always mounted. When a user creates a data set, he gives it a data set name and assigns it data set attributes. Subsequently, that data set is referenced by name, and the data management system is given responsibility for locating the data set and providing access to it. The system also protects the data set from being accessed by other users, unless the owner of the data set allows it to be shared. Data sets on public storage are always cataloged.

Private storage refers to the use of private volumes on devices allocated to private use. The user requests a private volume when he defines a data set; the system then requests that the operator mount the specified volume if it is not already mounted. Private volumes may contain cataloged or uncataloged data sets; if a cataloged data set is stored on a private volume, then the serial

---

*That is, partitioned data sets.

number of the volume is kept in the catalog, in addition to the "private" attribute. When the user requests a cataloged data set on a private volume by data set name alone, the operator is requested automatically to mount the appropriate storage volume.

Operating and time sharing systems are either private-storage oriented or public-storage oriented. In a private storage environment, the user may specify a specific volume or a nonspecific volume (i.e., any volume in the system). If a data set resides on a specific volume and it is not cataloged, the user must define a private volume as follows:

//MFILE DD DSNAME=MATH.LIB,UNIT-2314,DISP=OLD,
            VOLUME=(PRIVATE,,,SER=449795)

This data definition statement requests that a specific volume (namely the volume serial number 449795) be mounted by the system operator and also implicitly specifies that the volume be demounted after the job terminates. In this example, record formats need not be specified because they are recorded in the data set control block of the data set. An example of a data definition statement for a data set that will reside on a nonspecific volume is given as follows:

//NFILE DD DSNAME=LEFT.OUT,UNIT=2314,
            DISP=(NEW,CATLG),
            DCB=(RECFM=FB,LRECL=140,BLKSIZE=840),
            SPACE=(CYL,(10,2))

In this case, the record format and space requirements are specified because the data set is new. Also, the operator is requested to mount a new volume for the data set. In a private storage environment, public storage is normally used only for temporary data sets, and the standard "use attribute" for data sets is "private."

In a public storage environment, a data set is always assigned public storage when it is created—i.e., unless the user specifically requests a private storage volume. Page-oriented data management lends itself to the use of public storage, since the pages (i.e., page-sized blocks) that comprise a data set need not necessarily occupy contiguous direct-access storage and may be scattered across several storage volumes. When defining a data set on public storage using virtual storage methods, the process of data definition is simplified to include the following parameters:

1. Data definition name (ddname).
2. Data set name (dsname).
3. Data set organization.
4. DCB parameters.

Figure 9.1 suggests the manner in which data sets are cataloged and accessed in a virtual storage environment.

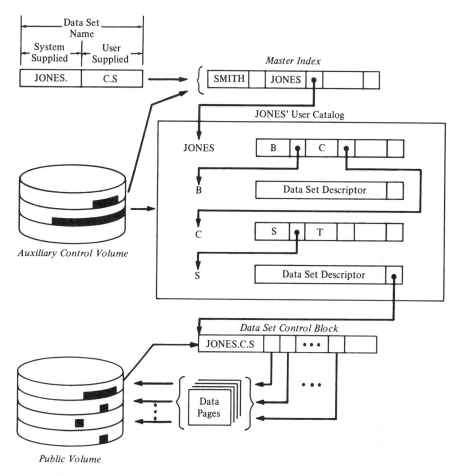

Figure 9.1   Data set cataloging and access in a virtual storage environment.

VIRTUAL STORAGE ACCESS METHODS

Virtual storage access method data sets are stored as page-size* blocks so that they can be accessed by the system paging programs. Virtual storage access method data sets are organized in three ways: (1) virtual sequential, (2) virtual indexed sequential, and (3) virtual partitioned. The *virtual sequential access method* (VSAM) is designed for data sets that are written and read sequentially. The access method uses an "external page map" that is stored along with the data set. When a VSAM data set is opened, the "external page map" is brought into main storage to form an External Storage Correspondence Table. The External Storage Correspondence Table is used by the access routines, located

---

*A typical page size is 4096 bytes.

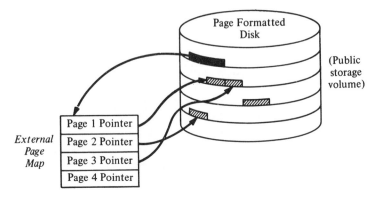

Figure 9.2 Conceptual view of virtual sequential data set organization.

in a task's virtual memory, to transfer VSAM pages between the storage unit and public storage. A VSAM data set is suggested by Figure 9.2.

The *virtual indexed sequential access method* (VISAM) is the virtual storage counterpart of the indexed sequential access method considered previously. VISAM data set include three kinds of pages: (1) directory pages, (2) data pages, and (3) overflow pages. The *directory page* serves as the master index to the data set and contains one entry for each page of the data set. That entry includes the lowest key on the page and the relative location of the page in public storage. Each *data page* includes the keys and the data records contained in that page. The keys entries are maintained in collating sequence so that a binary search can be made as required. Because of additions, deletions, and insertions, data records are not necessarily maintained in any specific order. When an insertion is made to the data set that would cause a page overflow, an *overflow page* is used. An overflow page is located by a key entry in a data page. A VISAM data set is depicted in Figure 9.3.

The *virtual partitioned access method* (VPAM) is analogous to the previously mentioned partitioned data set organization. VPAM data sets permit both virtual sequential members and virtual indexed sequential members; they are frequently used for program libraries stored as either object modules or source modules. A VPAM data set includes directory pages and member pages. The *directory page* gives the page location of each member of VPAM data set. *Member pages* take the form of either VSAM or VISAM pages, discussed previously. The form of the VPAM data set is suggested by Figure 9.4.

Virtual data sets are a convenience from both the user's point of view and the system's point of view. Space on public storage volumes (i.e., direct-access volumes) is allocated in page-size extents. Thus, external storage management

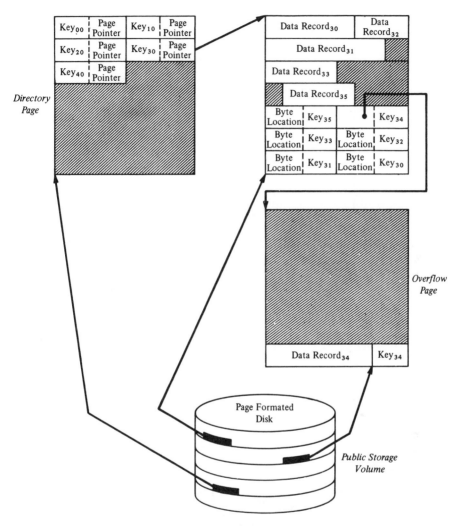

Figure 9.3   Conceptual view of virtual indexed sequential data set organization.

is simplified and a data set (or even parts of it) need not occupy contiguous tracks. The reader should refer to Figures 9.2, 9.3, and 9.4 here and note that pages of a virtual storage access method data set are always located through an "external page map" or a "directory page." As a result, the user need not specify primary and secondary allocations and a data set can grow in size, as required.

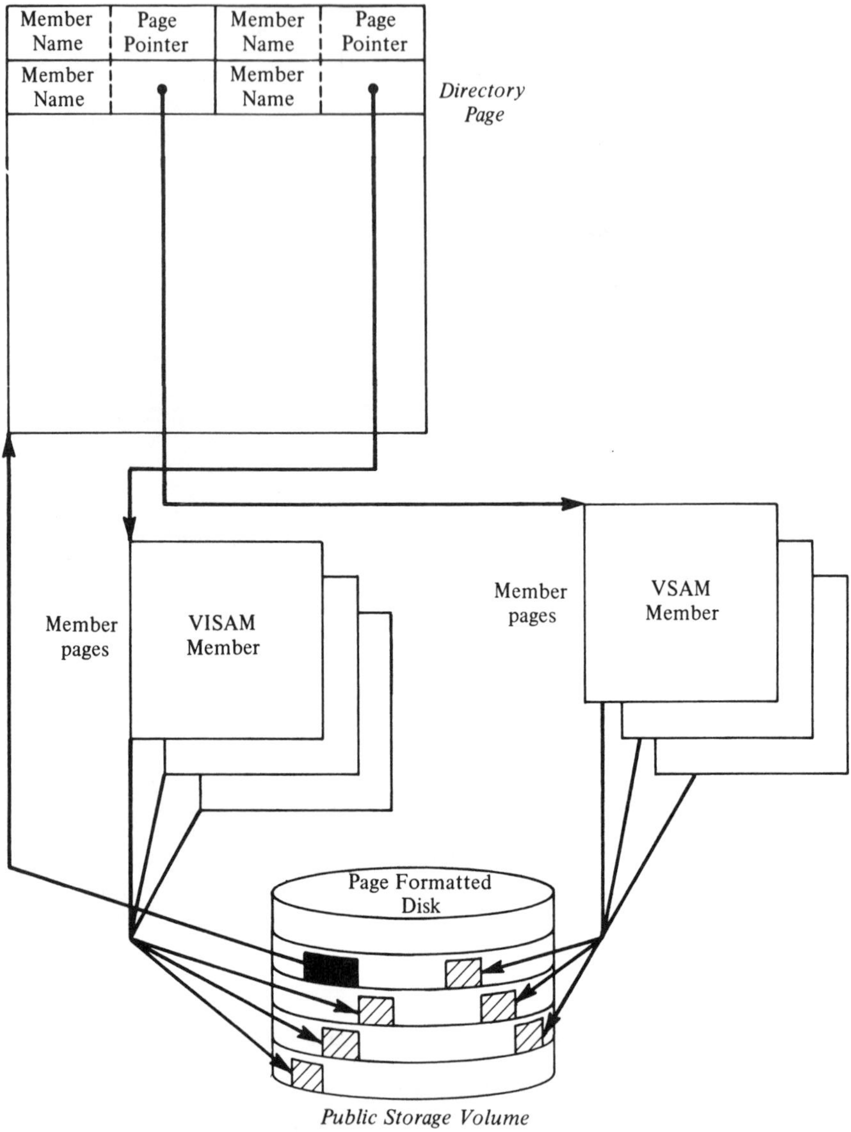

Figure 9.4   Conceptual view of virtual partitioned data set organization.

RECORD FORMATS AND DATA SET ACCESS

Record formats in page-oriented data management systems are a logical extension to the concepts presented earlier. Fixed-length, variable-length, and undefined-length records are defined for VSAM and VISAM data sets. (This

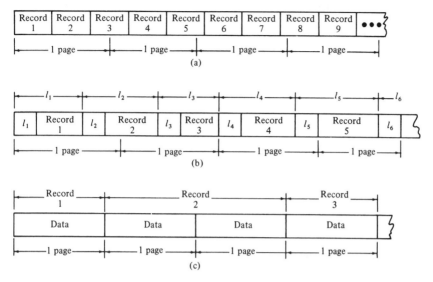

Figure 9.5   VSAM record formats. (a) Fixed-length records. (b) Variable-length records. (c) Undefined-length records.

obviously includes VPAM data sets that can have VSAM and VISAM members.) Figure 9.5 depicts VSAM record formats. For fixed-length and variable-length records, the data management system automatically keeps track of overlap across page boundaries. An undefined-length record must consist of an integral number of pages and always begins on a page boundary.

Figure 9.6 depicts VISAM record formats. The system automatically provides directory pages. Records cannot exceed page boundaries; however, the user can specify the percentage of data pages that are to be initially filled (see Figure 9.3). If many record insertions are anticipated, input/output processing time can be decreased by minimizing the number of overflow pages that will eventually be needed. VISAM records can have initial or embedded keys and can assume fixed-length and variable-length formats.

The *access methods* used for input and output processing are included as part of the task's virtual storage and use the Supervisor for actual input and output operations.   The access methods are used with assembler language macro instructions or by equivalent machine code generated by a compiler. In general, logical records are retrieved using either the move mode or the locate mode, and special macro instructions are available for use with VISAM and VPAM for performing input and output processing characteristic to those access methods. Explicit input and output buffering is not used with virtual access methods since it is inherent in the page-sized blocks and the manner in which the system does input and output.

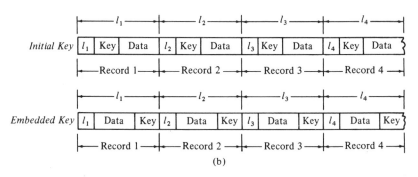

Figure 9.6 VISAM record formats (VISAM records cannot exceed page boundaries).
(a) Fixed-length records. (b) Variable-length records.

EXTERNAL STORAGE ALLOCATION

External storage allocation involves the allocation of space on direct-access volumes used for external storage. Allocation facilities fall into two classes: conventional direct-access storage space allocation and virtual storage access method allocation. Conventional space allocation is performed through the VTOC for a given volume, as covered previously.

Virtual storage access method allocation can be used with public or private volumes. Virtual storage access method volumes are divided into fixed-size blocks called pages. Each volume includes a Page Assignment Table that is located through the volume label and specifies the status of each page on the volume. The status of a page on a virtual storage access method volume can be one of the following:

1. Assigned as a data set page.
2. Unassigned.
3. Assigned as a data set control block.
4. Defective and unavailable for assignment.

Public volumes are located through a Public Volume Table maintained by an

External Storage Allocation routine. The Public Volume Table contains the volume identification of all volumes designated as public storage.

A page in public storage is located with an external page address that consists of a relative volume number and a relative page number on that volume. The relative volume number is an index to the Public Volume Table and the relative page number is an index into the "assigned page" part of the Page Assignment Table. A list of private virtual storage access method volumes is also maintained by the system so that all virtual storage access method data sets can be processed in the same manner.

VIRTUAL INPUT AND OUTPUT PROCESSING

Virtual storage access method input and output processing is performed in a similar manner to the way in which physical input and output processing is performed—except for the actual input/output operations. Each data set used by a task requires a data definition and a data control block (DCB). The DCB is included as part of a task's virtual storage and is completed when the data set is opened. One of the control blocks built during open processing is an External Storage Correspondence Table, which is a logical counterpart of the Data Extent Block, covered previously. The External Storage Correspondence Table contains the external page map of a virtual storage access method data set. The virtual storage access method orders the pages of a data set by relative page number from the beginning of the data set, and the external page map contains both the relative volume number (in the public/private volume table) and the relative external storage page number (on that volume) for each page in the data set. The format of the External Storage Correspondence Table entry for each data set page is given in Figure 9.7. The External Storage Correspondence Table entries are ordered by data set relative page number.

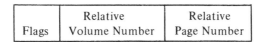

Flags	Relative Volume Number	Relative Page Number

Figure 9.7 Format of an External Storage Correspondence Table entry for one virtual storage access method data set page.

A virtual storage access method input operation proceeds as follows (see Figure 9.8):

1. The External Storage Correspondence Table is constructed in a task's virtual storage during open processing.
2. The task requests that a record is read into virtual memory by using a virtual storage access method.

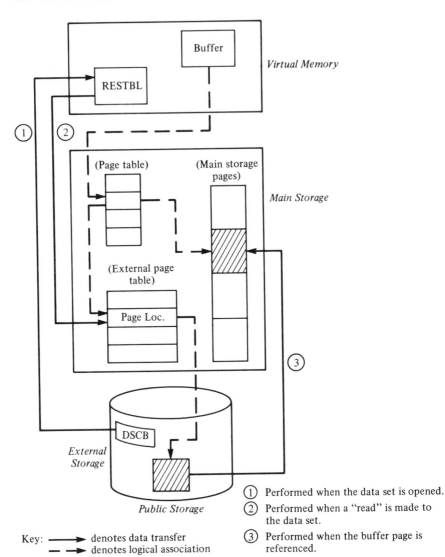

Figure 9.8 Data flow during a virtual storage access method input operation.

3. A page-sized buffer is obtained by the access method in virtual storage.
4. The external address of the data set page (containing the record) is obtained from the External Storage Correspondence Table and placed in the External Page Table entry of the buffer page. The data set page has not moved as yet, but its physical location on external storage is in the task's External Page Table. The buffer page is marked as not being in storage.

5. When the record is addressed in the virtual storage buffer, a relocation interruption occurs and the data set page is brought into storage from external storage by the paging routines.

The end result, obviously, is that only the needed pages of a data set are brought into the storage unit of the computer, and the input and output operations are performed efficiently by the paging routines. Virtual storage access method output processing operates in a analogous fashion.

The objective has been to introduce the concept of a virtual storage access method and how it operates. The complete process is indeed more sophisticated and includes much of the detail associated with physical input and output. Virtual storage access methods perform blocking, deblocking, and most of the other input/output operations that are ordinarily available with a physical access method. In short, the primary difference between the two techniques involves data set organization and the manner in which actual input and output operations are performed.

REFERENCES

Katzan, H., *Operating Systems: A Pragmatic Approach*, New York, Van Nostrand Reinhold Company, 1973.

Lett, A. S., "The approach to data management in Time Sharing System/360," *TSS/360 Compendium*, White Plains, N.Y., IBM Corporation, Data Processing Division, 1969.

OS/VS Virtual Storage Access Method (VSAM), *Planning Guide*, White Plains, N.Y., IBM Corporation, Form GC26-3799.

PART III DATA BASE TECHNOLOGY

10 | FOUNDATIONS OF DATA BASE TECHNOLOGY

DATA BASE ENVIRONMENT

Our interest in data base technology is considerably more than an intellectual excursion into new methods of organizing and accessing data. The modern era in computer technology is characterized by immediate access to integrated informational resources via telecommunications facilities. Inputs to the system are heterogeneous and occur at random intervals. Requests for information from the system are dynamic and time-dependent, so that queries and responses cannot be prepared beforehand. Files are large; thus, redundant data must be factored out to reduce the time required to access desired information. And, information must be current and up-to-date to meet the needs of a modern society. Therefore, an informational change must be reflected immediately in all associated files. Because these requirements are so widely known, it is often forgotten how they evolved and why they constitute a distinct departure from conventional data management techniques.

Conventionally, a data file is regarded as a set of related data records; similarly, a record is regarded as a set of related fields. In the absence of data management facilities, however, both file organization and data organization are identical, as depicted in Figure 10.1. The lack of data management facilities is also characterized by the fact that data organization is reflected in the logic of a program and is "committed" to a single device type. Changes to data organization, device type, or both require modification of the application program. Moreover, files

File
Organization

Data
Organization

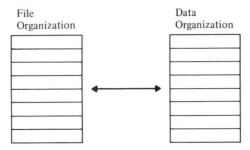

Figure 10.1 Without conventional data management facilities, file and data organization are synonymous.

of this type are normally limited to the set of computer applications for which
the data is organized.

With the use of data management facilities, a distinction is made between file
organization and both data organization and data access. Input and output
operations, device control, and direct-access space allocation are managed by
data management routines so that data is not bound to a particular set of
programs or applications. As shown in Figure 10.2, data can be organized as
non-contiguous extents for which several forms of data access is provided.
Records can be formatted to achieve operational efficiency and files can be
assigned to programs symbolically. Modern data management facilities greatly
extend the file processing capabilities of current systems and are extensive in
scope and complexity. However, data management, as we know it today, is
lacking in the requirement given earlier: fast access to large, integrated files that
are designed to be updated dynamically in a real time operational environment.

File Organization   Data Organization

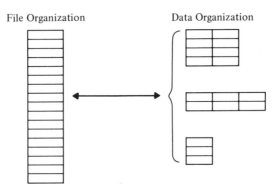

Figure 10.2 With data management facilities, file and
data organization are distinct, and data is
not "committed" to a particular set of
programs and applications.

File Organization   Data Base

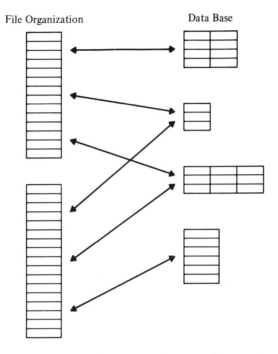

Figure 10.3 In a data base environment, files can be
defined over the totality of data in the
information space.

Future data base requirements involve a capability, as depicted in Figure 10.3,
wherein files can be defined over the totality of data in the information space.
Systems of this type require more than a simple arrangement of data items in
storage. File definition involves the reference to objects and relationships as
they exist in the real world through a complex arrangement of data mappings,
structural relationships, and complicated graph structures. *One way of character-
izing a data base is: it is the process of taking the knowledge about data that is
implicitly built into programs and making it explicitly available in a formal
manner at the systems level.*

DATA INDEPENDENCE

One of the key issues in data base technology is the degree to which data is
independent of the manner in which it is stored and of the programs that use it.
Obviously, both extremes—i.e., total data independence and total data depen-
dence—exist. However, flexibility impacts overhead and performance, while
rigidity impacts applicability.

Normally, data independence implies that data access is handled interpretively, as compared to the use of compiled code. Data management systems that are in current use involve interpretation and conversion during each data access to provide device independence and flexibility with regard to record formats. The architecture of data base systems go one step further and provides:

1. Tables of descriptors and interrelationships that are stored independently of the data.
2. Facilities for accessing data directly, indirectly through pointers, or via any decoding or conversion process that is required.
3. The capability of utilizing data items, regardless of the associations inherent in storage organization.

One of the major differences between data base systems is the degree to which data independence is achieved.

STORAGE AND DATA

Information in a data base is stored on volumes of secondary storage—such as magnetic disk or in rare cases, magnetic tape. The information is accessible by programs utilizing the data base system. Inputs to and outputs from the system take the conventional forms found in most computing, data processing, or information management applications: questions, transactions, and raw data for input and computed results, reports, updated files, and answers for output. In order to take advantage of the data base concept, however, it is absolutely necessary to make a distinction between data and storage.

With storage, we are dealing with bits and bytes and are further concerned with physical attributes of a storage device. Main storage is normally characterized by the fact that it is directly addressable and the unit of storage is a bit, byte, or word. A unit of secondary storage is the physical record that may be recorded between gaps on magnetic tape or as blocks on a direct-access device.

With regard to data, it is necessary to distinguish between applications-oriented data and system-oriented data. Applications-oriented data are depicted in Figure 10.4 and consist of fields, logical records, and files. A field is the smallest

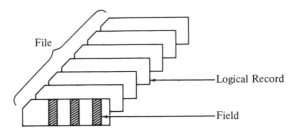

Figure 10.4   Conceptual view of units of applications data.

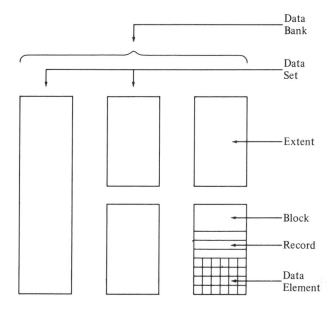

Figure 10.5   Conceptual view of system-oriented data.

unit of data and would lose its meaning if broken down further. A logical record, in its most simple form, has the same fields for each occurrence in a file. Obviously, more complex records exist where the fields are not necessarily the same for all records in a file.

Informational services are provided to a user through a system of some type—operating, data management, or data base. Thus, system-oriented data establishes an interface between applications-oriented data and units of storage. System-oriented data are depicted in Figure 10.5. The entire data base is divided into data banks that are composed of related data sets. As covered earlier, data sets are composed of extents that are subdivided into blocks. Blocks are composed of records and records are composed of data items—the lowest level of recognizable data that is usually taken to be a collection of bits. Clearly, the concepts of storage class, storage organization, and storage access—used in conventional data management—are defined in terms of system-oriented data.

ENTITIES, ATTRIBUTES, AND VALUES

The terms *entity, attribute,* and *value* are used to describe information, so that a blue suit in the real world would be represented, in the realm of information, by the entity "suit" wherein the value of its color attribute is "blue." As data, the color attribute corresponds to a data element for which an agreed upon interpretation for one of its data items is "blue." Thus, to sum up:

1. A *property* is associated with an *entity* in the real world.
2. A *value* is associated with an *attribute* in the realm of information.
3. A *data item* is associated with a *data element* in the domain of data.

The reason that these concepts, i.e., of entity, attribute, value, etc., are being emphasized is that collectively they are the mechanism by which information is recorded. Recall here that we are storing a symbolic representation of an event in the computer and not the event. When using conventional data management facilities, simple values are recorded with little or no regard to the overall process of storing information and what it means. In a data base environment, a more fundamental approach is needed to eliminate redundancy and provide accessibility.

DATA MAPS

It is important to recognize what the process of recording information entails. First, a fact that is a relationship between the members of two sets, as in the following list:

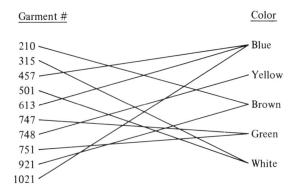

In this case, garment numbered 457, which could represent a suit, has the color value "blue." This is a fact. In this example, "Garment #" and "Color" are attributes and the numbers 210, 315, 457, etc. and the colors blue, yellow, etc., are values of their respective attributes. Stated in a slightly different manner, sets are attributes, and members of the sets are values.

A relationship, of this type, between two sets is known as a *data map*. One of the two sets is an identity attribute, so that an attribute/value pair (referred to as an *identifier* in Chapter 1) uniquely identifies an entity. The second set is an attribute associated with the same set of entities. More specifically, a data map is a mapping of a set A into a set B; symbolically, the relationship is written A→B. The mapping A→B, assigns zero, one, or more elements of set B to each element of set A. Sets A and B may be the same or different sets. Obviously, these definitions apply to a wide range of functional relationships. The defining characteristic of a data map is that the sets in a mapping are attributes of the same entity set and that one of the sets is an identity set. Data maps are classified according to the type of attribute sets involved and by the complexity of the mapping.

Two types of attribute sets are used in data maps—identity attribute sets and attribute sets that do not serve as identifiers. Let V denote a set of either type, let E denote an identity attribute, and let W denote attribute sets that do not serve as identifiers. A data map has the general form E→V and is classified as simple or complex. Each element of E can be related to no more than one element of V in a simple mapping. In a complex mapping, an element of E can be related to many elements of V.

A simple data map represents a simple fact and has the form E→W. Figure 10.6 gives an example of a simple data map. Complex data maps of the form

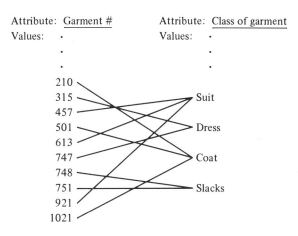

Figure 10.6   A simple data map representing a simple fact.

E→E and E→E′ are structural data maps that represent structural facts, since the sets E and E′ are both identity attributes. The map E→E establishes a relation between entities in the same set, such as the hierarchical relationship among people in an organization. The map E→E′ represents a structural relationship between identity attributes (i.e., entities) of different sets. A complex data map representing structural facts is shown in Figure 10.7; in this case, a mapping exists between entities identified by "garment #" and entities identified by "warehouse #." The three forms of mappings are summarized in Figure 10.8. One means of equating the concept of a data map to a real world situation is to consider its "rough analogy" with the "keyed" method of data organization and

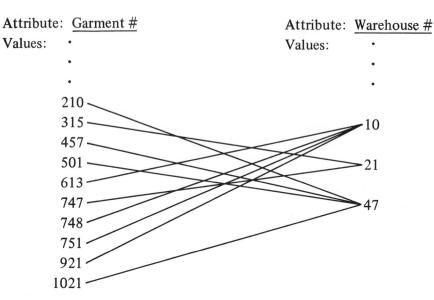

Figure 10.7   A complex data map representing structural facts.

Factual Relationship	E━━━━➤W
Relationship with another entity set	E━━━━➤E
Relationship with another entity in the same set	E━━━━➤E

Key: E denotes an identity attribute
       W denotes an attribute set that
          does not serve as an identifier

Figure 10.8   Three forms of data mapping.

the indexed sequential access method. Keyed organization takes the form of a simple mapping between a set of keys and a set of stored records. The set of keys is analogous to the identity attribute set, and the set of stored records is analogous to an attribute set.

An inverse data mapping has the form V→E and does not change the information content of the relationship. An inverse data mapping is "roughly analogous" to an inverted file structure, wherein a set of index values forms a complex data map for a particular attribute value. Using the data map in Figure 10.6 as an example, the inverse mapping from the attribute value "suit" forms the index set <457,613,921>.

There are four possible types of mappings, described as follows:

	Map	*Inverse Map*
1.	Simple	Simple
2.	Simple	Complex
3.	Complex	Simple
4.	Complex	Complex

Clearly, these mappings take the forms: 1-to-1, n-to-1, 1-to-n, and n-to-n in the order given. Examples of data mappings for the cases E→W, E→E', and E→E are given in Figure 10.9.

DATA BASE ORGANIZATION

Through the use of the concept of a data map, data base definition and organization becomes essentially a process of establishing, storing, and maintaining data maps. The concepts also apply to some extent to conventional data management and this fact is evident from the following discussion.

A fact, that is, an item of information, is represented by a data map—a relation between two attribute sets. Four things are necessary to define an item of information:

1. An identity attribute name.
2. An entity identifier.
3. A data attribute name.
4. An attribute value—i.e., the data item.

Normally, the "names" are omitted in a data system because they require extra storage space. The situation can be likened to the use of positional and keyword parameters in computer languages. It follows that each fact to be recorded about an entity consists of a pair of values: an entity identifier, such as a part number, and an attribute value, such as a color. Pairs are grouped by entity identifier so that all but one entity identifier can be eliminated. Thus, we are

Form of data map. E→V	Map is simple; inverse map is simple.	Map is simple; inverse map is complex.	Map is complex; inverse map is simple.	Map is complex; inverse map is complex.
E——→W	Employee # → Social Security Number	Policy # → Billing Date	School # → Student # of students in school	Garment # → Warehouse # where garments are stored
E——→E'	Department # → Employee # of supervisor of department	Student # → School # of students		Part # → Part # of component parts
E——→E	Employee # → Employee # of spouse	Employee # → Employee # of supervisor	Employee # → Employee # of subordinate employees	

Figure 10.9   Examples of the 12 possible types of data maps.

Attributes

Attribute Values	A_1	A_2	A_3	. . .	A_m
E_1	$V_{1,1}$	$V_{1,2}$	$V_{1,3}$		$V_{1,m}$
E_2	$V_{2,2}$	$V_{2,2}$	$V_{2,3}$		$V_{2,m}$
E_3	$V_{3,1}$	$V_{3,2}$	$V_{3,3}$		$V_{3,m}$
.	.				.
.	.				.
.	.				.
E_n	$V_{n,1}$	$V_{n,2}$	$V_{n,3}$		$V_{n,m}$

Entities

Figure 10.10   Data organization can be viewed conceptually as an entity/attribute matrix.

left with one entity identifier, which is an attribute value in itself, and one or more attribute values. The resultant organization can be viewed conceptually as an "entity/attribute" matrix, such as the one given in Figure 10.10. An entity/ attribute matrix is also known as an *entity record set*; the significance of the latter terminology will become apparent in subsequent chapters.

The information represented in an entity/attribute matrix can be stored in several ways. The manner in which the information is stored is normally referred to as data organization. For example, if the information in the matrix were stored by rows, the organization would correspond to a conventional data record, such as an employee's record in a payroll file. This is referred to as "regular" organization and is represented by data maps of the form E→V. Similarly, if the information were stored by columns, the organization would

Garment #	Class	Quality Level	Color	Location (Rack #)	Order #
9451	Suit	A	Brown	34	2984
10114	Coat	B	Blue	41	0032
10115	Coat	A	Beige	41	0032
11125	Suit	C	Black	34	6321
12532	Dress	A	White	55	1794
12611	Pants	B	Green	39	2984
13001	Suit	B	Brown	34	3009
15539	Coat	B	Blue	41	0032
16327	Dress	C	Black	55	6321
17199	Dress	C	White	55	6321
18777	Pants	A	White	39	1794
18778	Pants	A	White	39	2984
18779	Pants	A	White	39	0032

Figure 10.11   Sample data set conceptualized as an entity/attribute matrix.

Attribute	*Value*	*Identifier(s)*
Class ⟶	Suit	9451, 11125, 13001
	Coat	10114, 10115, 15539
	Dress	12532, 16327, 17199
	Pants	12611, 18777, 18778, 18779

Quality level ⟶	A	9451, 10115, 12532, 18777, 18778, 18779
	B	10114, 12611, 13001, 15539
	C	11125, 16327, 17199

Color ⟶	Brown	9451, 13001
	Blue	10114, 15539
	Beige	10115
	Black	11125, 16327
	White	12532, 17199, 18777, 18778, 18779
	Green	12611

Location ⟶	34	9451, 11125, 13001
	39	12611, 18777, 18778, 18779
	41	10114, 10115, 15539
	55	12532, 16327, 17199

Order # ⟶	0032	10114, 10115, 15539, 18779
	1794	12532, 18777
	2984	9451, 12611, 18778
	3009	13001
	6321	11125, 16327, 17199

Figure 10.12   Inverted form of the sample data set of Figure 10.11.

correspond to an inverted file structure. In the latter case, however, it would be necessary to include entity identifiers with data records since the entities involved would not otherwise be identified. Inverted organization is represented by data maps of the form V→E. Sample data conceptualized as an entity/attribute matrix is given in Figure 10.11. Information is normally stored according to the collating sequence of the values of one of the attributes and gives rise to the various forms of file organization: sequential, indexed sequential, random, etc. Clearly, the data is redundant in the sense that several values are replicated. *In general, data redundancy can be reduced by making the data structure more complex; conversely, the complexity of a data structure can be reduced by adding replications of data elements.*

DATA BASE UTILIZATION

An obvious consideration in data base structure is the manner in which the data is to be accessed. When records are processed sequentially or inquiries are made about specific entities, such as an employee with the entity identifier "employee #," a regular storage organization such as sequential, indexed sequential, or random is frequently appropriate. However, when inquiries are made with regard to particular attribute values, such as "list the employees that are over 40 years of age and have children," then a form of inverted structure is more appropriate. The major consideration here is time, or more accurately, access efficiency.

Figure 10.12 gives an inverted form of the sample data set conceptualized in Figure 10.11. Clearly, the regular form is more appropriate for a conventional data processing operation, such as a file update according to batch transaction records. However, the preparation of a list of all records where the class attribute was "suit" would require that the processing program pass over the complete data set. Thus, the inverted form is more useful for data requests of the latter type from the viewpoint of access efficiency.

Another problem is change. The modification of the value of an attribute for data stored in regular form requires only that a specific field be changed.* With inverted organization, an entity identifier must be moved from one list to another causing difficulties in list maintenance. In general, update is a problem of complex data maps regardless of the method of file organization.

REFERENCES

Chapin, N., "Common file organization technqiues compared," *Proceedings of the 1969 Fall Joint Computer Conference,* AFIPS Volume 35, pp. 413–422.

CODASYL Systems Committee, "Introduction to Feature Analysis of Generalized Data Base Management Systems,"' *Communications of the ACM,* Volume 14, No. 5 (May 1971), pp. 308–318.

Engles, R. W., *A Tutorial on Data Base Organization,* IBM Corporation, Presented to the SHARE Organization, March 1970.

Hayden, G., *Data Base Structures,* Federal Reserve Bank of New York, 1970.

---

*Frequently, subfiles are created from a master file to achieve access efficiency. When the master is changed, subfiles must also be updated. This simple fact leads to much of the file processing that is performed in the data processing industry.

Lyon, J. K., *An Introduction to Data Base Design*, New York, John Wiley and Sons, Inc., 1971.

Meltzer, H. M., *Data Base Concepts and Architecture for Data Base Systems*, IBM Corporation, Presented to the SHARE Organization, August 1969.

Wright, K. R., "Information Description and Relationships," *Managing the Impact of Generalized Data Bases*, A Special Seminar Held at the National Computer Conference, June 7 and 8, 1973, Sponsored by AFIPS, pp. 93–103.

11 | DATA BASE STRUCTURE AND REPRESENTATION

INTRODUCTION

In order to facilitate the updating of inverted files or in general, complex data maps, some consideration must be given to the manner in which information is represented and organized in storage. The most obvious conclusion to draw at this stage is to use pointers to chain related information, and in many cases, this is the technique that is actually used. However, it is useful to consider chaining as an implementation technique and to view representation at a higher and more conceptual level.

The complex data map given in Figure 11.1 is used as an example to demonstrate three basic methods of representation: the "connection matrix," "value pairs," and "variable list" techniques. (The data map should be considered to be of the form: *letter→digit*.) The objective is to establish a representation that achieves a viable trade-off between search, update, and storage requirements. For any particular application, the "best" method is dependent upon the "needs" of the data base system.

If the number of values in the attribute sets of the data mapping is small, then a convenient method of representing the mapping is to use a *connection matrix*, as shown in Figure 11.2. A mapping between two elements is denoted by a value of one placed at the intersection of the appropriate row and column. A conventional mapping corresponds to examination of the matrix by rows. An inverse mapping corresponds to examination of the matrix by columns. A connection matrix can also be used to represent an entity/attribute matrix as

179

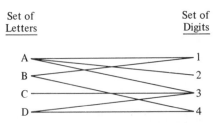

Figure 11.1 A data map of the form *letters→ digits* used to demonstrate three methods of representation.

	1	2	3	4
A	1	1	1	0
B	1	0	0	1
C	0	0	1	0
D	0	0	1	1

Figure 11.2 Representation of a data map by a connection matrix.

shown in Figure 11.3. Because the total number of bits in the connection is small, which is a defining characteristic for its use, the matrix can be stored as a bit map followed by the set of attribute values that correspond to one bit.

If the number of values in the attribute sets is large but the mappings for individual values is small, then *value pairs* is a suitable representation. With this method, the pairs of attribute values that comprise a mapping (i.e., a fact as

Attributes

	A_1	A_2	A_3	A_4
E_1	1	1	0	1
E_2	1	0	0	1
E_3	0	0	1	0
E_4	0	0	1	1

Entities

(Connection Matrix)

| 1 | 1 | 0 | 1 | 1 | 0 | 0 | 1 | 0 | 0 | 1 | 0 | 0 | 0 | 1 | 1 | $v_{1,1}$ | $v_{1,2}$ | $v_{1,4}$ | $v_{2,1}$ | $v_{2,4}$ | $v_{3,3}$ | $v_{4,3}$ | $v_{4,4}$ |

Bit map representing connection matrix (by rows.) ⎫ Corresponding attribute values (by rows of the connection matrix).

Figure 11.3 A connection matrix can also be used to represent an entity/attribute matrix. It is stored as a bit map followed by a set of attribute values.

A   1
A   2
A   3
B   1
B   4
C   3
D   3
D   4

Figure 11.4 Value pairs representation of
the data map of *letters→digits*
given in Figure 11.1.

defined earlier) are simply listed. Thus, the complete data mapping exists as a
list of pairs of values, as shown in Figure 11.4, which is a "value pairs" representation of the data map of Figure 11.1.

When a convenient limitation cannot be placed on the number of values in the
attribute sets or in individual mappings, then the method of *variable lists* is useful
because argument values in the mappings are not repeated, as shown in Figure
11.5. A variable list consists of a value followed by a list of the values to which
it is mapped.

A 1 2 3, B 1 4, C 3, D 3 4.

Figure 11.5 Variable lists representation of
the data map of *letters→digits*
given in Figure 11.1.

The above methodology has a definite orientation to simple data maps and
complex data maps (with inverses that are not complex). The reason is that data
maps of this type represent tree structures, and tree structures model many real-
life situations. For example, tree structures can be used to describe: the organizational structure of a business; the breakdown of a written report into section,
paragraph, and sentence; an accident reporting system organized by policy,
accident, and claim; and the static structure of a computer program.

A *tree* is defined recursively as a finite set T of nodes structured as follows:
(1) one node is designated as the root of the tree (T); and (2) the remaining
nodes are partitioned into disjoint sets $T_1, T_2, \cdots, T_n$, each of which is a tree.
The trees $T_1, T_2, \cdots, T_n$ are known as *subtrees* of the tree T. If a node has no
subtrees, it is referred to as a *terminal node*. A nonterminal node is referred to
as a *branch node*. In the tree depicted in Figure 11.6, node A is the root of the
tree, nodes B and C are branch nodes, and nodes D, E, F, G, H, I are terminal
nodes. Figure 11.7 gives an example of department, employee, and dependent
data represented as a tree structure.

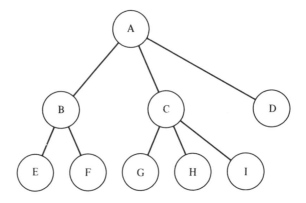

Figure 11.6   A tree structure.

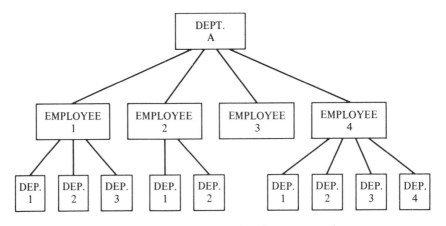

Figure 11.7   Department, employee, and dependent data represented as a tree structure.

A tree can be described by a complex data map with an inverse that is a simple data map.

HIERARCHICAL STRUCTURE

Hierarchical organization is a method of representing a tree in storage while maintaining its structural properties.   Hierarchical organization achieves its greatest utility from the fact that it is possible to store a tree without the use of pointers.   Consider the tree structure in Figure 11.8 which could represent the department/employee/dependent data mentioned previously.   Each node of the tree would ordinarily exist as a collection of data elements recording facts about a single entity.   One method of storing this information is to replicate all nodes

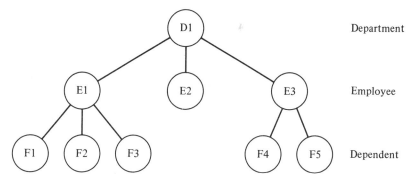

Figure 11.8 An example of information that lends itself to a hierarchical structure.

for all paths through the tree from a terminal node to the root. Thus, as a conventional file structure, the information content of Figure 11.8 would be stored as:

$$
\begin{array}{lll}
\text{D1} & \text{E1} & \text{F1} \\
\text{D1} & \text{E1} & \text{F2} \\
\text{D1} & \text{E1} & \text{F3} \\
\text{D1} & \text{E2} & \\
\text{D1} & \text{E3} & \text{F4} \\
\text{D1} & \text{E3} & \text{F5}
\end{array}
$$

Obviously, this type of representation is not efficient for large files. A method of storing trees that avoids unnecessary replication is to use a *linear representation*, expressed symbolically as:

D1(E1(F1,F2,F3),E2,E3(F4,F5)),D2. . .

Linear representation gives rise to a storage technique known as *contiguous hierarchical data organization* in which data elements corresponding to a predefined subtree occupy contiguous storage locations. Figure 11.9 gives an example of contiguous hierarchical storage organization for two departments D1 and D2 that exists as subtrees of a tree representing the total organization of an enter-

D1 *data*	E1 *data*	F1 *data*	F2 *data*	F3 *data*	E2 *data*	E3 *data*	F4 *data*	F5 *data*	
D2 *data*	E4 *data*	F6 *data*	F7 *data*	E5 *data*	F8 *data*	E6 *data*	F9 *data*	F10 *data*	F11 *data*

Figure 11.9 Contiguous hierarchical storage organization for the two departments D1 and D2, employees E*i*, and dependents F*i*.

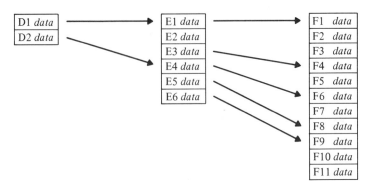

Figure 11.10   Noncontiguous hierarchical storage organization for the two
departments D1 and D2, employees E*i*, and dependents F*i*.

prise.   Actual implementation of contiguous hierarchical storage organization
would probably utilize numeric codes to denote the level of each node and the
number of corresponding subordinate nodes.

The preceding examples utilize data maps of the form E→E′, which means that
two entity sets are involved.   When this is the case, it is frequently desirable to
process the data of an entity set independently of its hierarchical structure.
Thus, for example, it may be desirable to process all employee records without
regard to the departments. *Noncontiguous hierarchical organization,* as shown
in Figure 11.10, permits records for departments, employees, and dependents to
be accessed without scanning unneeded information.   Some of the disadvantages
of noncontiguous hierarchical storage organization are that subordinate records
must contain unique identifiers (e.g., each employee must have a unique
employee #, and corresponding records must be sequenced in some manner)
along with an indicator denoting the record of which it is a descendent (e.g.,
each employee record would probably contain a department code).   In actual
practice, therefore, noncontiguous hierarchical storage organization would normally be implemented through an index that points to each subordinate record.

Frequently, contiguous and noncontiguous hierarchical organizations are used
in combination with each other, and in combination with other methods, such
as ring structures (covered later), to store the information of an enterprise.

COMPLEX DATA MAPS

Hierarchical structures are satisfactory for representing data maps of the form
A→B and B→C where the inverse data maps are not complex—in other words,
tree structures.   Complex data mappings of the form A→C and B→C cannot be
represented by hierarchical structures and must be represented by networks.   (A
network is a set of nodes with relationships between the nodes.   Figure 11.11
depicts a simple network that can be used to represent a complex data map.)

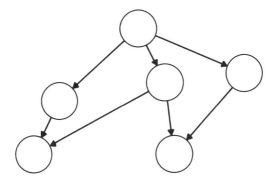

Figure 11.11   An example of a simple network that can
be used to represent complex data maps.

In a complex data mapping of the form A→C and B→C, the physical ordering
of information must be based on the entity set into which the mappings are
made—i.e., the set C in this case. (This is a distinct departure from hierarchical
storage organization in which the physical ordering is based on the entity set
from which the mappings are made. In the previous department/employee/
dependent examples; the employee records, for example, were based on depart-
mental order.) This is a logical consequence because if we consider the inverse
mappings C→A and C→B, the physical ordering must be based on C.

In a complex data mapping of the form A→C and B→C where the physical
ordering is based on set C, several methods, including the connection matrix,
value pairs, and variable lists methods given previously, can be used to represent
the mapping.

There is no reason to avoid the use of pointers further and the two methods
introduced here utilize the concept of records that are linked together. Two
convenient methods representing networks are "chained list organization" and
"variable pointer list organization". Examples of these methods use the familiar
case of departments, job, and employees with complex mappings of the form:
Department→Employees and *Job→Employees.*

One method of associating related employees is by job and department.
Records for employees with the same job code are chained together as a linked
list. A "job record" serves as the head of the list. Similarly, records for
employees in the same department are chained together as a linked list and a
"department record" serves as the head of the list. Thus, each employee record
contains two pointers, as demonstrated in Figure 11.12. This technqiue is known
as *chained list organization.* The concept of chained list organization can be
extended further; employee records (in this case) can contain fields that serve as
pointers for other linked lists and also as heads of subordinate lists.

Two of the stated disadvantages of chained list organization involve the

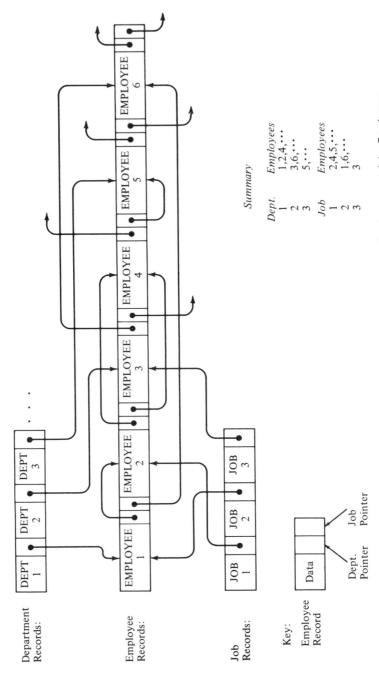

Figure 11.12 Chained list for a data mapping of the form: *Department→Employees* and *Job→Employees*.

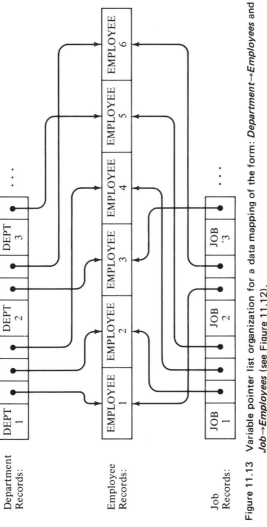

Figure 11.13   Variable pointer list organization for a data mapping of the form: *Department→Employees* and *Job→Employees* (see Figure 11.12).

following:

1. If a pointer field is lost, the remainder of the chain is not recoverable.
2. It is a time consuming process to follow a linked list on secondary storage because most records will be located in different areas and require separate input/output operations before they can be accessed.

These disadvantages are relieved somewhat with *variable pointer list organization*, which is characterized by the fact that the pointers are kept with the records of the set from which the mappings are defined. Variable pointer list organization is depicted in Figure 11.13.

Chained list and variable pointer list organization are both integrated data base structures for representing complex data mappings. Another approach is to utilize separate data structures, dependent upon the data requests that are made. Assume that employee records are stored using a conventional direct organization technique—such as indexed sequential—wherein records are ordered by a unique identifier, such as employee number. A means of representing complex

Employee #	Name	Dept #	Job #
1		1	2
2		1	1
3		2	3
4		1	1
5		3	1
6		2	2

Conventional Data Organization

Dept #	Name	Employee #	Name	Employee #	Name	Employee #	
1		1		2		4	. . .
2		3		6	. . .		
3		5	. . .				

Secondary Indexes

Job #	Name	Employee #	Name	Employee #	Name	Employee #	
1		1		4		5	. . .
2		3		6	. . .		
3		5	. . .				

Figure 11.14 The use of secondary indexes can be used to represent complex data mappings.

data mappings is to create secondary indexes as shown in Figure 11.14, which contain employee numbers (and perhaps names) of employees in each department and with a particular job classification.

RING STRUCTURES

The preceding discussion has been concerned with conceptual and practical methods for the representation of simple and complex data mappings. Implementation techniques necessarily include tables and lists that utilize both consecutive and linked organization. Linked list structures can be singly linked, doubly linked, or may include any number of links and/or pointers. Regardless of the method of implementation, these structures represent only a data mapping and not its inverse.

A *ring structure* is a linked list in which the last element of a list points to the head of the list—hence the name "ring structure." Figure 11.15 depicts a ring

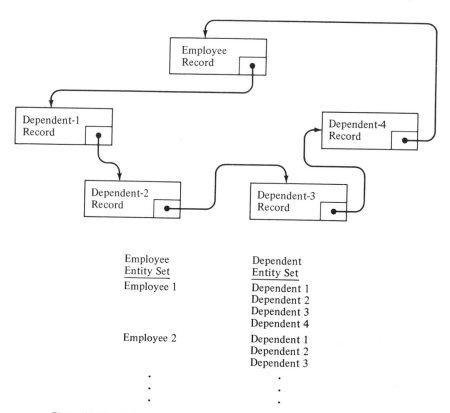

Figure 11.15 A ring structure representing a data mapping and its inverse.

structure for an employee and his dependents. The use of ring structures in data base technology has several distinct advantages:

1. A ring structure represents a data mapping and its inverse.
2. The technique provides a means of processing the records in one ring and the capability for branching off and processing the records in a subordinate ring. When the processing of the subordinate ring is complete, processing of the primary ring can be continued.
3. Nesting of ring structures can be implemented to any level and a single record can be a member record of several ring structures.
4. Ring structures may also include backward pointers and/or pointers to the head of the list—referred to as the owner record.

Thus when using ring structures, any record can simultaneously be the "owner" of a ring of subordinate records and a member of another ring structure.

ORGANIZATION AND MANAGEMENT

Data base organization is and should be a management concern rather than a problem of systems analysis and programming. This concern stems from the desire to share data by multiple applications. The requirement for sharing implies data independence—that is, an organization and description of data that is independent of a particular application. However, if an enterprise is concerned with operational and informational efficiency, data description and organization cannot be completely independent of all computer programs.

For example, the efficiency of informational requests is dependent upon data organization. An *attribute request* is a query to obtain the attribute values of one or more entities. If the data is stored using a regular organization (such as random direct or indexed sequential), then this type of request normally can be satisfied in an efficient manner—relatively speaking. If the data is stored using only an inverted organization, then an attribute request would be relatively inefficient. On the other hand, a *classification request* is a query to obtain entity identifiers for entities that possess certain attributes. A classification request would be relatively efficient for a file with inverted organization and inefficient for a file with a regular organization. (This is so because an exhaustive search is required with regular organization.)

Another aspect of data organization and efficiency concerns the time at which the attributes of data are associated with the operational characteristics of a program. The process of performing this association is known as *binding,* which can occur at several points in the development process: coding, compilation, linkage edit or loading, opening of a file, and at data access time. In very general terms, the earlier that binding takes place, the more efficient the execution of the program will be; however, late binding is related to versatility and data independence. The consideration of binding also requires descriptive techniques for defining a data base so that it can be referenced by different programs.

Data base organization and description along with binding are data base management problems. The current thinking on data base management is that it should be performed by a combination of human procedures and software facilities. The person involved with data base management is called the *Data Base Administrator* (DBA), and some corporate executives have predicted that in the near future, some organizations will have Vice Presidents of data base management. The software required for data base management is known as the *Data Base Manager* (DBM), which operates under the direction of the data base administrator to establish the structure of the data base and control the manner in which it is used and by whom.

The data base administrator communicates with the data base manager with a language known as the *Data Description Language* (DDL). The data base administrator can define the structure of the data base, assign names to entities, attributes, records, and files, and can specify the necessary privacy and data security measures that must be taken during access control. The user communicates with the data base manager using a *Data Manipulation Language* (DML) that opens and closes files and performs input and output operations. When a user requests access to a file through the data manipulation language, the data base manager uses the description of the file provided in the data description language by the data base administrator to access the correct information, perform editing and conversion as required, and provide the requested service.

A data base and all of its components and facilities must be sensitive to change. Users and applications change as do attributes, values, entities, and entity/attribute relationships. For any collection of data, attributes may be added or deleted. An example of the latter is adding of ZIP codes to mailing addresses, which was instituted in the not-to-distant past. In a similar manner, the use of integrated management information and control systems has reduced the need for data not directly relevant to the operation of an enterprise resulting in the reduction in the amount of data actually recorded. At the same time, advanced analysis techniques have created the need for "summary statistics" that serve as entity attributes; these are normally added to the data base on a dynamic basis.

A FINAL REMARK

The design, development, and use of a data base is a complicated process that is usually accompanied by a certain amount of trial-and-error, frustration, and reworking. Because a data base, by definition, contains the information known to an enterprise, it is not a system that can be developed "overnight" and not without an extensive amount of coordination and planning. The computer programs necessary for operating a data base are normally available from hardware or software vendors. However, a thorough background in data base technology is needed in order to put these systems to use. The objective of this chapter is to present an introduction to data base technology without "binding" the presentation to any particular system or design philosophy. Subsequent chapters deal with more specific topics ranging from the design of real systems to theoretical concepts in data base technology.

REFERENCES

Engles, R. W., *A Tutorial on Data Base Organization,* IBM Corporation, Presented to the SHARE Organization, March 1970.

Hayden, G., *Data Base Structures,* Federal Reserve Bank of New York, 1970.

Lyon, J. K., *An Introduction to Data Base Design,* New York, John Wiley and Sons, Inc., 1971.

Meltzer, H. M., *Data Base Concepts and Architecture for Data Base Systems,* IBM Corporation, Presented to the SHARE Organization, August 1969.

12 | DESCRIPTIVE TECHNIQUES

INTRODUCTION

In the design, development, and analysis of a data base, much of the thinking is done at the logical level. Analysts are concerned primarily with the logical relationships of data—called data structure—as opposed to storage structure that involves physical considerations. The objective of this chapter is to introduce techniques for describing data structures—other than through the use of a programming language—so that concepts can be discussed without the repeated use of examples.

One of the by-products of "descriptive techniques" is that an alternate approach to the introduction of data base concepts is presented. The goal of this book is to cover the current thinking on the subject of data base technology, and it is necessary to mention that computerists are not always referring to the same concept when they use the words "data base." Many readers of this volume will be preparing lectures and seminars on the subject matter and a viable method of introduction is the use of descriptive techniques.

GENERIC STRUCTURE

A data base is comprised of different types of structures, each with its own defining set of attributes. The structures of one type are constructed from structures of another type. The generic types from which a data base is constructed are listed as follows:

Item
Group
Group Relation
Entry
File
Data Base

The interrelationship of the generic types is given in Figure 12.1.

Within each of the above structures, it is important to distinguish between a component [of that structure] type and an occurrence of that structure type. In a file definition, for example, only one description of a particular record may exist. In the actual data file, however, any number of occurrences of that record may exist.

Structure	Component Structures
Item	No component structures
Group	Item, Group
Group Relation	Group
Entry	Group, Group Relation
File	Entry, Group Relation
Data Base	File, Group Relation

Figure 12.1   Component structures of generic structure types.

ITEMS

The basic type of structure is the data item that usually corresponds to the field in the realm of storage structures. The principal attribute of a data item is its *value*, which may be an element of arithmetic data, string data, or program control data. Other attributes that normally apply to data items are:

1. *Name*, which is used to refer to the data item.
2. *Value existence indicator,* which indicates the presence or absence of a valid value.
3. *Access lock* (privacy lock), which is used to control access to the data item.

Attributes that describe the type of data being considered are referred to as *data attributes.* For arithmetic data, data attributes include base, scale, mode, and precision. For string data, data attributes include the length of the string and type of string element—usually taken to be character or bit.* Program control data includes labels, addresses, and implementation-defined data concerned

---

*An alternate type of data to bit string would be logical data that can assume the values "true" or "false."

with the execution of a program. The class of address-values, frequently referred to as pointers, is the primary type of program control data that is of concern in data base technology.

Other attributes can be defined for use within a given programming language or operation environment. Some of the more familiar of these are: the date and time of the last change to the data item; units in which values are expressed (feet, pounds, etc.); editing and conversion masks; synonym lists (such as MALE for "M"); multiple valued items—such as arrays or arrays of structures; justification and synchronization of data values within storage boundaries; and indicators to indicate whether a data item is still contained in the data base and has not been deleted.

Data items are normally of concern within the data definition facility of a data base system.

GROUPS

A *group* is a set of items and other groups. A group is "simple" if it contains only items. A group is "compound" if it contains at least one group. A *simple group* is designed to be a means of collecting dissimilar items that are logically related. For example, Figure 12.2 gives the schema* for a simple group. The

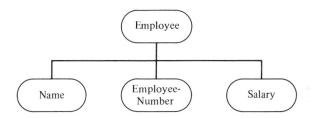

Figure 12.2 A schema (i.e., a structure diagram) representing a simple group.

group includes the items: *name, employee number,* and *salary,* which are logically related to an *employee;* the group schema corresponds to a COBOL group item of the form:

```
02 EMPLOYEE.
   03 NAME PICTURE. . . .
   03 EMPLOYEE-NUMBER PICTURE. . . .
   03 SALARY PICTURE. . . .
```

*A *schema* is a diagrammatic presentation of a concept, such as a structure diagram or an organization chart.

or a PL/I structure declaration, such as:

```
DECLARE 1 ...
    2 EMPLOYEE,
        3 NAME PIC ...
        3 EMPLOYEE-NUMBER PIC ...
        3 SALARY ... ;
```

An occurrence of a simple group includes one realization of each constituent item.

A group schema is represented symbolically by an expression of the form:

$$group\text{-}name = \{member, \ldots\}$$

where "member" is either an item or another group. The schema in Figure 12.2 is represented symbolically as:

EMPLOYEE = {NAME, EMPLOYEE-NUMBER, SALARY }

(This notation pertains only to this chapter and is not used throughout the book.)

A *compound group* is a means of collectively representing items and other dissimilar groups that are logically related. If, for example, the group:

JOB= {CODE,TITLE}

were added to the above EMPLOYEE group, the result would be the compound group:

EMPLOYEE- {NAME,EMPLOYEE-NUMBER,SALARY,JOB= -{CODE,TITLE}}

A schema representing a compound group EMPLOYEE is given as Figure 12.3 and corresponds to a COBOL group item of the form:

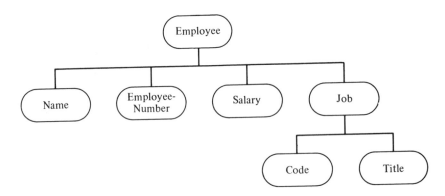

Figure 12.3   A schema representing a compound group.

```
02 EMPLOYEE.
    03 NAME PICTURE ...
    03 EMPLOYEE-NUMBER PICTURE ...
    03 SALARY PICTURE ...
    03 JOB.
        04 CODE PICTURE ...
        04 TITLE PICTURE ...
```

or a PL/I structure declaration, such as:

```
DECLARE 1 ...
    2 EMPLOYEE,
    3 NAME PIC ...
    3 EMPLOYEE-NUMBER PIC ...
    3 SALARY PIC ...
    3 JOB,
        4 CODE PIC ...
        4 TITLE PIC ... ;
```

Items that comprise a group are referred to as *principal items*, as compared to items that are members of component groups. Similarly, a group that is a member of a compound group is referred to as a principal group. Thus, in the compound group:

EMPLOYEE= {NAME,EMPLOYEE-NUMBER,SALARY,JOB= {CODE,TITLE}}

for example, the items NAME, EMPLOYEE-NUMBER, and SALARY are principal items and the group JOB is a principal group. A principal group schema may be simple or compound, so that groups may be nested.

A principal group schema may be singular (non-repeating) or multiple (or repeating). With a singular group schema, one occurrence of the group may exist. With a multiple group schema, several occurrences of a group may exist. A multiple group schema corresponds to a group item defined with an OCCURS clause in COBOL or an array of structures in the PL/I language. Figure 12.4 depicts an occurrence of a compound group schema that incorporates a multiple group schema.

Group attributes are primarily concerned with definition and utilization, compared with item attributes that are operationally oriented. Group schema usually include the following attributes:

1. A *name* attribute that is used during definition.
2. An *identifier* attribute that uniquely identifies an entity and is frequently used for sequencing and retrieval.
3. *Access locks* that control group utilization.
4. *Date and time indicators* that specify when the group was created.
5. *Monitoring* attributes that record frequency data on group utilization.

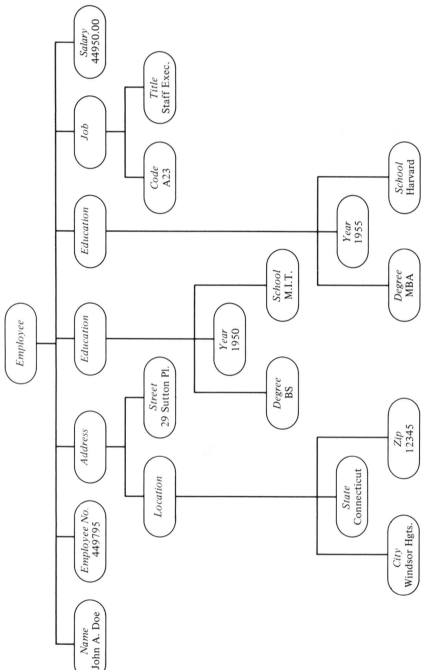

Figure 12.4   An occurrence of a compound group schema that incorporates multiple principal groups (*Education*).

The manner in which a group schema is used by a data base system is dependent upon the physical attributes of the system.* Data mappings are established between groups that correspond to records (in the conventional sense) or between areas of contiguous storage in systems that are not record oriented.

GROUP RELATIONS

A *group relation* is a mapping between two groups—or more precisely, between two sets whose elements are group occurrences. Most data base systems employ the mapping concept and provide a means of assigning names and attributes to group relations. A graphic diagramming technique has been developed for displaying the structural relationship among groups; it is described in this section and is referred to as a "structure diagram." An application of structure diagrams to storage structures is given later in this chapter.

A group relation consists of one or more group schemas and a mapping between the schemas or from the group schema to itself. A group schema is represented by a rectangle and the mapping is denoted by the arrow, as shown in Figure 12.5. Figure 12.6 employs the technique to represent a one-to-many

Group Schema   Arrow Representing

Figure 12.5 Basic symbols for representing structure diagrams.

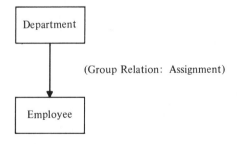

(Group Relation: Assignment)

Figure 12.6 An example of a group relation between the department and employee groups.

*For example, in COBOL, a group is known as a group item; in the DBTG system, a group is known as a record; and in IMS, a group is known as a segment.

(1:n) relationship between two group schemas: the "department" and the "employee." The "employee" group would normally represent several employees for each occurrence of a department. The arrowhead points to the subordinate (or dependent) group and the tail of the arrow leaves the master (or parent) group. The arrow is frequently labeled with the name of the group relation. The parent/dependent relationship may also be viewed as an owner/ member set of groups. Figure 12.7 illustrates an occurrence of the group relation schema given in Figure 12.6. The differences between a group relation and a compound group are twofold: (1) in a group relation, a group may be subordinate to several groups (an n:1 relationship), whereas in a compound group, a group may be subordinate to a single item; and (2) in a group relation, a subordinate group retains its identity, whereas in a compound group, subordinate items do not possess unique names.

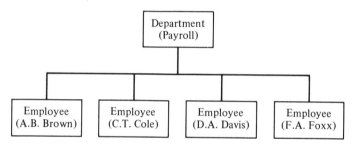

Figure 12.7   An occurrence of the group relation schema given in Figure 12.6.

A mapping of a group schema onto itself is represented by a solid arc, as shown in Figure 12.8 that represents a relationship between an employee and his spouse. When attached to a subordinate group schema, the arc specifies a ring structure (Figure 12.9).

Structure diagrams can also be used to represent group relation schemas for a multilevel hierarchy, as illustrated in Figure 12.10. In this case, the following data mapping exists: *Department→Employee→Dependent*.

In data management, a file can contain more than one type of detail record. Similarly, a group relation schema can have multiple subordinate group schemas. The group relation schema in Figure 12.11 depicts a simple tree structure that

Figure 12.8   The mapping of a group onto itself. This schema represents a relationship between an employee and his spouse.

Figure 12.9 Group schema for a ring structure.

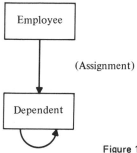

Figure 12.10 Group relation schema for a multilevel hierarchy.

represents a hierarchical relationship. (Each individual relationship in Figure 12.11 is a 1:n mapping.)

A network is a form of an n:1 relationship. A typical example is that of an employee group that would normally be subordinate to two "parent" groups: a department group and a group that represents "job classification." Figure 12.12 illustrates a group relation schema for a network of this general type. (Again, each relationship is a 1:n mapping.)

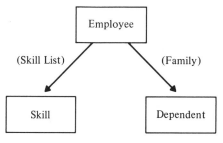

Figure 12.11 A structure diagram of a hierarchical relationship.

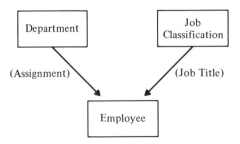

Figure 12.12   A structure diagram of a simple
network.

Typical group relation attributes are: name, access locks, and placement criteria for group insertions—such as first, last, or by ordering sequence.

ENTRY, FILE, AND DATA BASE

An *entry* is a set of groups and group relations in which only one group is not contained in or is not subordinate to another group. This group is known as the *entry defining group* that roughly corresponds to a data record in data management. Typical attributes of an entry are: name, access locks, and date and time information denoting when the entry was created.

A *file* is set of independent entries, so that a *data base* is a collection of files. Files are identified by name and can be composed of entries that are unrelated or related. Files containing unrelated entries or entries related only by ordering are referred to as *unlinked files*. Files with entries that are related explicitly are known as *linked files*.

In general, the descriptive methodology does not apply beyond the group and group relation classifications. Moreover, the techniques apply only to the logical organization of data. An instance of the schema of an integrated file structure that can be viewed as a data base is illustrated in Figure 12.13.

DESCRIPTION OF STORAGE STRUCTURES—AN EXAMPLE OF THE METHODOLOGY

One of the most useful examples of the use of structure diagrams involves the concepts of external storage structures.* Structures of this type are characterized by the fact that entities exist with a specific relationship to each other. For example, a track is a subunit of a cylinder, a cylinder is a subdivision of a disk volume, and so forth.

---

*See: C. W. Bachman, "The evolution of storage structures," *Communications of the ACM*, Vol. 15, No. 7 (July 1972), pp. 628–634.

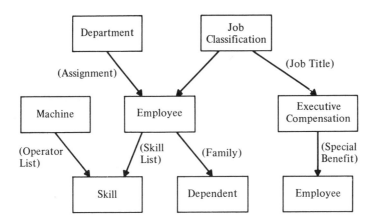

Figure 12.13   Schema of a data base. MACHINE, DEPARTMENT, and JOB CLASSIFICATION are entry defining groups that are analogous to files in conventional data management.

A conventional file structure is illustrated in Figure 12.14. It is interpreted to denote that there are three classes of entities: files, records, and fields; they are related in the following manner: (1) for each occurrence of the FILE entity class, there exists a 1:n relationship with many occurrences of the RECORD entity class; and (2) for each occurrence of the RECORD entity class, there exists a 1:n relationship with many occurrences of the FIELD entity class. The dashed line without an arrowhead between STORAGE DEVICE and FILE indicates a sometime 1:1 relationship between the two entities; "sometime" is defined as

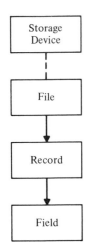

Figure 12.14   Structure diagram of a conventional file structure. (See Bachman, p. 632.)

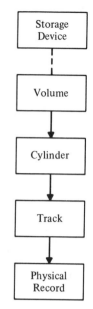

Figure 12.15   Structure diagram of a removable disk volume. (See Bachman, p. 632.)

times when the file is mounted on the storage device. A disk volume is represented in Figure 12.15 and the same concepts are used.

A permanent 1:1 relationship between the occurrence of two or more entities is denoted by a "wide" box containing more than one entity name. In Figure 12.16, a fixed-head magnetic drum is represented wherein the relationship between STORAGE DEVICE, VOLUME, and CYLINDER is permanently fixed. In a similar manner, the relationship between VOLUME, CYLINDER, and TRACK is permanently fixed for magnetic tape as illustrated in Figure 12.17.

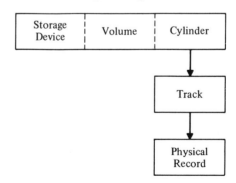

Figure 12.16   Structure diagram of a fixed-head magnetic disk. (See Bachman, p. 632.)

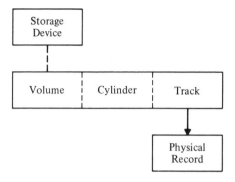

Figure 12.17 Structure diagram of a magnetic
tape volume.   (See Bachman,
p. 632.)

Data base technology is primarily concerned with logical data structures such as logical files, pages, records, and fields, and the manner in which they are related.   Figure 12.18 gives a structure diagram of logical data structures; and its interpretation parallels that given in the preceding discussion: a logical file is comprised of one or more pages, which contain one or more logical records, and so forth.

Bachman's extension to the structure diagram is a useful descriptive technique that can be used to represent the following kinds of structures:

1. Mapping a logical file structure onto magnetic tape.
2. Mapping a logical file structure onto removable disk storage.

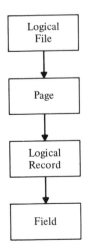

Figure 12.18 Structure diagram of logical data structures.   (See
Bachman, p. 633.)

3. Correspondence between blocks in an indexed sequential file.

4. The representation of complex mappings.

The structure diagram is a powerful conceptual tool that can be used to describe the interrelationships of a data base without "binding" it to a particular data base management system. Additional insight on how the technique can be used is available from the Bachman paper that served as the basic reference for this section.

REFERENCES

Bachman, C. W., "The evolution of storage structures," *Communications of the ACM*, Volume 15, No. 7 (July 1972), pp 628–634.

CODASYL *Data Base Task Group (DBTG) Report,* April 1971. Available from the Association for Computing Machinery.

CODASYL Systems Committee Technical Report, *Feature Analysis of Generalized Data Base Management Systems,* May 1971. Available from the Association for Computing Machinery.

Lyon, J. K., *An Introduction to Data Base Design,* New York, John Wiley and Sons, Inc., 1971.

Schubert, R. F., "Basic concepts in data base management systems," *Datamation,* Volume 18, No. 7 (July 1972), pp 42–47.

13 | DBTG REPORT

INTRODUCTION

The DBTG report is a recommendation of the Data Base Task Group to its parent committee—the CODASYL Programming Language Committee.* The subject matter concerns data base management systems and the report proposes three associated concepts and languages: a data description language for describing a data base, a data description language for describing the part of a data base known to a program, and a data manipulation language.

The objectives of the Data Base Task Group were manyfold:**

1. Allow data to be structured in the manner most suitable to each application, regardless of the fact that some or all of that data may be used by other applications—such flexibility to be achieved without requiring data redundancy.
2. Allow more than one run-unit to concurrently retrieve or update the data in the database.
3. Provide and permit the use of a variety of search strategies against an entire database or portions of a database.
4. Provide protection of the database against unauthorized access of data, and from untoward interaction of programs.

*CODASYL is an acronym for "Committee on Data Systems Languages."
***DBTG Report*, p. 6.

5. Provide for centralized capability to control the physical placement of data.
6. Provide device independence for programs.
7. Allow the declaration of a variety of data structures ranging from those in which no connection exists between data-items to network structures.
8. Allow the user to interact with the data while being relieved of the mechanics of maintaining the structural associations which have been declared.
9. Allow programs to be as independent of the data as current techniques will permit.
10. Provide for separate descriptions of the data in the database and of the data known to a program.
11. Provide for a description of the database which is not restricted to any particular processing language.
12. Provide an architecture that permits the description of the database, and the database itself, to be interfaced by multiple processing languages.

The DBTG concepts can be classed as a host language system which means that a self-contained language is not being defined but rather an enhancement of an existing system. In this case, the host language is COBOL; however, the data description language for describing a data base does not necessarily require a host language. Thus, the data base can be accessed through other programming languages that can utilize the data base description.

The emphasis in this chapter is placed on the overall DBTG concept so that some topics are covered lightly and others are omitted completely. A case in point is that of data security. It is an important area and has become a major subject in its own right. For information on this and other topics, the reader is referred to the original DBTG report.*

SYSTEMS CONCEPTS

A *data base management system* is intended to be utilized in an operating system environment that contains conventional data management facilities, manages auxiliary storage,** and provides traditional language capabilities. The data base management system (DBMS) exists as a set of operational programs— analogous to the control programs of an operating system. The exact design of the DBMS is a function of the implementation of the DBTG concepts.

The data description languages (DDL's) permit a data base or a part of a data base to be defined, and exist as language structures. The data description lan-

*CODASYL Data Base Task Group Report (April 1971), available from the Association for Computing Machinery (ACM), New York, and the IFIP Administrative Data Processing Group, Amsterdam.

**Auxiliary storage is also referred to as "secondary storage" and "external storage." For example, disk storage is auxiliary storage while large capacity storage (LCS) is not.

guages recognize a collection of applications-oriented data structures that allow the user, at the programmer level, to communicate with the data base management system. These data structures are defined in Figure 13.1. Each subschema has an independent identity of its own and can be utilized by any number of programs.

The *data manipulation language* is used to transfer data between the data base and a program. The data manipulation language is intended to be imbedded in a host language; collectively, the data description languages and the data manipulation language provide, to the host language, the declarations and the procedure for data base processing.

The manner in which a data base management system functions in a general operating environment is conceptualized in Figure 13.2. A request for a data

Data Item	The smallest unit of named data. An occurrence of a data item represents an operational value.
Data Aggregate	A named collection of data items occurring in a record. There are two types of data aggregate, vectors and repeated groups. A vector is a linear array of homogeneous data items. A repeated group is a collection of data items, vectors, and repeated groups that may occur one or more times in a record occurrence.
Record	A named collection of data items or data aggregates. A data base may contain only one record definition of a specified type; however, any number of "occurrences" of that record type may exist.
Area	A named subdivision of the data base that permits the management and efficient utilization of a data base. An area may contain occurrences of records, sets, and parts of sets and may be assigned on a temporary, permanent, or shared basis.
Data Base	The collection of record occurrences, set occurrences, and areas that are defined and controlled by a particular schema. One schema exists for each data base and the contents of each data base are disjoint.
Schema	A complete description of a data base that exists as DDL entries. It includes the names and descriptions of all data items, data aggregates, record occurrences, set occurrences, and areas that are part of the data base.
Subschema	A description of that portion of the data base known to one or more particular programs. The subschema also exists as DDL entries.

Figure 13.1   Application-oriented data structures in a DBTG environment.

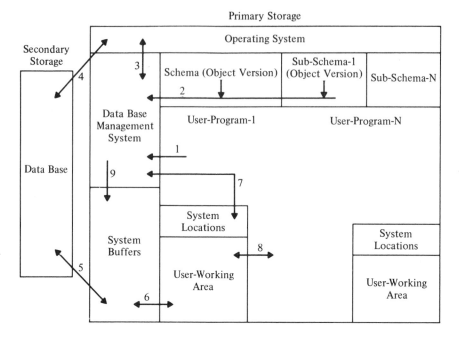

Figure 13.2 Functional organization of a conceptual data base management system.

transfer operation between the data base and the user-working area (UWA) is made by a user program. Each user program has a user-working area that is used by the data base management system in the following manner:

1. All data provided in response to a call to the data base management system is delivered to the user-working area.
2. All data to be picked up by the data base management system is placed in the user-working area.

A user-working area is established by the data base management system as a consequence of the subschema definition and can be addressed through the user program's host language. Program and data flow in Figure 13.2 are denoted by numbered arrows that are explained below:

1. A data request is made in the DML to the DBMS. (All communications between a user program and the DBMS are made in the DML.)
2. The data request is analyzed by the DBMS and the arguments of the data request statements are supplemented with information about the data itself that is contained in the object versions* of the schema of the data base, and the relevant subschema for the program.

*The object versions of the schema and the subschema are analogous to object code for programs. This is introduced later.

3. Using the arguments of the data request and the information from the schema and subschema, the DBMS initiates physical input/output operations through the operating system to access the data base on auxiliary storage.
4. The operating system initiates, controls, and manages physical input/output operations.
5. Data is transferred between the data base on auxiliary storage and the system buffers by the input/output system and the operating system.
6. The required data is transferred between the UWA of the calling program and the system buffers by the DBMS. The DBMS also performs transformations, editing, and conversions to compensate for data representation in the data base and user requirements as reflected in the UWA.
7. Status information on the data request is provided by the DBMS to the calling program.
8. The user program may perform data manipulation operations on the data in its UWA, as required.
9. The utilization of the system buffers are managed and controlled by the DBMS, and are shared by all user programs serviced by the DBMS.

Clearly, a user program's only interface with the data base is through the data base management system. The user working area is used as a loading and unloading zone for data transfer operations to and from the data base, and may be accessed by the host language. As a result, the host language provides the operational environment for the data manipulation language—which serves as the operational interface with the data base management system. Conceptually, statements from the data manipulation language are intermixed with host language statements, as is the case with conventional data management operations. The data manipulation language introduced later in the chapter is COBOL-oriented so that special "exit" or "enter" statements from one language to the other are not required. Operational conventions for other host languages would have to be worked out.

SCHEMA AND SUBSCHEMA

A schema is a description of the entire data base and a subschema is a description of a subset of a data base known to a user program. This concept has several distinct advantages:

1. The programmer need not be concerned with the entire data base but only those portions of it that are relevant to his needs.
2. Portions of the data base may be shared among different user programs.
3. A user program is limited to the subset of the data base specified in its subschema. This convention is a useful security and integrity feature.
4. Data independence between a data base and a user program can be achieved

because the subschema may differ from the schema. Thus, changes can be made to the data base without necessarily impacting user programs.

Language facilities for defining schema and subschema are given later. In general, however, a subschema must be a consistent and logical subset of the schema over which it is defined.

Implementation of schema and subschema is through compilation. The source code for schema and subschema is compiled independently and the object version is stored in a library. All schema and subschema are named and any number of subschema may be defined on the same schema. A user program invokes a particular subschema and only the data items, records, sets, and areas defined therein may be referenced in the program. Any number of user programs may use the same subschema.

The centralization of data base facilities requires human activity for modeling the data needs of an enterprise and establishing compromise agreements between conflicting user groups. This activity is referred to as the *data administration function* which involves organizing the data base, monitoring its use, and performing reorganization in response to a dynamically changing environment. The data administrator essentially assigns names, establishes privacy keys, allocates devices and media, synthesizes data structures, and makes reassignments, as required.

The DBTG concept of data base management is record oriented so that each record possesses a unique identifier/attribute known as a *data base key*. A data base key is assigned by the data base management system when a record is stored for the first time in the data base. Data base keys are used for accessing the data base and are mapped by the data base management system into physical addresses. The methodology for mappings of this sort are implementation defined. However, the schema data description language provides facilities for the relative placement of records so that record occurrences can be placed in the same area or "near some other records" to increase the efficiency of the system.

RECORDS AND SETS

Schema record definition is independent of any particular host language and includes definitional facilities for the following units of user data: (1) arithmetic and string data items, (2) data base keys, (3) implementation-defined data types, (4) vector and repeating group data aggregates, and (5) records. A record is described in a machine-independent manner so that a record in the data base does not necessarily correspond to a physical record in the storage structure. Moreover, a physical record may include control information that is not explicitly described in the schema data description language.

The content and structure of a record described in a subschema is a subset of the corresponding record described in the data base schema. In addition, data attributes between the two schemas may differ and the data base management system is responsible for performing the required conversions during a data request. Subschema records are defined relative to a user program's user working area; i.e., the data description entries describe formats and characteristics of data items as they appear in the UWA. Because subschema definitional facilities are COBOL-oriented, they necessarily include the following data description entries: (1) level numbers, (2) elementary data items, (3) group items, (4) arrays, (5) repeating groups, (6) condition names, and (7) index names. Each data item in a subschema record must correspond to a data item or data aggregate for the corresponding record in the schema.

A *set* is a named collection of record types that contains one owner record type and one or more member records. Any number of sets may be declared in a schema in accordance with the following concepts:

1. Any record type may be defined as being the owner record type of a set.
2. Any record type may be defined as being a member record type of one or more sets.
3. Any record type may be defined as being the owner record type of a set and a member record type of one or more different sets.
4. The occurrence of a set in a data base may include an occurrence of its owner record, and an arbitrary number of occurrences of each of its member records.

A set is declared in a data base schema that includes a "set order." The *set order* controls the logical order of the member records of a set and utilizes the following methods:

1. Sorted on the basis of a sort key, which may be the record's unique identifier.
2. In an order that results from inserting new records in *first, last, next,* and *prior* positions.

A record type can exist as a member record in two sets and have a different set order for each set. The manner in which a record occurrence participates in a set is referred to as the *type of set membership* that can be automatic, manual, mandatory, or optional. *Automatic* membership denotes that a set inclusion is established by the data base management system when a record is stored in the data base. *Manual* membership indicates that a stored record does not automatically become a member of a set; set membership must be established in an executing program with an INSERT command. *Mandatory* membership means that once a stored record is included in a set, the membership is permanent and the record cannot be deleted; however, the record occurrence can be changed with the MODIFY command. The *optional* type of set membership indicates that set membership is not necessarily permanent. With the optional type, the set membership of a record occurrence can be discluded with the REMOVE command and established in another set with the INSERT command or excised from the data base with the REMOVE or DELETE commands.

Set mode refers to the manner in which a set is implemented as a storage structure and involves an operational trade-off between access time and space utilization. Two modes are defined in the DBTG report: chain and pointer array; however, the schema data description language allows other set modes to be defined by the implementor of the DBTG concept. Sets declared with a set mode of *chain* are stored with linked organization so that serial access is provided to all record occurrences in the set. Actual implementation of the linked organization is optional and pointers may or may not be imbedded in the records themselves. The owner record of a set points to the first record, which points to the second record, etc. The last record points back to the owner record forming a ring structure. Figure 13.3 depicts a chain structure with forward

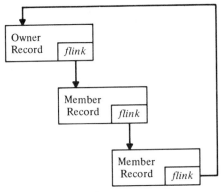

flink — forward pointer.

Figure 13.3   A chain structure with forward
(next) imbedded pointers.

imbedded pointers. (It is implemented as a singly-linked list.) A singly-linked list of this type can be processed in the forward (or next) direction only. If it is desired to process a set in the backward (or prior) direction, the attribute LINKED TO PRIOR must be used and backward pointers are established by the data base management system as shown in Figure 13.4. In addition, any of a set's member record types may be optionally linked to the owner record with the LINKED TO OWNER attribute. Figure 13.5 depicts a chain structure that includes forward (next), backward (prior), and owner pointers.

The unique record identifiers are used as data base pointers; thus, all data requests require the services of the data base management system. Space for at least one pointer is assigned to each record by the data base management system

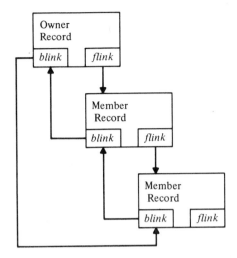

flink — forward pointer.
blink — backward pointer.

Figure 13.4   A chain structure with forward (next) and backward (prior) imbedded pointers.

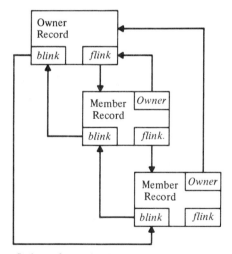

flink   — forward pointer.
blink   — backward pointer.
Owner — pointer to owner.

Figure 13.5   A chain structure with forward (next), backward (prior), and owner imbedded pointers.

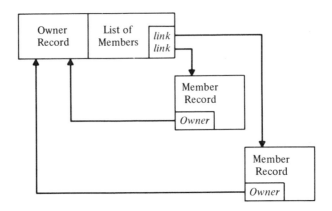

Figure 13.6   A   pointer   array   structure   with   imbedded   owner
pointers.

for each chain that the record participates in as an owner or as a member record. Additional pointers are generated by the data base management system when the set has the LINKED TO PRIOR attribute or member records are assigned the LINKED TO OWNER attribute.

Sets declared as *pointer arrays** are organized through a list of member record occurrences stored with the owner record. Figure 13.6 depicts a pointer array structure in which member records contain owner pointers, which are optional. The relations of "prior record" and "next record" are inherent in the contiguous list of pointers to member record occurrences stored in the owner record. A member record of a pointer array structure may be the owner record of either a pointer array structure or a chain structure.

Records are referenced in the data base through the data base management system with the data manipulation language. The following conventions govern the accessing of records from a data base:

1. The design of the data manipulation language requires that a distinction be made between the selection of a record and its delivery to an executing program.
2. A record is selected with a FIND command and an appropriate "record selection expression." An executing program has a "current" record that is defined as the most recently selected record.
3. The GET command is used to transfer the data items of the current record to a program's user-working area.

---

*The DBTG report also includes a *dynamic pointer array* structure of which any member record in the data base is a potential member. This is an advanced concept and the reader is referred to the original DBTG document.

4. The manner in which data items in the user-working area are interpreted is dependent upon the subschema invoked by the executing program.

The selection of a record can be based on the unique record identifier, on the current status information, and on the position of a record relative to the current record. Record selection based on the unique *record identifier* assigned by the data base management system capitalizes on the fact that an identifier is invariant for the life of the record. Record selection based on *currency* utilizes the fact that the data base management system maintains status indicators for each executing program that include: current record name, current set name, and current area name. Record selection based on position uses the current record indicator and allows the prior, next, first, last, owner, or the nth record occurrence to be retrieved.

Location of a data base record is analogous to data access in a data management environment. The "location mode" of a record occurrence is specified with the LOCATION MODE attribute for a record entry. Three access methods are provided: direct, calculation, and via set name. *Direct access* utilizes the unique record identifier mentioned previously; the unique record identifier of the current record is made available to an executing program by the data base management system and is therefore available for subsequent access. Retrieval based on *calculation* uses data items declared as CALC keys. The data base management system transforms the values of the CALC keys into the unique record identifier for data access. Retrieval based on *set name* involves two steps: selection of the required set, and selection of the desired record occurrence in the selected set. A set is selected through its owner record and a record occurrence is selected on the basis of a specified value for a data item or by positional record selection.

DATA STRUCTURES

Redundancy in a data base environment is minimized through data structures that model the data needs of an enterprise. Through the use of the set concept, introduced earlier in this chapter, the following data structures can be represented: sequential structures, tree structures, and networks. A list, as introduced in Chapter 4, is an example of a sequential data structure. Figure 13.7 gives three representations of a sequential data structure as a singly-linked list, a doubly-linked list, and as a ring structure. By definition, a single set occurrence is a representation of a sequential data structure with elements that are records. A structure diagram* of a sequential data structure is given as Figure 13.8; it has the following characteristics:

1. The arrow points from the owner record type to the member record type.

*See Chapter 12 for an introduction to descriptive techniques and structure diagrams.

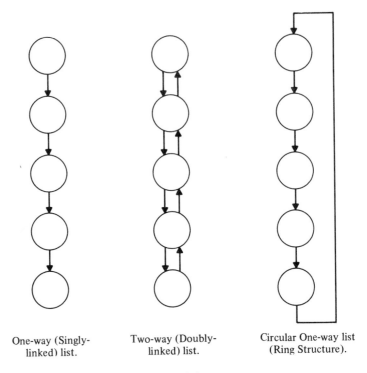

One-way (Singly-
linked) list.

Two-way (Doubly-
linked) list.

Circular One-way list
(Ring Structure).

Figure 13.7   Sequential data structures.

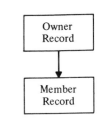

Figure 13.8   Structure diagram for a sequential data structure.

2. There may be any number (i.e., n) occurrences of the owner record type.
3. There is a 1-to-n relationship between owner records and member records, i.e., for each occurrence of an owner record, there may be n occurrences of the corresponding member record.

A *tree structure* is a hierarchically organized set of elements in which each element is related to only one element above it and n elements below it—as depicted in Figure 13.9. In a tree structure, each set contains one or more different record types—each of which represents a 1-to-n relationship. A struc-

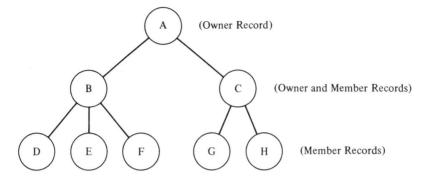

Figure 13.9   Tree structure.

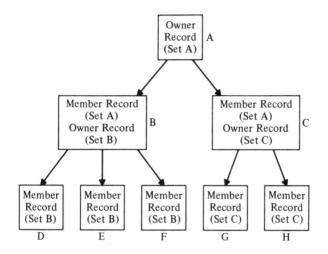

Figure 13.10   Structure diagram for a tree structure.

ture diagram for the tree structure of Figure 13.9 is given as Figure 13.10. In the latter diagram, each of the record types (i.e., A,B,C, . . .) is interpreted as being distinct.

A *network* is a data structure in which an *n*-to-*n* relationship can exist between elements. The set concept wherein a 1-to-*n* relationship exists between owner and member records applies to network structures so that complicated structures can be synthesized.* Figure 13.11 depicts a simple network structure and Figure 13.12 gives its structure diagram.

*A *cycle* is an occurrence in which the last record type in a structure is the owner record of a set in which the first record type is a member. This topic is treated in the DBTG report.

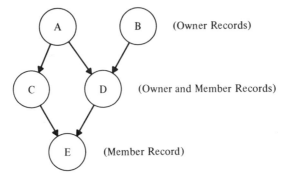

Figure 13.11   A network structure.

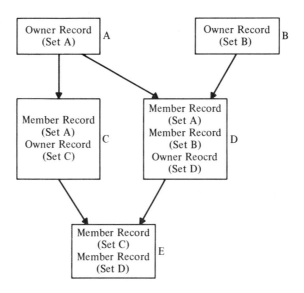

Figure 13.12   Structure diagram for a network structure.

Viewed in a collective sense, the notions of schema, subschema, record, set, and data structure provide only a means of modeling the data needs of an enterprise. Notions do not solve data base problems; systems and languages do. The structure and operation of a data base management system is dependent upon the implementor.

Language facilities have been specified in the DBTG report and are the subject of the remainder of this chapter. Entry skeletons, general formats, and functional descriptions are presented for each feature of the language. The objective is to give an overview of the data description and data manipulation languages without requiring that the reader "wade through" a myriad of details and operational conventions. For these, the reader is referred to the DBTG report or the reference manual for any implementation of the system.

SYNTAX NOTATION

The entry skeletons and general formats for the DBTG languages reflect the following syntactical conventions:

1. The elements of which a syntactical description is composed consist of upper-case words, lower-case words, special symbols, and special characters.
2. Underlined upper-case words are required when the format, of which they are a part, is used.
3. Upper-case words that are not underlined are optional and may be elided.
4. Lower-case words are generic terms that must be replaced by names or values selected by the programmer.
5. Special symbols in an entry skeleton are interpreted as follows:

$$\begin{bmatrix} a \\ b \\ c \end{bmatrix}$$ *Option.* At least no occurrence and at most one occurrence of the enclosed syntactical units.

$$\begin{Bmatrix} a \\ b \\ c \end{Bmatrix}$$ *Selection.* At least one occurrence and at most one occurrence of the enclosed syntactical units.

$$\left\| \begin{matrix} a \\ b \\ c \end{matrix} \right\|$$ *Multiple selection.* At least one occurrence and at most one occurrence of each of the enclosed syntactical units.

Three periods in succession, i.e., . . . , represents the ellipsis symbol that denotes that repetition is permitted. Repetition applies to the preceding syntactical unit. (A syntactical unit enclosed in brackets, braces, or the double stroke symbol are treated as a single syntactical unit.)

COBOL language specifications are used for the following language elements: character set, words,* literals,** and punctuation.

SCHEMA DATA DESCRIPTION LANGUAGE

The schema data description language is ostensibly independent of a host language and could be implemented as such. In general, however, the entry skeletons and general formats closely resemble those of the COBOL language.

---

*The definition of a COBOL word includes reserved words, names, qualification, and subscripting.

**The definition of a COBOL literal includes nonnumeric and numeric literals.

A schema written in the data description language consists of four types of entries:

1. The *schema entry* used to identify the schema.
2. The *area entry* used to define areas.
3. The *record entry* used to define records.
4. The *set entry* used to define sets.

The following rules apply to the construction of a schema:

1. The schema entry must be the first entry. There must be only one schema entry in a schema.
2. A separate entry is required for each area, record type, and set type in the schema.
3. An area entry must precede the record entries for records in that area.
4. A set entry must follow the record entries for records included in that set.

(Item 4 appears to be incorrect but is not. The order is based on the sequence in which data base elements are defined.) Each entry consists of one or more clauses that give the attributes of that type of entry.

The *schema entry* is used to identify the schema of a data base. The schema entry skeleton, given in Figure 13.13, consists of two clauses: (1) the SCHEMA

SCHEMA NAME IS schema-name

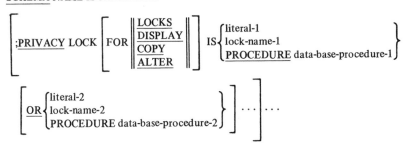

Figure 13.13   Schema entry skeleton of the schema data description language.

clause used to name the schema, and (2) the PRIVACY clause used to specify the privacy locks that apply to the use of the data base.

An *area entry* is used to name and specify the attributes of an area in a data base. The area entry skeleton, given in Figure 13.14, consists of four clauses: (1) the AREA clause used to name an area in a data base, (2) the TEMPORARY clause used to specify to the data base management system that the area is temporary, (3) the PRIVACY clause used to specify the privacy locks that apply to the use of an area, and (4) the ON clause used to specify the procedure to be executed when an area is opened or closed.

AREA NAME IS area-name-1

[;AREA IS TEMPORARY]

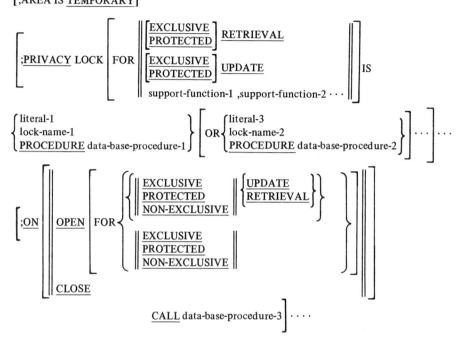

Figure 13.14   Area entry skeleton of the schema data description language.

A *record entry* is used to name and give attributes of records and their sub-ordinate data items. A record entry skeleton is composed of two major components: a record subentry and a data subentry. The record subentry skeleton, given in Figure 13.15, specifies the information necessary for record processing and includes the follwoing clauses: (1) the RECORD clause used to name a record type, (2) the LOCATION clause used to specify to the data base management system the criteria established for selecting a record occurrence and for placing a record occurrence in a particular area, (3) the WITHIN clause used to specify to the data base management system the area in which a record occurrence is to be placed, (4) the ON clause used to specify the procedure to be executed when given data manipulation language commands are preformed on a data item or data aggregate in the record, and (5) the PRIVACY clause used to specify the privacy locks that apply to the use of a record and the privacy locks that collectively apply to the use of data items or data aggregates contained in a record.

The data subentry skeleton, given in Figure 13.16, gives the attributes of the

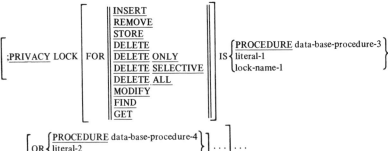

RECORD NAME IS record-name-1

Figure 13.15   Record subentry skeleton of the record entry of the schema data description language.

data items and data aggregates contained in a record and includes the following clauses: (1) the *data name* clause, used to name a data item or a data aggregate and to indicate its level number that is used to structure the element in the record; (2) the PICTURE clause, used to describe the structural characteristics of a data item or element of a data aggregate; (3) the TYPE clause, used to specify the base, scale, mode, and precision of a data item or element of a data aggregate; (4) the OCCURS clause, used to define a vector or repeating group in a record; (5) the RESULT clause, used to specify a procedure to be executed that involves the associated data item and to specify whether or not the result of the procedure is to be physically stored in the record; (6) the SOURCE clause, used to specify the data item that is to be used as a source value by the data base management system for implicitly establishing the value of the defined data item and to specify whether or not the value is to be physically contained

[level-number] data-base-data-name-1

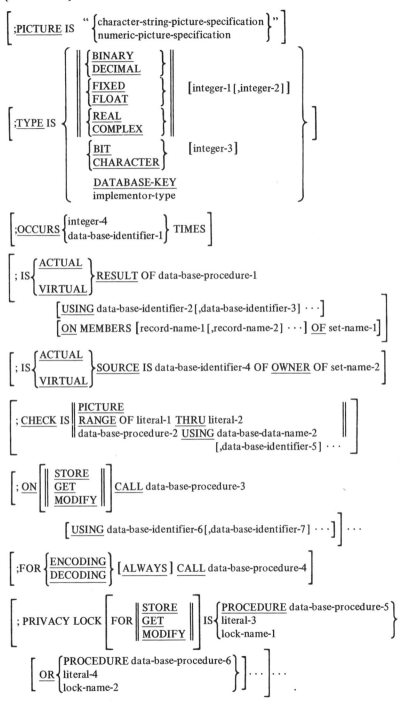

Figure 13.16 Data subentry skeleton of the record entry of the schema data description language.

in the record; (7) the CHECK clause, used to control data conversion and to establish a validity-checking procedure that is executed when the value of the defined data item is changed or added to the data base; (8) the ENCODING/ DECODING clause, used to specify the procedure to be executed when a data item requiring conversion, in lieu of the standard procedure, is retrieved from the data base or is updated; (9) the ON clause, used to specify the procedure to be executed when given data manipulation language commands are performed on a data item or data aggregate; and (10) the PRIVACY clause, used to specify the privacy locks that apply individually to the use of the defined data item or data aggregate.

A *set entry* is used to name and given the attributes of sets defined in the data base. A set entry skeleton is composed of two major components: a set subentry and a member subentry. The set subentry skeleton, given in Figure 13.17(a), specifies the structural attributes of a set and includes the following

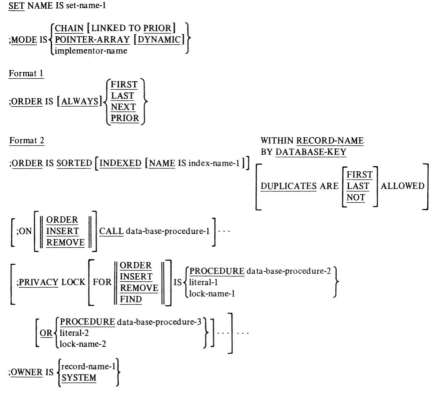

Figure 13.17(a) Set subentry skeleton of the set entry of the schema data description language.

MEMBER IS record-name-1 $\left\{ \begin{matrix} \text{MANDATORY} \\ \text{OPTIONAL} \end{matrix} \right\}$ $\left\{ \begin{matrix} \text{AUTOMATIC} \\ \text{MANUAL} \end{matrix} \right\}$ [LINKED TO OWNER]

[DUPLICATES ARE NOT ALLOWED FOR data-base-identifier-1

[,data-base-identifier-2] · · ·] · · ·

$\left[\begin{matrix} \text{ASCENDING} \\ \text{DESCENDING} \end{matrix} \right\}$ [RANGE] KEY IS data-base-identifier-3[,data-base-identifier-4] · · ·

$\left[\text{DUPLICATES ARE} \begin{bmatrix} \text{FIRST} \\ \text{LAST} \\ \text{NOT} \end{bmatrix} \text{ALLOWED} \right]$

;SEARCH KEY IS data-base-identifier-5[,data-base-identifier-6] · · ·

$\left[\text{USING} \left\{ \begin{matrix} \text{CALC} \\ \text{INDEX [NAME IS index-name-1]} \\ \text{data-base-procedure-1} \end{matrix} \right\} \right]$ DUPLICATES ARE [NOT] ALLOWED $\Big]$ · · ·

Format 1

;SET OCCURRENCE SELECTION IS THRU

$\left\{ \begin{matrix} \text{CURRENT OF SET} \\ \text{LOCATION MODE OF OWNER} \end{matrix} \right.$

$\left[\begin{matrix} \text{USING data-base-identifier-7[,data-base-identifier-8]} \cdots \\ \{\text{ALIAS FOR data-base-identifier-9 IS data-base-data-name-1}\} \cdots \end{matrix} \right] \Big\} \Big]$.

Format 2

;SET OCCURRENCE SELECTION IS THRU set-name-2 USING

$\left\{ \begin{matrix} \text{CURRENT OF SET} \\ \text{LOCATION MODE OF OWNER} \\ \qquad \text{[ALIAS FOR data-base-identifier-10 IS data-base-data-name-2]} \cdots \end{matrix} \right\}$

$\left\{ \text{set-name-3} \left\{ \begin{matrix} \text{USING data-base-identifier-11[,data-base-identifier-12]} \cdots \\ \{\text{ALIAS FOR data-base-identifier-13 IS data-base-data-name-3}\} \cdots \end{matrix} \right\} \right\} \cdots \Big]$.

Figure 13.17(b)   Member subentry skeleton of the record entry of the schema data description language.

clauses: (1) the SET clause, used to name a set type and to specify the generic name of all occurrences of that set type in the data base; (2) the MODE clause, used to specify the type of storage organization used to represent the set; (3) the ORDER clause, used to specify the criteria to be used for inserting a record occurrence in the set occurrence and implicitly defining the sequential order of set members; (4) the ON clause, used to specify the procedure to be executed when given data manipulation commands are performed on a set; (5) the PRIVACY clause, used to specify the privacy locks that apply to the use of a set; and (6) the OWNER clause, used to specify the owner record of a set and for which each occurrence of that record establishes a set occurrence.

The member subentry skeleton, given in Figure 13.17(b), gives the operational procedures to be utilized with the record occurrences of a set and includes the following clauses: (1) the ASC/DES clause,* used to specify the sort control keys for the member records of a set to be maintained in sorted order; (2) the SEARCH clause, used to establish that an index is required for all member records of a set and to indicate the type of indexing that is required; and (3) the SELECTION clause, used to establish the operational rules that control the selection of a set occurrence for the purpose of inserting or accessing a record occurrence.

COBOL SUBSCHEMA DATA DESCRIPTION LANGUAGE

The description of a COBOL subschema consists of two divisions:

1. The Subschema Identification Division that identifies the subschema.
2. The Subschema Data Division that defines the areas, records, and sets included in the subschema.

The *subschema identification division* must precede the subschema data division, and consists of the single entry given in Figure 13.18. The subschema identification division consists of three clauses: (1) the SUBSCHEMA NAME clause, used to name a subschema and specify its associated schema; (2) the PRIVACY LOCK clause, used to specify the privacy locks that apply to the use of the subschema; and (3) the PRIVACY KEY clause, used to specify the key for accessing a schema (for the development of a subschema) that is defined with a privacy lock.

The *subschema data division* consists of four sections that must appear in the following order:

1. Renaming section.
2. Area section.
3. Record section.
4. Set section.

*ASC/DES is an abbreviation for ASCENDING/DESCENDING.

SUB-SCHEMA IDENTIFICATION DIVISION.

SUB-SCHEMA NAME IS sub-schema-name OF SCHEMA NAME schema-name

$$
\left[\underline{\text{PRIVACY}} \text{ LOCK} \left[\text{FOR} \left\| \begin{array}{l} \underline{\text{LOCKS}} \\ \underline{\text{DISPLAY}} \\ \underline{\text{COMPILE}} \\ \underline{\text{ALTER}} \end{array} \right\| \right] \text{IS} \left\{ \begin{array}{l} \text{literal-1} \\ \text{lock-name-1} \\ \underline{\text{PROCEDURE}} \text{ data-base-procedure-1} \end{array} \right\} \right.
$$

$$
\left[\underline{\text{OR}} \left\{ \begin{array}{l} \text{literal-3} \\ \text{lock-name-2} \\ \underline{\text{PROCEDURE}} \text{ data-base-procedure-2} \end{array} \right\} \right] \cdots \left. \right] \cdots
$$

$$
\left[\underline{\text{PRIVACY KEY}} \text{ FOR COPY IS} \left\{ \begin{array}{l} \text{literal-5} \\ \text{implementor-name-1} \end{array} \right\} \right].
$$

Figure 13.18   Identification division skeleton for the COBOL subschema data description language.

The renaming and set sections are optional. As in COBOL, the sections consist of entries consisting of one or more clauses that specify the attributes of the associated entry.

The *renaming section* skeleton, given in Figure 13.19, is used to equate names in the subschema to names in the schema for operational purposes, for convenience, and to relate the naming conventions of the schema to the host language.

The *area section* is used to list the areas of a schema that are included in the subschema. Areas of the schema not specified in the area section are not

RENAMING SECTION

[AREA NAME area-name-1 IN SCHEMA IS CHANGED TO area-name-2
         [,area-name-3 TO area-name-4] ···] ···

[RECORD NAME record-name-1 IN SCHEMA IS CHANGED TO record-name-2
         [,record-name-3 TO record-name-4] ···] ···

[DATA NAME data-base-identifier-1 IN SCHEMA IS CHANGED TO data-base-data-name 1
         [,data-base-identifier-2 TO data-base-data-name-2] ···] ···

[SET NAME set-name-1 IN SCHEMA IS CHANGED TO set-name-2
         [,set-name-3 TO set-name-4] ···] ···

[IMPLEMENTOR NAME implementor-name-1 IN SCHEMA IS CHANGED TO implementor-name-2
         [,implementor-name-3 TO implementor-name-4] ···] ··· .

Figure 13.19   Renaming section skeleton of the subschema data division for the COBOL subschema data description language.

AREA SECTION

Format 1

COPY area-name-1 [,area-name-2] · · ·

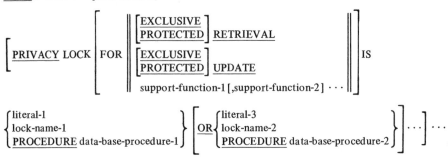

Format 2

COPY ALL AREAS.

Figure 13.20 Area section entry skeleton of the subschema data division for the COBOL subschema data description language.

accessible through the defined subschema.   The area section entry skeleton, given in Figure 13.20, consists of two clauses: (1) the COPY AREA clause, used to list all areas that are to be included in the subschema; and (2) the PRIVACY clause, used to give the privacy locks that apply to the use of an area.

The *record section* is used to specify the records and their subordinate data items from the schema that are included in the subschema. Records defined in the schema that are not specified in the record section are not accessible through the defined subschema.   The record section skeleton is given in Figure 13.21; it consists of three entries: the record control entry, the data description entry, and the condition-name entry. The *record control entry* specifies the areas in which a record occurrence is located. Its entry skeleton is given in Figure 13.22 and consists of three clauses: (1) the *record name* clause, used to specify the name of a record type to be included in the subschema; (2) the WITHIN clause, used to specify the areas in which record occurrences are to be located for the defined subschema; and (3) the PRIVACY clause, used to specify the privacy

RECORD SECTION

Record Control Entry.
[Data Description Entry. [Condition-name Entry.] · · ·] · · ·

Figure 13.21 Record section skeleton of the subschema data division for the COBOL subschema data description language.

01 record-name-1

[;<u>WITHIN</u> area-name-1 [,area-name-2] · · ·]

$$
\left[\;\text{;}\underline{\text{PRIVACY}}\ \text{LOCK}\ \left[\text{FOR}\ \left\|\begin{array}{l}\text{INSERT}\\ \text{REMOVE}\\ \underline{\text{STORE}}\\ \underline{\text{DELETE}}\\ \text{DELETE}\ \text{ONLY}\\ \text{DELETE}\ \underline{\text{SELECTIVE}}\\ \text{DELETE}\ \text{ALL}\\ \underline{\text{GET}}\\ \underline{\text{MODIFY}}\\ \underline{\text{FIND}}\end{array}\right\|\right]\ \text{IS}\left\{\begin{array}{l}\underline{\text{PROCEDURE}}\ \text{data-base-procedure-1}\\ \text{literal-1}\\ \text{lock-name-1}\end{array}\right\}\right.
$$

$$
\left[\underline{\text{OR}}\left\{\begin{array}{l}\underline{\text{PROCEDURE}}\ \text{data-base-procedure-1}\\ \text{literal-3}\\ \text{lock-name-2}\end{array}\right\}\right]\ \cdots\ \Big]\ \cdots\ \Big. .
$$

Figure 13.22   Record control entry skeleton of the record section of the subschema data division for the COBOL subschema data description language.

level-number   data-base-data-name-1

$$
\left[\;\text{;}\left\{\begin{array}{l}\underline{\text{PICTURE}}\\ \underline{\text{PIC}}\end{array}\right\}\text{IS character-string}\right]
$$

$$
\left[\;\text{;}\ [\underline{\text{USAGE}}\ \text{IS}]\left\{\begin{array}{l}\underline{\text{COMPUTATIONAL}}\\ \underline{\text{COMP}}\\ \underline{\text{COMPUTATIONAL-n}}\\ \underline{\text{COMP-n}}\\ \underline{\text{DISPLAY}}\\ \underline{\text{DATABASE-KEY}}\end{array}\right\}\right]
$$

$$
\left[\;\text{;}\ [\underline{\text{SIGN}}\ \text{IS}]\left\{\begin{array}{l}\underline{\text{LEADING}}\\ \underline{\text{TRAILING}}\end{array}\right\}[\underline{\text{SEPARATE}}\ \text{CHARACTER}]\right]
$$

$$
\left[\begin{array}{l}\text{;}\underline{\text{OCCURS}}\ \text{integer-2 TIMES}\\ \quad[\underline{\text{INDEXED}}\ \text{BY index-name-1 [,index-name-2]}\ \cdots\ ]\\ \text{;}\underline{\text{OCCURS}}\ \text{integer-1}\ \underline{\text{TO}}\ \text{integer-2 TIMES}\\ \quad\underline{\text{DEPENDING}}\ \text{ON data-base-data-name-3}\\ \quad[\underline{\text{INDEXED}}\ \text{BY index-name-1 [,index-name-2]}\ \cdots\ ]\end{array}\right]
$$

$$
\left[\text{;}\underline{\text{PRIVACY}}\ \text{LOCK}\ \left[\text{FOR}\left\|\begin{array}{l}\underline{\text{STORE}}\\ \underline{\text{GET}}\\ \underline{\text{MODIFY}}\end{array}\right\|\right]\ \text{IS}\left\{\begin{array}{l}\underline{\text{PROCEDURE}}\ \text{data-base-procedure-3}\\ \text{literal-1}\\ \text{lock-name-1}\end{array}\right\}\right.
$$

$$
\left[\underline{\text{OR}}\left\{\begin{array}{l}\underline{\text{PROCEDURE}}\ \text{data-base-procedure-4}\\ \text{literal-3}\\ \text{lock-name-2}\end{array}\right\}\right]\ \cdots\ \Big]\ \cdots\ \Big. .
$$

Figure 13.23   Data description entry skeleton of the record section of the subschema data division for the COBOL subschema data description language.

locks for given data manipulation language commands that apply to the use of a record and that collectively apply to the use of data items or data aggregates contained in the record.

The *data description entry* is used to define and give the attributes of data items and data aggregates that are subordinate to a record. Its entry skeleton is given in Figure 13.23 and consists of the following clauses: (1) the *data name* clause, used to select desired data items and data aggregates from a record defined in the schema and to specify the hierarchical structure within the record of the data items and data aggregates selected; (2) the PICTURE clause, used to describe the characteristics of a data item as it appears in the user-working area (UWA); (3) the USAGE clause, used to specify the internal format of a data item and to implicitly denote conversions between a data item as it is defined in the schema and its format in the user-working area; (4) the SIGN clause, used to indicate the form and position of the operational sign of a data item; (5) the OCCURS clause, used to define arrays and repeating groups based on schema declarations and to supply information necessary for the use of subscripts; and (6) the PRIVACY clause, used to specify the privacy locks that apply individually to the use of subordinate data items or data aggregates in a record.

The *condition-name* entry is used to specify a conditional name for particular values of a data item; this entry must follow the entry to which it applies. The entry skeleton for a condition-name entry is given as Figure 13.24 and consists of two clauses: (1) the *condition-name* clause, used to give the name of a particular condition; and (2) the VALUE clause, used to define the values associated with a condition name.

The *set section* is used to list and describe the sets of a schema that are to be included in the subschema. Sets of the schema not specified in the set section are not accessible through the defined subschema. The set section skeleton, given in Figure 13.25, consists of three clauses: (1) the COPY SET clause, used to list all sets from the schema that are to be included in the subschema; (2) the SET OCCURRENCE SELECTION clause, used to establish the operational rules that control the selection in a subschema of a set occurrence for the purpose of inserting or accessing a member record occurrence; and (3) the PRIVACY

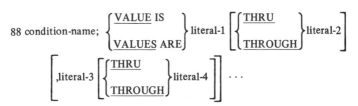

Figure 13.24   Condition-name entry skeleton of the record section of the subschema data division for the COBOL subschema data description language.

SET SECTION.

Format 1

<u>COPY</u> set-name-1 [,set-name-2] · · · .

Format 2

<u>COPY ALL SETS</u>.

Format 3

<u>COPY</u> set-name-3

SET <u>OCCURRENCE</u> SELECTION FOR MEMBER record-name-1 IS THRU set-name-4 <u>USING</u>

$$\begin{Bmatrix} \underline{CURRENT}\ SET \\ \underline{LOCATION}\ MODE\ OF\ OWNER\ [\underline{ALIAS}\ FOR\ data\text{-}base\text{-}identifier\text{-}1\ IS \\ \qquad data\text{-}base\text{-}data\text{-}name\text{-}1]\ \cdots \end{Bmatrix}$$

$$\begin{Bmatrix} set\text{-}name\text{-}5 \begin{Bmatrix} \underline{USING}\ data\text{-}base\text{-}identifier\text{-}2[,data\text{-}base\text{-}identifier\text{-}3]\ \cdots \\ \{\underline{ALIAS}\ FOR\ data\text{-}base\text{-}identifier\text{-}4\ IS\ data\text{-}base\text{-}data\text{-}name\text{-}2\}\cdots \end{Bmatrix} \end{Bmatrix}\ \cdots$$

$$\left[\underline{PRIVACY}\ LOCK\ \left[FOR\ \left\| \begin{matrix} ORDER \\ \underline{FIND} \\ \underline{REMOVE} \\ \underline{INSERT} \end{matrix} \right\| \right]\ IS \begin{Bmatrix} literal\text{-}1 \\ lock\text{-}name\text{-}1 \\ \underline{PROCEDURE}\ data\text{-}base\text{-}procedure\text{-}1 \end{Bmatrix} \right.$$

$$\left. \left[OR \begin{Bmatrix} literal\text{-}3 \\ lock\text{-}name\text{-}2 \\ \underline{PROCEDURE}\ data\text{-}base\text{-}procedure\text{-}2 \end{Bmatrix} \right] \cdots \right] \cdots \ .$$

Figure 13.25   Set section skeleton of the subschema data division for the COBOL sub-schema data description language.

clause, used to specify the privacy locks that apply to the use of a set occurrence.

The similarity between the schema and subschema data description languages is to be expected. The purpose of the subschema is to specify a subset of a schema that is of interest to a user program, and the association between the two descriptions is achieved through appropriate entries and the use of identical names. It necessarily follows that characteristics and attributes that apply to schema entries would also apply, to some extent, to corresponding subschema entries. In many cases, subtle differences between the corresponding entry skeletons exist that are significant from an operational point of view.

COBOL DATA MANIPULATION LANGUAGE

The data manipulation language (DML) is an extension to COBOL to handle data bases. The DML affects the identification, data, and procedure divisions of a COBOL program.

IDENTIFICATION DIVISION.
PROGRAM–ID.

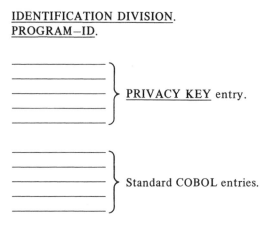

Figure 13.26   Extended skeleton for the Identification Division of the extension to COBOL to handle data bases.

The extended skeleton of the Identification Division is given in Figure 13.26. The PRIVACY clause is the only entry involved with the data base extension; its entry skeleton is given in Figure 13.27. The PRIVACY clause is used to establish the authority of the executing program to execute data manipulation language commands with regard to the privacy locks specified in the schema or subschema.

The extended skeleton for the Data Division is given in Figure 13.28. The first section of the data division must be the *schema section,* which has been added to handle data bases. The schema section is used to reference a previously defined subschema and to supply information to the data base management system for establishing appropriate user-working areas. The INVOKE clause is the only entry used in the schema section; its entry skeleton is given in Figure 13.29. The INVOKE clause is used to specify the predefined subschema that provides the data known to the program. It is also used to implicitly cause the data base management system to create the necessary user-working areas in the executing program.

The COBOL data manipulation language includes imperative statements that allow the user to utilize the data base described in the schema. These statements, frequently referred to as data base commands, may be intermixed with standard COBOL imperative statements in the Procedure Division. A short description of each of the data base imperative statements is given in the following paragraphs.

The OPEN statement is used to gain access to an area and involves the verification of privacy conditions and a specification of the executing program's usage mode, which can be EXCLUSIVE/PROTECTED or RETRIEVAL/UPDATE.

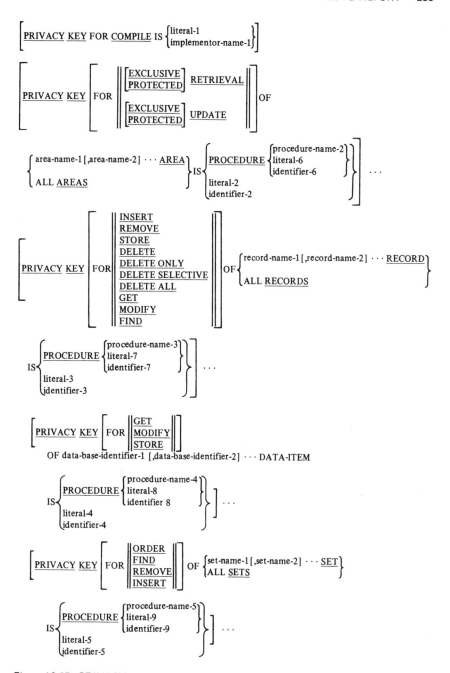

Figure 13.27   PRIVACY clause skeleton for the Identification Division of the extension to COBOL to handle data bases.

DATA DIVISION.
SCHEMA SECTION.
INVOKE clause

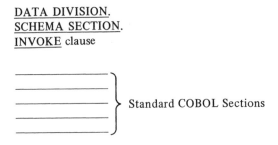

} Standard COBOL Sections

Figure 13.28 Extended skeleton for the Data Division of the extension to COBOL to handle data bases.

INVOKE SUB-SCHEMA sub-schema-name OF SCHEMA schema-name

Figure 13.29 INVOKE clause skeleton for the Data Division of the extension to COBOL to handle data bases.

Format 1

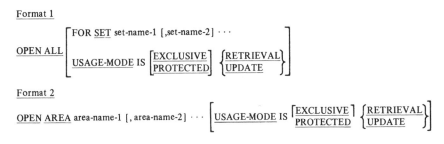

Figure 13.30 OPEN statement of the COBOL data manipulation language.

The format of the OPEN statement is given in Figure 13.30. The EXCLUSIVE phrase prevents concurrently executing programs from interacting with the same area. The PROTECTED phrase prevents concurrent update but allows concurrent retrieval.

The FIND statement is used to establish (i.e., locate) the record occurrence specified by a "record selection expression" as one of the following: (1) the current record of the executing program, (2) the current record of the area in which the desired record occurrence is located, (3) the current record of a record name, or (4) the current record of a set for all set occurrences in which the record participates as a member. The statement also can optionally be used to suppress the establishment of record occurrences in any of the above structures. The format of the FIND statement is given in Figure 13.31. The format of a *record selection expression* is given in Figure 13.32; it is used to give the operational characteristics of the desired record occurrence.

The GET statement is used to transfer the contents of data items (specified

$$\underline{\text{FIND}} \text{ rse} \left[\underline{\text{SUPPRESS}} \left\{ \left\| \begin{matrix} \underline{\text{ALL}} \\ \underline{\text{RECORD}} \\ \underline{\text{AREA}} \\ \left\{ \begin{matrix} \underline{\text{SET}} \\ \text{set-name-1} \, [\text{,set-name-2}] \cdots \end{matrix} \right\} \end{matrix} \right\| \right\} \underline{\text{CURRENCY}} \ \underline{\text{UPDATES}} \right]$$

Figure 13.31   FIND statement of the COBOL data manipulation language.

Format 1

[record-name-1] USING identifier-1

Format 2

$$[\underline{\text{OWNER}} \text{ IN set-name-3 OF}] \ \underline{\text{CURRENT}} \text{ OF} \left\{ \begin{matrix} \text{record-name-2 } \underline{\text{RECORD}} \\ \text{set-name-4 } \underline{\text{SET}} \\ \text{area-name-1 } \underline{\text{AREA}} \\ \underline{\text{RUN-UNIT}} \end{matrix} \right\}$$

Format 3

$$\left\{ \begin{matrix} \underline{\text{NEXT}} \\ \underline{\text{PRIOR}} \\ \underline{\text{FIRST}} \\ \underline{\text{LAST}} \\ \text{integer-1} \\ \text{identifier-2} \end{matrix} \right\} [\text{record-name-3}] \ \underline{\text{RECORD}} \text{ OF} \left\{ \begin{matrix} \text{set-name-5 -}\underline{\text{SET}} \\ \text{area-name-2 } \underline{\text{AREA}} \end{matrix} \right\}$$

Format 4

OWNER RECORD OF set-name-6 SET

Format 5

[NEXT DUPLICATE WITHIN] record-name-4 RECORD

Format 6

record-name-5 VIA [CURRENT OF] set-name-7
    [USING data-base-identifier-3 [data-base-identifier-4] ···]

Format 7

NEXT DUPLICATE WITHIN set-name-8
    USING data-base-identifier-5 [,data-base-identifier-6] ···

Figure 13.32   Format of the Record Selection Expression used with the FIND statement.

Format 1

GET [record-name]

Format 2

GET record-name; data-base-identifier-1 [,data-base-identifier-2] ···

Figure 13.33   GET statement of the COBOL data manipulation language.

Figure 13.34   STORE statement of the COBOL data manipulation language.

in the subschema) from the indicated record occurrence to the user-working area. The format of the GET statement is given in Figure 13.33. The GET statement essentially makes a defined data record available for use by the executing program. Thus, a typical sequence of data base input operations would be OPEN, FIND, and then GET.

The STORE statement establishes the specified record as the current record of the executing program, area, record-name, or set name. It causes one or more of the following actions to be performed: (1) acquires storage space and a unique data base key for a new record occurrence in the data base, (2) causes the values of data items of the defined record in the user-working area to be contained in the occurrence of the specified record in the data base, (3) inserts the specified record into all sets of which it is specified as a member, and (4) establishes a new set occurrence for each set defined to have the specified record as an owner record. The format of the STORE statement is given in Figure 13.34. The statement format also optionally provides the capability of suppressing the above action on specified structures.

The MODIFY statement is used to replace values in the specified record with values from the user-working area and to alter set membership relations through the USING option in the set section. The format of the MODIFY statement is given in Figure 13.35.

The INSERT statement is used to include the specified record as a member of the specified sets. The format of the INSERT statement is given in Figure 13.36. The specified record must be defined as an optional, automatic, or a manual member of the set names used in the statement. If the "record-name"

Format 1

MODIFY [record-name] [USING data-base-identifier-1 [,data-base-identifier-2] · · ·]

Format 2

MODIFY record-name; data-base-identifier-3[,data-base-identifier-4] · · ·
        [USING data-base-identifier-5[,data-base-identifier-6] · · ·]

Figure 13.35   MODIFY statement of the COBOL data manipulation language.

Format 1

INSERT [record-name] INTO set-name-1 [,set-name-2] · · ·

Format 2

INSERT [record-name] INTO ALL SETS

Figure 13.36   INSERT statement of the COBOL data manipulation language.

option is not selected, then the current record of the executing program is used in the object record.

The REMOVE statement is used to cancel the membership of the specified record occurrence from the specified sets. The format of the REMOVE statement is given in Figure 13.37; if the "record-name" option is not selected, then

Format 1

REMOVE [record-name] FROM set-name-1 [, set-name-2] · · ·

Format 2

REMOVE [record-name] FROM ALL SETS

Figure 13.37   REMOVE statement of the COBOL data manipulation language.

the current record of the executing program is used as the object record. A record that is removed from a set occurrence is not deleted from the data base. It may be accessed through other sets of which it is a member or with the CALC mode when given as the location mode.

The DELETE statement effectively eliminates the specified or current record occurrence from the data base. The format of the DELETE statement is given in Figure 13.38. The various options in the statement format provide the

$$\text{DELETE} \quad [\text{record-name}] \quad \begin{bmatrix} \text{ONLY} \\ \text{SELECTIVE} \\ \text{ALL} \end{bmatrix}$$

Figure 13.38   DELETE statement of the COBOL data manipulation language.

following facilities: (1) make the record unavailable for further processing, (2) remove the record from all set occurrences of which it is a member, (3) delete all record occurrences that are mandatory or optional members of sets owned by the deleted record, and (4) prevent deletion of the record if it owns member records—this is the unqualified form.

The FREE statement is used to cancel the effect of a previous KEEP statement for the current record of the executing program. The format of the FREE statement is given in Figure 13.39.

FREE [ALL]

Figure 13.39   FREE statement of the COBOL data manipulation language.

The MOVE statement provides a means of saving the currency status indicators in an executing program and a means of obtaining the area name corresponding to a data base key. The format of the MOVE statement is given in Figure 13.40.

The IF statement provides a conditional facility based on data base conditions. The format of the IF statement is given in Figure 13.41.

The ORDER statement is used to sort the specified set in an ascending or descending order on the basis of the given keys. The format of the ORDER statement is given in Figure 13.42.

Format 1

$$\underline{\text{MOVE}} \ \underline{\text{CURRENCY}} \ \underline{\text{STATUS}} \ \underline{\text{FOR}} \left\{ \begin{array}{l} \text{RUN-UNIT} \\ \text{record-name } \underline{\text{RECORD}} \\ \text{area-name } \underline{\text{AREA}} \\ \text{set-name } \underline{\text{SET}} \end{array} \right\} \underline{\text{TO}} \ \text{identifier-1}$$

Format 2

$$\underline{\text{MOVE}} \ \underline{\text{AREA-NAME}} \ \underline{\text{FOR}} \left\{ \begin{array}{l} \text{RUN-UNIT} \\ \text{record-name } \underline{\text{RECORD}} \\ \text{area-name } \underline{\text{AREA}} \\ \text{set-name } \underline{\text{SET}} \\ \text{identifier-2} \end{array} \right\} \underline{\text{TO}} \ \text{identifier-3}$$

Figure 13.40   MOVE statement of the COBOL data manipulation language.

Format 1

$$\underline{\text{IF}} \ \text{set-name-1} \ \underline{\text{SET}} \ [\underline{\text{NOT}}] \ \text{EMPTY}; \left\{ \begin{array}{l} \text{statement-1} \\ \underline{\text{NEXT}} \ \underline{\text{SENTENCE}} \end{array} \right\} \left[; \underline{\text{ELSE}} \left\{ \begin{array}{l} \text{statement-2} \\ \underline{\text{NEXT}} \ \underline{\text{SENTENCE}} \end{array} \right\} \right]$$

Format 2

$$\underline{\text{IF}} \ \underline{\text{RECORD}} \ [\underline{\text{NOT}}] \left[\begin{array}{l} \underline{\text{MEMBER}} \\ \underline{\text{OWNER}} \end{array} \right] \text{OF} \left\{ \begin{array}{l} \text{set-name-2} \\ \underline{\text{ANY}} \end{array} \right\} \underline{\text{SET}}; \left\{ \begin{array}{l} \text{statement-3} \\ \underline{\text{NEXT}} \ \underline{\text{SENTENCE}} \end{array} \right\}$$

$$\left[; \underline{\text{ELSE}} \left\{ \begin{array}{l} \text{statement-4} \\ \underline{\text{NEXT}} \ \underline{\text{SENTENCE}} \end{array} \right\} \right]$$

Figure 13.41   IF statement of the COBOL data manipulation language.

Format 1

$$\underline{\text{ORDER}} \text{ set-name-1 } \underline{\text{SET}} \left[\text{FOR } \underline{\text{RUN-UNIT}}\right] \left\{\begin{matrix}\underline{\text{ASCENDING}}\\\underline{\text{DESCENDING}}\end{matrix}\right\} \text{KEY IS}$$

$$\left\|\begin{matrix}\underline{\text{RECORD-NAME}}\\\underline{\text{DATABASE-KEY}}\\\text{data-base-identifier-1 } [\text{,data-base-identifier-2}] \cdots\end{matrix}\right\| \cdots$$

Format 2

$$\underline{\text{ORDER}} \text{ set-name-2 } \underline{\text{SET}} \left[\text{FOR } \underline{\text{RUN-UNIT}}\right]$$

$$\left\{\underline{\text{FOR}} \text{ record-name-1 } \left\{\begin{matrix}\underline{\text{ASCENDING}}\\\underline{\text{DESCENDING}}\end{matrix}\right\} \text{KEY is} \left\|\begin{matrix}\underline{\text{DATABASE-KEY}}\\\text{data-base-identifier-3}\end{matrix}\right\|\right\} \cdots\right\} \cdots$$

Figure 13.42   ORDER statement of the COBOL data manipulation language.

The KEEP statement is used to inform the data base management system that the program will re-access the current record. The format of the KEEP statement is given in Figure 13.43.

<u>KEEP</u>

Figure 13.43   KEEP statement of the COBOL data manipulation language.

The CLOSE statement is used to release control over records, sets, and areas so they may be accessed by other executing programs that may be in a delay-status waiting for access to one of the specified units. The format of the CLOSE statement is given in Figure 13.44.

Format 1

<u>CLOSE ALL</u> [FOR <u>SET</u> set-name-1 [,set-name-2] $\cdots$]

Format 2

<u>CLOSE AREA</u> area-name-1 [,area-name-2] $\cdots$

Figure 13.44   CLOSE statement of the COBOL data manipulation language.

The USE statement is used to inform the data base management system of procedures that should be executed when specified error conditions arise. The format of the USE statement is given in Figure 13.45.

Without question, the above formats are of limited value without detailed information on the operational characteristics of the various statements. This is the function of the DBTG report and the reference manual for an implementation of the language and associated concepts. The above presentation does give,

USE IF ERROR-STATUS [IS integer-1 [,integer-2] ...]

Figure 13.45   USE statement of the COBOL data manipulation language.

however, an indication of the scope and complexity of the DBTG report. It also provides for users planning to design a data base system an indication of some of the factors involved with design and implementation.

REFERENCES

CODASYL *Data Base Task Group (DBTG) Report*, October 1969. (Superseded by the April 1971 *Report*.)

CODASYL *Data Base Task Group (DBTG) Report*, April 1971. Available from the Association for Computing Machinery.

CODASYL Systems Committee Technical Report, *Feature Analysis of Generalized Data Base Management Systems*, May 1971. Available from the Association for Computing Machinery.

Engles, R. W., "An analysis of the April 1971 Data Base Task Group Report," *Data Description, Access and Control*, edited by E. F. Codd, and A. L. Dean, 1971 ACM SIGFIDET Workshop, pp. 69–91. Available from the Association for Computing Machinery.

14 | GUIDE/SHARE DATA BASE MANAGEMENT SYSTEM REQUIREMENTS

INTRODUCTION

GUIDE and SHARE are IBM user groups. This chapter is a summary of a document produced by a joint committee of these groups stating their position on the definition of long-range requirements for data base management systems. The report does not describe an existing system, but does present a viable operating environment in which a data base management system can be expected to operate. The significance of the report lies in the fact that it represents the data base requirements of a large class of influential and knowledgeable users. Further information may be obtained from the Chairman of the Data Base Requirements Subcommittee, whose name and address can be obtained from your local IBM representative.*

The derived data base management system requirements are developed in light of a set of basic objectives, listed as follows:

1. Data independence.
2. Data relatability.
3. Data non-redundancy.
4. Data integrity.
5. Security.
6. Performance.
7. Compatibility with existing concepts.

*At the time the report was written, Mr. W. D. Stevens, Skelly Oil Company, P. O. Box 1650, Tulsa, Oklahoma 74102, was the chairman of the subcommittee.

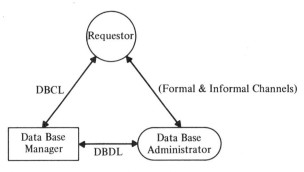

Key: DBCL – Data Base Command Language
     DBDL – Data Base Descriptive Language

Figure 14.1   Communication among the three principal functions of the data base management system.

Most of the objectives are introduced in earlier chapters and are not covered further; however, any differences in meaning of the above objectives are easily absorbed in the generality of the requirements.

The objectives lead in a straightforward manner to three principal functions and two data base language concepts. The three principal functions are: (1) the user—referred to as the Requestor, (2) the Data Base Administrator—an individual responsible for the organization and utilization of the data base, and (3) the Data Base Manager—a combination of hardware and software facilities. The two data base languages are: (1) a Data Base Descriptive Language—used to define the data in a precise and formal manner, and (2) the Data Base Command Language—used to access the data base and its descriptors.

The Requestor communicates with the Data Base Administrator to establish a means of accessing data in the data base. Effectively, the Data Base Administrator maintains control over the accessing of data on a system-wide basis. The Data Base Administrator communicates with the Data Base Manager using the Data Base Descriptive Language to establish the manner in which data is stored and is accessed, and to delineate the data that can be accessed by a specific user. The Requestor communicates with the Data Base Manager using the Data Base Command Language to access data that has been authorized by the Data Base Administrator. The relationships between the Requestor, Data Base Administrator, and the Data Base Manager are depicted in Figure 14.1, along with the languages used for communication.

FUNCTIONS OF THE REQUESTOR

The primary function of the Requestor is to make the data in the data base available to members of the enterprise. The obvious implication here is that the needed data is stored in the data base using the necessary level of independence, relatability, and non-redundancy. Thus, the storage structures representing the needed data may not hold the data in a form that is immediately useful. In fact, the methodology allows the Data Base Administrator to change the physical representation of data without impacting the applications programs.

In accessing the data base, the Requestor communicates with the Data Base Administrator to determine if the needed data is available and to specify its logical characteristics—as viewed by the Requestor. The function of the Data Base Administrator is to make the needed data available to the Requestor, if possible, by logically reorganizing appropriate portions of the data base or by adding portions or all of the needed data. The Requestor also specifies operational considerations, such as privacy and security rules, time constraints, and performance indicators. The latter information along with logical and physical data characteristics are communicated to the Data Base Manager by the Data Base Administrator using the data base descriptive language.

The Requestor uses the data base command language to describe the data formats, and to access the portion of the data base that has been defined on his behalf by the Data Base Administrator. Typical statement types in the Requestor's repertoire are OPEN, RETRIEVE, REPLACE, ADD, DELETE, and CLOSE. The data base subcommittee also conceptualizes a descriptive facility, taking the form of a limited subset of the data base descriptive language that could be used by the Requestor for defining logical data relationships. One such relationship might be for temporary files, that would exist for short periods of time and would not be generally available to other users.

FUNCTIONS OF THE DATA BASE ADMINISTRATOR

The primary function of the Data Base Administrator is to establish and maintain management control over the data base. The fact that a data base serves as a repository for the informational resources of an enterprise requires that careful attention be given to the manner in which data is used throughout the organization. The importance of the Data Base Administrator is attested to by the fact that it has been predicted by several people in the field that the position will become eventually a high-level management position in the organization. It is also likely that many of the functions will be assumed by a staff of people under the direction of the Data Base Administrator.

The functions of the Data Base Administrator are listed as follows:

1. Description of data.
2. Definition of relationships.
3. Definition of mappings.
4. Establishment of data security rules.
5. Specification of performance measurement procedures.

Data description involves assigning names and levels of qualification to data units; describing entity types and associated logical and physical data; and describing physical data structures, such as data sets, records, and data elements. The Data Base Administrator is effectively defining the following structures:

Structure	*Examples:*
Physical data structures	Data sets, physical records, and data elements.
Entity types	Entity constructs, entity record types, entity relationships, and entity fields.
Logical data structures	Files, logical records, logical relationships, and data items.

Data description is accomplished through statements in the data base descriptive language that are supplied to the Data Base Manager by the Data Base Administrator. The Data Base Manager derives data descriptors from the statements, and stores the descriptors in a data base directory for use during access by the Requestor.

Relationships are defined for entity types, logical data, and physical data. The relationships that can be established between physical data, entities and entity types, entity fields and entity records, and between logical records, are inherent in the data base description language.

The *definition of mappings* allows the data base manager to derive logical data from physical data, as suggested in Figure 14.2. The physical mappings can be viewed as access strategies that are used by the Data Base Manager for storing and retrieving data. The logical mappings define logical structures as a subset of the total amount of information about a particular entity set that is available in the data base.

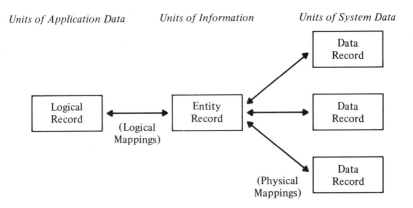

Figure 14.2   Logical and physical mappings in a data base environment.

Data security is established through rules supplied by the Data Base Administrator that specify how the Data Base Manager should enforce the security needs of the user and the requirements of the data base system. These rules constitute a security system that recognizes two dimensions of the security problem: The *right-to-know* and the *need-to-know*. The security system operates through the use of security profiles constructed from the rules specified by the Data Base Administrator.

Performance measurement procedures that the data base system should perform during its operation are specified with the data base description language. The Data Base Administrator specifies the functions and resources that must be monitored and subsequently evaluates the system on the basis of the results obtained.

FUNCTIONS OF THE DATA BASE MANAGER

The Data Base Manager is a collection of hardware and software resources that serve as the interface between the data base and its users. All data descriptions enter the data base system through the Data Base Manager and all data entering or leaving the data base system also pass through it.

The primary function of the Data Base Manager is to manipulate data which includes accessing the data base in response to user statements in the data base command language, and transforming data to compensate for differences in the logical and physical structures. Thus, the user can subordinate the details of data base utilization to the Data Base Manager. An overview of the data manipulation function and its relationship to a user program, access routines, and the data base is given in Figure 14.3.

In order to accomplish its primary function, the Data Base Manager must manage system resources in its domain, which necessarily includes device and auxiliary storage allocation. In addition to allocating storage space for data structures, the Data Base Manager is also in a position to select the most appropriate data organization and storage technique, and to migrate data from one device type to another.

Other functions placed in the domain of the Data Base Manager are: (1) data base checkpoint and restart facilities, (2) recording of performance data, (3) enforcing data security, (4) insuring the integrity of data stored in the data base,

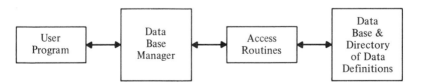

Figure 14.3 Overview of the data manipulation function.

and (5) providing a common interface with conventional data management facilities to achieve compatibility, insure security, and to permit optimum performance.

DATA BASE DESCRIPTIVE LANGUAGE

The data base descriptive language is a non-procedural extensible language that permits the Data Base Administrator (and also the Requestor) to specify his data requirements to the data base management system and, in particular, to the Data Base Manager component. The data base descriptive language is conceptualized as a language facility, independent of any host language (such as COBOL or PL/I). But, at the same time, it could be incorporated into host language compilers, and would allow users to specify logical data definitions to the data base management system. The Data Base Descriptive Language is viewed by the committee as including the means of communicating a wide range of functional capabilities that are supplemented by a set of default options to facilitate its use. The functional capabilities of the language include but are not limited to the following:

1. A means of describing the logical and physical properties of data structures.
2. A means of describing relationships.
3. A means of describing mapping rules.
4. A means of specifying security procedures and access rules.
5. A means of subsetting the data base to minimize access times and control costs—this is an operational function that differs from the concept of defining a logical data structure that is a subset of a universal data structure.
6. A means of specifying monitoring requirements.

Statements in the data base descriptive language are used to specify descriptors that are stored by the data base management system in data base directories, which are stored with the data base. The primary user of the data base descriptive language is the Data Base Administrator who uses the language facilities contained therein to define logical descriptors, entity descriptors, and physical descriptors. Within each category, the facility for adding, changing, deleting, and for maintaining several versions of each descriptor is defined. In general, the process of specifying a data descriptor involves a unique name assignment and the definition of relationships. Clearly, the facilities of the data base descriptive language parallel the functions of the Data Base Administrator.

Logical descriptors are effective at the application program level and permit the following types of structures to be named and defined: data items, logical records, files, and logical relationships. Data items are defined by establishing a correspondence with an entity field and by assigning data attributes (such as base, scale, mode, precision, and installation-defined properties) along with possible alternate attributes and the conditions under which they apply. The concept of a logical data relationship is presented in its most general sense, and allows you to distinguish between the following:

1. Between two data items at the same level.
2. Between data units at different hierarchical levels.
3. Between a data item and an entity field.
4. Between a data item and its corresponding value.

Logical data relationships may or may not be known to an application program that uses the corresponding data. Other requirements stated by the data base committee as being necessary, include:

1. The facility to define conditional and unconditional relationships.
2. The facility to define hierarchical relationships including the definition of repeating group and elementary data items.
3. The facility for specifying membership rules (for records in files).
4. The facility for denoting operational rules for file operations (i.e., additions, deletions, etc.).
5. The facility for specifying sequencing rules.
6. The facility for defining logical relationships between files.
7. The facility for establishing logical data relationships from entity descriptors.
8. The facility to support, supplement, and not to conflict with host language characteristics and relevant data structures.

An *entity descriptor* describes the mapping between physical and logical data; the concept is similar to that of a "fact" that is a relationship between two sets—as defined earlier. More specifically, an entity descriptor relates a logical data request of an application program to a physical data structure, and represents a description of data in terms of entities. While an entity exists as a person, place, thing, or event of interest to an enterprise, entity data is never materialized and exists as "abstract data." Much like the definition of logical data, the Data Base Administrator may choose to name fields, record types, constructs,* and relationships that exist at the entity level, and to assign appropriate synonyms. Moreover. the facility should exist to specify one or more entity fields as unique identifiers of entity records and to define the type of function implied by the existence of an entity field. Typical function attributes denote that the field serves to link, identify, order, etc. The concept of entity data involves the following definitional requirements at the entity level:

1. The facility to distinguish between real and virtual fields.
2. The facility of defining an entity to be simultaneously a component of two

---

*An *entity construct* is defined collectively as entity record types and the relationship that connects them.

or more entity groups, constructs, record types, or any combination thereof.
3. The facility for specifying ordering attributes.
4. The facility of defining mappings and relationships between units of entity data.
5. The facility of associating operational functions with physical data structures.
6. The facility for describing hierarchical structures.

Lastly, *physical descriptors* are used to describe the organization of data on auxiliary storage devices and permit the conventional descriptive facilities of naming, specification of identifier fields, specification of data attributes and formats, notation of storage requirements, and the definition of operational attributes that determine the function served by a data element.

Essentially, the Data Base Administrator uses the data description language to describe data sets that exist as one or more extents; this process necessarily involves a whole class of specifications that are similar to conventional data management facilities, primarily because physical storage structures are involved. Physical descriptors also include the facility for describing the following attributes or characteristics:

1. Initial, default, or null values.
2. Compaction algorithms.
3. Ordering attributes for elements in records and records in data sets or extents.
4. Indexes.
5. Conditions under which a specific record becomes a member of an extent or a data set.
6. Physical data set attributes, such as block size, access method, space allocation, and device allocation.
7. Retrieval strategies and mapping facilities.
8. Identifying redundant data.
9. Derived data elements.

The three types of descriptors, i.e., logical, entity, and physical, are obviously very similar in outward appearance; however, they each serve different purposes in a data base management system. Clearly, this presentation of the scope and function of the various descriptors is a summary of the original report, which serves as the best reference. Even in the original report, however, the concepts are very general to allow as much leeway as is possible.

Three other features that are available to the Data Base Administrator through the data base description language deal with data security, data integrity, and performance and control. The *data security* features permit the following: system security requirements; user identification; the source of user identification data (i.e., through job control language, password, job status, etc.); unique security requirements that apply to individual commands; security requirements that apply at the logical, entity, and physical levels; and security requirements that are dependent upon data values, environmental conditions, and logical relationships. Through the data base description language, the Data Base Administrator may also control the manner in which security procedures are enforced by specifying special conditions and actions that should be taken when security precautions are violated.

Data integrity is concerned with protecting stored data from being contaminated through misuse or by accident. Data is contaminated when an inappropriate value is assigned to a data item. Data integrity requirements are enforced in two ways: through exclusive and shared control, and by imposing restrictions on the values that can be assigned to records and on records that can be assigned to files. Data integrity also applies to cases where an application program terminates part way through an update procedure. The Data Base Administrator should have the facility for reversing the effect of changes to the data base.

Performance and control requirements include facilities for the specification of conditions and events that should be monitored, including: security and integrity violations; usage statistics; and operational conditions, such as user identifications, hardware and software units, and job and task indicators.

In summary, the data base descriptive language allows the Data Base Administrator to describe data and to control the operation of the data base management system. Information supplied by the Data Base Administrator is stored in a data base directory and is used by the Data Base Manager in responding to Requestor commands in the data base command language.

DATA BASE COMMAND LANGUAGE

The data base command language is a procedural language that allows the Requestor to access the data base. The language operates only at the logical data level. In general, the data base command language permits conventional file operations, such as open, read, update, close, etc., along with the facility to share files and create temporary files. Data security and data integrity restrictions are applicable to commands issued in the data base command language and are enforced by the data base management system, from information stored in the data base directory.

Commands are divided into two categories: primitive and compound. *Primitive commands* perform basic data base manipulation functions, including the following:

1. Condition the system to forthcoming data requests—i.e., OPEN.*

---

*The words OPEN, RETRIEVE, etc. are not given in the report. They are included to further explicate the material even though they may not apply directly.

2. Retrieve logical records—i.e., RETRIEVE.
3. Return logical records to the data base system—i.e., RETURN.
4. Add logical records to the data base—i.e., INSERT.
5. Delete logical records from the system—i.e., DELETE.
6. Complete access requirements—i.e., CLOSE.

Command format includes a parameter list providing operational data, qualifiers, and default conditions. The parameter list is used to specify the record or file involved, the data desired, error conditions and returns, and supplementary record and file descriptions. Logical records may be accessed by an identifier or by a sequence indicator specified as a qualifier to the command. Typical sequence qualifiers are: next, previous, unique, first, last, etc. Typical lists also necessarily include Boolean and relational operations, such as: and, or, not, between, equal to, not equal to, greater than, less than, greater than or equal to, and less than or equal to. Lastly, defaults may be specified at the system level or the user can specify his own defaults. Clearly, the options available are dependent upon the command used.

Certain sequences of commands are frequently used. Common examples in conventional data management are: an OPEN statement followed by a READ statement. In a data base command language, sequences of commands of this sort are referred to as *compound commands*. In a comprehensive data base command language, a facility for defining compound commands is of prime importance because of the wide scope of applicability of the language. In a data base environment, typical operations synthesized as compound commands are: "read," which would be comprised of an OPEN command (if the file hasn't been opened) followed by a RETRIEVE command; and "update," comprised of a RETRIEVE followed by a RETURN.

Collectively, primitive and compound commands provide the same facilities in a data base environment that familiar input and output statements provide in an environment that uses conventional data management.

IMPLEMENTATION

An aspect of a data base system that is nearly as important as its functional capability is the method of implementation. *Implementation* primarily refers to the Data Manager component that should be designed with the following characteristics in mind: modularity, extensibility, reconfigurability, and the capability of operating within a network of data base management systems. *Modularity* is related to the system generation process and involves facilities for selecting a viable subset of data base management functions. Thus, the Data Base Administrator can structure and restructure his data base management system to meet the needs of his installation. *Extensibility* refers to a design methodology that allows evolutionary changes to the system itself without requiring substantial conversion in the area of application programs.

Reconfiguration is a hardware function. A viable data base management system should allow the Data Base Administrator to perform hardware reconfiguration without affecting the information stored in the data base and the applications programs that use it. The concept of a *network* of data base management systems communicating with each other is certainly within the realm of technical feasibility. Currently, networks of computers are practically commonplace. Some of the problems involved with networks of data base management systems involve security and integrity measures and countermeasures. Essentially, the key point is that a data base management system operating in a network must have the capability of establishing and maintaining the security and integrity requirements of the home installation.

SUMMARY

The joint GUIDE-SHARE requirements obviously do not represent an operational data base management system; moreover, there is no indication of how representative these requirements actually are of the class of users that are involved in data base technology. Yet, in spite of the great generality of the requirements and the limitations just discussed, the document does reflect an extensive analysis of the data base concept as it is known today. The joint GUIDE-SHARE data base requirements give functional capabilities; the mode or method of implementation is not discussed except to a limited extent. Thus, for example, there is no mention given of the use of: linked lists, pointer fields, storage allocation, device management, and so forth—except for the fact that these are generally regarded as, or related to, Data Base Manager functions.

The key point is that the data base management system can be implemented using the latest concepts in data base technology.

REFERENCES

Everest, G. C., and E. H. Sibley, "A critique of the GUIDE-SHARE DBMS requirements," *Data Description, Access and Control*, edited by E. F. Codd and A. L. Dean, 1971 ACM SIGFIDET Workshop, pp. 93–112. Available from the Association for Computing Machinery.

Joint GUIDE-SHARE Data Base Requirements Group, *Data Base Management Systems Requirements*, New York, Share Inc., November 11, 1970.

15 | A RELATIONAL DATA BASE MODEL

INTRODUCTION

One of the goals of a data base management system is to provide data independence such that an application program is independent of the manner in which the data is stored. The problem becomes important when a data base must be restructured due to growth in the size of the data base (i.e., its volume of data) and in the different kinds of data types. Thusfar, we have viewed the data stored in a data base at three levels: the applications level, the systems level, and the physical level. E. F. Codd of IBM has proposed a relational model of data that could be placed somewhere between the applications level and the systems level.* The relational model is based on the concept of a relation as discussed previously and is implemented by viewing a data base as a table of values. The use of the table, which exists as an entity/attribute matrix, has one overriding advantage: it provides a means of describing data with only its natural structure and without imposing any additional structure needed for logical or physical representation. The benefit to be derived from viewing the information in the data base as a rectangular array is that any ordering, indexing, and access path dependencies are removed—at least, at the level at which the user interacts with the system. A data base model based on relations is not necessarily dependent upon an entity/attribute matrix for its representation, but the tabular format of

*This is the author's viewpoint and not necessarily that of Codd.

254

ATTRIBUTES

EMPLOYEE	(employee-number	name	salary)
	346825	K. KING	16381.50
	221607	L. WEEK	9423.75
	346826	T. ABLE	17440.00
	449795	J. DOE	44950.00
	741109	P. RIDER	14657.40
	533412	M. FINI	32400.00

ENTITIES ↓

Figure 15.1   Example of an entity/attribute matrix for the EMPLOYEE relation.

the entity/attribute matrix is convenient and lends itself to the mathematical notion of a relation.

As an example of an entity/attribute matrix, consider the group schema:

EMPLOYEE = {EMPLOYEE-NUMBER,NAME,SALARY}

and the corresponding entity/attribute matrix given as Figure 15.1. The *employee-number* attribute is the entity identifier. A *relation*, as covered in a previous chapter on "Descriptive Techniques," is a mapping between the set represented as the idenitifier attribute, and the other attribute sets. The number of columns in the matrix is regarded as the degree of the relation. The EMPLOYEE relation in Figure 15.1, for example, is a relation of degree 3. In general, an entity/attribute matrix has the following properties:

1. Each row of the matrix represents an instance of the relation.
2. The columns are homogeneous in the sense that all entries in a selected column are of the same kind.
3. Each row of the matrix is distinct, at least as far as the identifier attribute is concerned, and the ordering of rows is not significant.*
4. Each column of the matrix represents an attribute and the ordering of columns is not important—i.e., unless two columns are labeled the same.

Codd gives several reasons why the entity/attribute matrix is preferred over the "linked list" approach for the user's model of data. Two of the most significant reasons are given here. First, access is not symmetric with the linked-list approach since a link from A to B implies that B is accessible from A, but the reverse is not true. Secondly, the use of linked structures to represent relations complicates system structure since relations of different degrees are treated differently and the growth of a relation to a higher degree is inconvenient to represent.

*It should be remembered here that we are dealing with a model of a data base and that physical storage structures and operations on those structures are not of immediate concern.

REPRESENTATION

Figure 15.1 is an example of a data structure in what is known as a preferred, or *normal form.* A data structure represented as an entity/attribute matrix in normal form has the characteristics given in the previous section along with one additional requirement: each item in the matrix is a simple number or character string. For simple groups,* the latter convention causes no problems. For compound groups, the convention requires that the data structure be normalized.

Figure 15.2 depicts the following compound group:

EMPLOYEE = {EMPLOYEE-NUMBER,NAME,SALARY,
JOB-SKILL = {JOB-CODE,JOB-TITLE},
EDUCATION = {DEGREE,YEAR,SCHOOL}}

The relations in this example are EMPLOYEE, JOB-SKILL, and EDUCATION. With his data base sublanguage, Codd uses the relation as a qualifier and uses the following notation for each relation:

EMPLOYEE (*employee-number*, name, salary, job-skill, education)
JOB-SKILL (*job-code*, job-title)
EDUCATION (*degree*, year, school)

Thus, the compound group exists as three simple interrelationships.

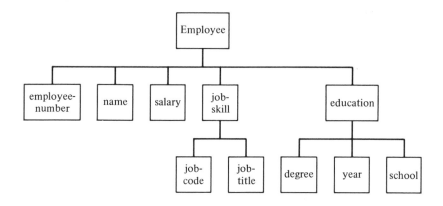

Figure 15.2   Compound group.

NORMALIZATION

The process of *normalization* involves eliminating the dependencies of a compound group without a loss of information. A set of schemas for the compound

---

*For a definition of "simple group," see Chapter 12, Descriptive Techniques.

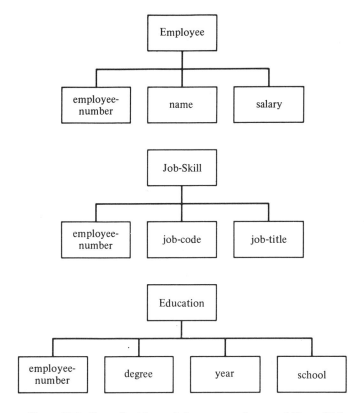

Figure 15.3   Normalized form of the compound group of Figure 15.2.

group of Figure 15.2 with dependencies removed is given as Figure 15.3, and a normalized set of corresponding relations is listed as follows:

EMPLOYEE (*employee-number*, name, salary)
JOB-SKILL (*employee-number*, *job-code*, job-title)
EDUCATION (*employee-number*, *degree*, year, school)

Codd gives the normalization procedure as follows:

Starting with the relation at the top of the tree [i.e., the tree corresponding to the compound group], take its primary key and expand each of the immediately subordinate relations by inserting this primary key domain [i.e., attribute value] or domain combination. The primary key of each expanded relation consists of the primary key before expansion augmented by the primary key copied down from the parent relation. Now, strike out from the parent relation all nonsimple domains [i.e., subordinate groups], remove the

Unnormalized Form

EMPLOYEE (*employee-number* name salary JOB-SKILL (*job-code* job-title) EDUCATION (*degree* year school))

employee-number	name	salary	job-code	job-title	degree	year	school
449795	JOHN A. DOE	44950.00	A23	Staff Exec.	BS	1950	M.I.T.
			F34	Mathematician	MBA	1955	Harvard
			G15	Actuary			
670042	L. K. SMITH	33619.50	L70	Personnel Man.	BBA	1950	Ohio
716832	S. BROWN	19500.00	F57	Systems Analyst	BS	1965	Pratt
					MS	1967	Pratt

Normalized Form

EMPLOYEE (*employee-number* name salary)

employee-number	name	salary
449795	JOHN A. DOE	44950.00
670043	L. K. SMITH	33619.50
716832	S. BROWN	19500.00

JOB-SKILL (*employee-number* *job-code* job-title)

employee-number	job-code	job-title
449795	A23	Staff Exec.
449795	F34	Mathematician
449795	G15	Actuary
670043	L70	Personnel Man.
716832	F57	Systems Analyst

EDUCATION (*employee-number* *degree* year school)

employee-number	degree	year	school
449795	BS	1950	M.I.T.
449795	MBA	1955	Harvard
670043	BBA	1950	Ohio
716832	BS	1965	Pratt
716832	MS	1967	Pratt

Figure 15.4 An occurrence of a compound group schema in unnormalized form and as a set of normalized relations.

top node of the tree, and repeat the same sequence of operation on each remaining subtree.*

Figure 15.4 gives an occurrence of a compound group schema in both unnormalized form and as a set of normalized relations. In the latter case, each normlized relation is stored as an entity/attribute matrix.

The above concepts are adequate for data that can be represented as tree structures. For more complex data structures, Codd also defines a second normal form and a third normal form. The references to the relational model also define operations on relations and include considerations of redundancy and consistency.

DATA BASE ACCESS

With the relational model, a data base exists as a collection of relations that are represented as entity/attribute matrices. The advantage of this approach is significant from an operational point of view. The matrices are not dependent upon pointers, hashing schemes, or indexing; thus they can be compressed, using an appropriate algorithm, and can also be transferred between data base systems as bulk data.

The data base is effectively partitioned by relation—or to be more precise—relation name, so that a data name takes the form:

$$R.a$$

where R is the name of a relation and a is the name of an attribute.** Data are accessed by name and are retrieved through a buffer area called a *workspace*. The workspace serves as an interface between a host language program and the data base, so at each point in time, it may contain an entire entity/attribute matrix for a given relation, or a portion thereof. An application may use several workspaces concurrently.

A data base sublanguage† is defined as that used to transfer information between the data base and a workspace; the sublanguage permits the following classes of data base operations:

Retrieve value or set of values.
Change value or set of values.
Insert value or set of values.
Delete value or set of values.
Establish a relation.
Delete a relation.

*E. F. Codd, "A relational model of data for large shared data banks," *Communications of the ACM*, Vol. 13, Number 6 (June 1970), p. 381.
**Codd uses the more general form $R(g).r.d$, where R is a relational name, g is a generation identifier, r is an optional role name, and d is a domain (i.e., attribute) name.
†The data base sublanguage is known as ALPHA or DSL ALPHA.

An introductory subset of the sublanguage is introduced in the next section. The examples use the data structure depicted in the group schema of Figure 15.5 and in normalized form in Figure 15.6.* The data structure represents information describing "job classes" and how they are used in an enterprise. For example, a company may employ managers, engineers, salesmen, and clerical personnel, so that corresponding entity/attribute matrices might exist as follows:

JOB	Job Code (JC)	Job Title (JT)	Quantity (Q)
	010	Manager	14
	020	Engineer	60
	030	Salesman	12
	040	Clerical	21

ASSIGNMENT	Job Code (JC)	Project Code (PC)	Quantity Needed (QN)
	010	100	5
	010	150	4
	010	200	5
	020	100	25
	020	150	15
	020	200	20
	030	100	7
	030	200	5
	040	100	10
	040	150	6
	040	200	5

PROJECT	Project Code (PC)	Project Name (PN)	Project Manager Number (PMN)
	100	COMPUTER DEV	447380
	150	FACILITY SURVEY	377199
	200	ROAD DESIGN	637768

The above relations demonstrate the notion of a "primary key." An attribute or combination of attributes that uniquely identify a row of an entity/attribute matrix is known as a *primary key*. Thus, for the JOB and PROJECT relations,

---

*Figure 15.6 depicts Codd's Second Normal Form. In normalizing the group schema, an entity/attribute matrix is developed in which the attributes "project name" and "project manager number" are not attributes of the primary key <job code, project code> but only of the <project code> component. Therefore, the attributes that pertain to the latter component are split into a third entity/attribute matrix.

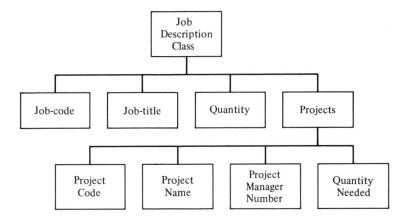

Figure 15.5 Group schema representing the assignment of personnel in an enterprise.

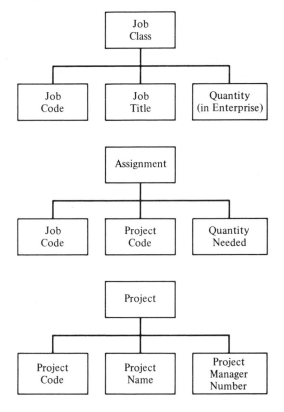

Figure 15.6 Normalized form of the group schema representing the assignment of personnel in an enterprise (see Figure 15.5).

the primary keys are *Job Code* and *Project Code*, respectively. For the ASSIGN-MENT relation, the primary key is a combination of the *Job Code* and *Project Code* attributes.

DATA BASE SUBLANGUAGE

The data base sublanguage exists as a set of statements that provide the basic operations listed in the preceding section. A statement consists of a combination of the following syntactical units:

A required operation name.
A workspace name used with most statements.
A list of variables representing data elements or relations.
An optional qualification expression.

The nature of the sublanguage is demonstrated through a variety of examples.

Data is retrieved from the data base with the GET statement, as in the following case:

GET WS (PROJECT.PC,PROJECT.PN)

This statement transfers the list of project code numbers and project names from the data base to the workspace named WS. A qualified retrieval uses a conditional expression as follows:

GET BIGA (ASSIGNMENT.JC,ASSIGNMENT.PC):(ASSIGNMENT.QN>5)

This statement transfers all job code and project code numbers to workspace BIGA for all entries in the ASSIGNMENT entity/attribute matrix where the quantity needed (QN) is greater than 5.

An update operation uses the HOLD and UPDATE statements as follows:

HOLD AREA1 (PROJECT.PMN):(PROJECT.PC=150)
AREA1.PMN=NEWMAN
UPDATE AREA1

The HOLD statement moves the data to be updated from the data base to the workspace AREA1, while retaining control information with which to perform the update. The second statement, in the host language, changes the project manager number (PMN) in the workspace. UPDATE returns the modified data to the workspace.

Insertion is performed by placing the values to be inserted into a workspace and by specifying the workspace name and an appropriate relation name in a PUT statement as follows:

PUT WS PROJECT

With an insertion operation, the data base system performs validity checking on the primary keys and maintains the ordering properties of the entity/attribute matrix.

The deletion operation excises entries (i.e., rows) from the entity/attribute matrix as in the following example:

$$\text{DELETE PROJECT:(PROJECT.PC=150)}$$

This statement deletes the entry from the entity/attribute matrix for the relation PROJECT where the project code is equal to 150. The DELETE statement can also utilize a list of values held in a workspace:

$$\text{DELETE JOB:(JOB.JC=AREA2.JC)}$$

This statement deletes entries from the entity/attribute matrix for the relation JOB whose job codes (JC) are contained in workspace AREA2.

A relation is established in a data base by placing its entity/attribute matrix in a workspace and by issuing a PUT statement with a unique "new" relation name as follows:

$$\text{PUT WS PAY}$$

This statement creates data base entries for the new relation PAY. A relation is deleted from a data base with the DROP statement as follows:

$$\text{DROP PAY}$$

This statement removes the entity/attribute matrix for the relation PAY from the data base.

The sublanguage is obviously more sophisticated in both scope and complexity. However, the concept is both powerful and flexible as demonstrated in the limited examples given here.

FINAL REMARK

It should be emphasized that the relational model has been the object of extensive theoretical development as well as practical implementation and this chapter presents only a brief overview. Most of the recent development is due to Codd, as mentioned previously. Earlier research in this area is referenced in several of his research papers.

REFERENCES

CODASYL Systems Committee, *Feature Analysis of Generalized Data Base Management Systems*, May 1971. Available from the Association for Computing Machinery.

Codd, E. F., "A relational model of data for large shared data banks," *Communications of the ACM*, Volume 13, No. 6 (June 1970), pp. 377–387.

Codd, E. F., "Further normalization of the data base relational model," published in *Data Base Systems*, edited by R. Rustin, Englewood Cliffs, N.J., Prentice-Hall Inc., 1971, pp. 33–64.

Codd, E. F., "Relational completeness of data base sublanguages," published in *Data Base Systems*, edited by R. Rustin, Englewood Cliffs, N.J., Prentice-Hall Inc., 1971, pp. 65–98.

Codd, E. F., "Normalized data base structure: a brief tutorial," published in 1971 ACM SIGFIDET WORKSHOP, *Data Description, Access and Control*, edited by E. F. Codd and A. L. Dean, pp. 1–17. Available from the Association for Computing Machinery.

Codd, E. F., "A data base sublanguage founded on the relational calculus," published in 1971 ACM SIGFIDET WORKSHOP, *Data Description, Access and Control*, edited by E. F. Codd and A. L. Dean, pp. 35–68. Available from the Association for Computing Machinery.

16 | INTEGRATED DATA STORE

INTRODUCTION

Integrated Data Store (IDS) is a data base management system developed in 1963 by the General Electric Company for their line of computing equipment, and is currently supported by Honeywell Information Systems, Inc. IDS can be viewed as a forerunner of the DBTG concept (i.e., an extension to the COBOL language in order to handle data bases) and is generally regarded as a significant development in the evolution of data base technology.

IDS is an operational system and one of the advantages of including a brief description of it is that topics related to implementation can be mentioned. The best sources of detailed information on IDS are the Honeywell reference manual and the two CODASYL reports listed at the end of the chapter.

SYSTEM STRUCTURE

IDS exists as an extension to COBOL in a conventional operating environment, and consists of five interdependent system components:

1. A *language extension* to COBOL (i.e., the IDS language).
2. A *translator* that translates a COBOL source program with IDS extensions to a conventional source program.
3. A *data base management system* (i.e., IDS itself) that accesses and manages storage and serves as the interface between the application program and the data base.

4. An *internal communications facility* whereby data specifications, formats, etc. can be transferred between the application program and the data base management system.

5. A *storage management facility* that provides a convenient method of storing and retrieving information in the data base.

The IDS language, which is covered in detail later in the chapter impacts the environment, data, and procedure divisions of a COBOL program. In the environment division, extensions involve the addition of an IDS-SPECIAL-NAMES paragraph to the CONFIGURATION SECTION, and a variation to the SELECT clause in the FILE-CONTROL paragraph. Data base structures are defined in the data division in the new IDS SECTION established for that purpose. IDS procedure statements may be used anywhere in the procedure division of a COBOL program. Each IDS sentence, which may be composed of one or more IDS imperative statements, must be preceded by an ENTER IDS and be terminated with a period.

The IDS translation and execution process is depicted in Figure 16.1. The *IDS translator* translates the source program into a combination of IDS/COBOL statements and assembler language statements. The assembler language statements are used during execution of the IDS program to supply information on the structure of the data base and work areas to be used during data base operation. The assembler language statements are preceded and followed by appropriate ENTER statements so that the source program exists as a valid IDS/COBOL program. The source program is then compiled*, loaded, and executed as a conventional application program.

The IDS data base management system exists primarily as a set of subroutines that are called as the result of an IDS imperative statement in a COBOL program. These subroutines then call other subroutines that perform the desired functions, manage the data base, update control blocks and tables, etc.

Information describing the structure of a data base file is passed between an application program and the data base management system through the use of control blocks that are assembled as part of the application program. Collectively, the control blocks are referred to as a *definition structure* that defines the relationship between master and detail records, the characteristics of chains (of records), and the attributes of each field in an IDS record.

Management of the data base storage space utilizes the notion of a page and a set of lines within a page. An IDS data record is assigned a unique line number within a page. Thus, a page number and a line number constitutes a reference code for a record; once a reference code is assigned to a record, it does not change for the duration of the life of that record. The data base management

*The Honeywell COBOL compiler produces assembler language output that is passed through the assembler program.

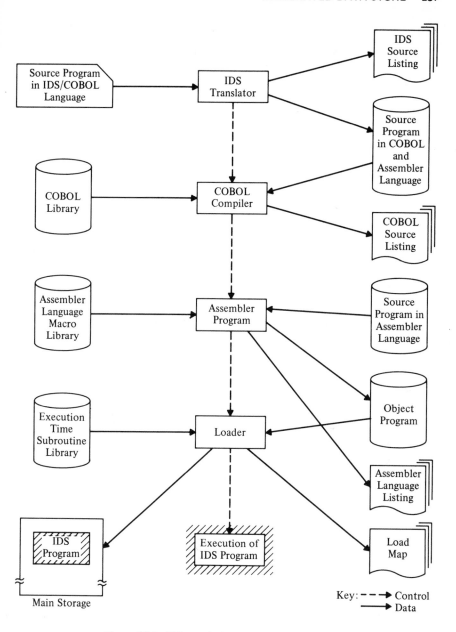

Figure 16.1   IDS translation and execution process.

system also uses a set of page buffers in main storage during system operation. One of the objectives of the IDS system is to keep as many active pages in main storage as possible. As a result, data base access time may be reduced considerably, based on the execution-time characteristics of an application program.

A description of the five components listed at the beginning of this section, along with the techniques used to structure and organize data constitute the remainder of this chapter. The amount of technical implementation information is minimized to allow the reader the greatest possible conceptual view of the system.

DATA STRUCTURE AND ORGANIZATION

The basic unit of data in IDS is the record; and files are composed of records in the conventional sense. Nonredundancy and consistency of information stored in the data base is achieved through the use of ring structures—or *chains*, as they are called in IDS. A chain consists of a master record and any number of detail records, as depicted in Figure 16.2. Through the effective use of chain structures, a record need be stored only once and update problems are minimized.

The types of relationships that can be represented by IDS chains include the following:

1. Simple group structure.
2. Compound group structure.
3. Hierarchical data structure.
4. Simple network structure.

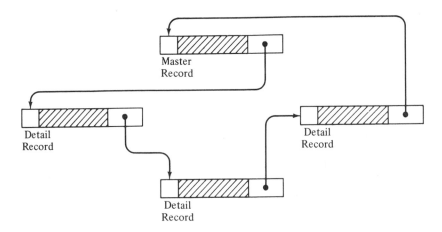

Figure 16.2   A simple chain structure in IDS.

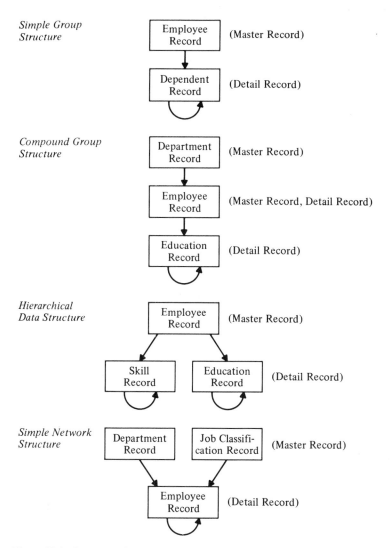

Figure 16.3 Structure diagrams for examples of data structures that can be stored in IDS.

Structure diagrams for examples of these relationships are given in Figure 16.3. A chain structure is developed by a user* to represent the relationship between

---

*A user can be a systems analyst, a programmer, a data administrator, etc. Because a data description is included in an IDS/COBOL program, the role of the data administrator is not explicitly defined. Another consideration is that IDS is an early system and the data administrator function has evolved to some degree.

data records in a data base. The following conventions govern the construction
and utilization of chain structures:

1. Each chain must have exactly one master record.
2. A chain may include any number of detail records.
3. All detail records in a chain are not restricted to be of the same type.
4. A record may simultaneously be a master record of one chain and a detail
   record in another chain.
5. A record may be the master record of two or more chains.
6. A record may be a detail record in two or more chains.
7. A detail record may not be stored unless its master record exists.
8. When a master record is deleted from a data base, the entire chain is also
   deleted.
9. A record may not be a detail record to itself, either directly or indirectly.

The structure of an IDS data record is given in Figure 16.4. When using IDS/
COBOL, the user defines a data record in the conventional manner and the iden-

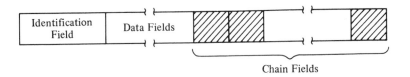

Figure 16.4   Structure of an IDS data record.

tification and chain fields are supplied by the IDS system. At least one chain
field exists for each chain in which the record participates as a member. A chain
field contains the reference code (i.e., page and line number) of the "next" record in the ring structure. The IDS/COBOL programming language also allows a
detail record to be linked to a prior record and to the master record for each
chain in which it participates. Figure 16.5 depicts an instance of an IDS chain in
its most general form.

An IDS data record is classed by the manner in which it is referenced, as specified in a data division record definition. Three classes are provided: primary
records, secondary records, and calculated records. A *primary record* is referenced through its unique reference code. When a primary record is created, the
unique reference code generated internally by the IDS system is made available
to the application program.* The reference code is then used as the key field for
subsequent storage and retrieval operations.

---

*The reference code generated by IDS is moved to the field in working storage specified
by the "RETRIEVAL VIA field-name" clause.

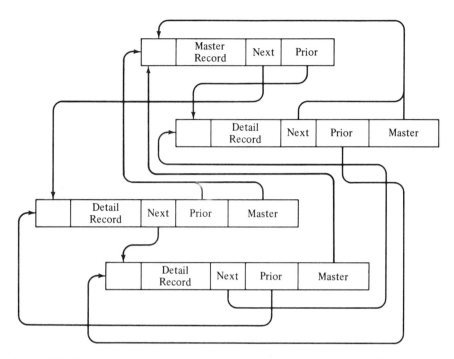

Figure 16.5   Chain structure depicting *next*, *prior*, and *master* pointer fields (i.e., reference codes).

A *secondary record* is referenced through its master record, by first locating that master record and subsequently sequencing through the chain to determine its location by comparison of data fields contained therein. A *calculated record* is located through an IDS-defined randomizing technique. The technique uses the contents of one or more data fields to determine a page location. During an initial storage operation, the record is stored on the designated page if space is available, or on the next successive page with available space. During a retrieval operation, the process is essentially reversed.

SYSTEM OPERATION

Detail records are normally stored and retrieved through a master record. A store operation involves storage allocation, chain selection, and record insertion. In general, a new detail record can be added to the chain currently being processed (i.e., the current master record) or to the chain of a unique master record. The manner in which a new detail record is added to a chain is dependent upon the data definition for that chain. Six options for the ordering of detail records are available through the CHAIN-ORDER clause of a chain definition:

1. Sorted by specified data fields.
2. Sorted by specified data fields within record type.
3. As the first detail record on the chain, relative to the master record.
4. As the last detail record on the chain, relative to the master record.
5. Before the "current" record on a chain.
6. After the "current" record on a chain.

As a chain is being processed by the IDS system, a record is kept of the current detail record, the prior detail record, the next detail record, and, of course, the master record. Thus, the system is able to perform the operations listed above as well as a variety of storage and retrieval functions, such as:

RETRIEVE PRIOR RECORD OF chain-name CHAIN
RETRIEVE NEXT RECORD OF CALC CHAIN

The manner in which a chain is linked determines how efficiently chain processing can be performed—especially when references must be made to prior and master records. As mentioned previously, linking structures are provided automatically by IDS depending upon how a chain is defined in the IDS section of the data division. The following definition,

```
01  DEPT-MAST-REC;
        TYPE IS 20;
        RETRIEVAL VIA DEPT CHAIN.
    02  DEPT-NO PICTURE 9(4).
    02  INFOR PICTURE X(25).
    98  DEPT CHAIN MASTER;
        LINKED TO PRIOR;
        CHAIN-ORDER IS SORTED.
    98  COMPANY CHAIN DETAIL;
        DESCENDING KEY IS DEPT-NO;
        SELECT CURRENT MASTER.
```

for example, describes the master record to a chain named DEPT. The level number of 98 denotes a chain specification that must follow the associated record description. Detail records in the chain DEPT are maintained in sorted order and include "prior" pointers (i.e., chain fields). The same record is also a detail record of a chain named COMPANY. Because no linking attributes are specified for the COMPANY chain, detail records including DEPT-MAST-REC contain only "next" pointers. In the next definition, a record which is related to the above record definition, is described:

```
01  EMPLOYEE-REC;
        TYPE IS 40;
        RETRIEVAL VIA CALC CHAIN;
        PAGE-RANGE IS 1 TO 750.
```

```
02  S-S-NO PICTURE 9(9).
02  NAME PICTURE X(25).
02  ADDR.
    03  NUMBER X(10).
    03  LOCATION X(15).
    03  ZIP 9(5).
02  RATE 9(5)V9(2).
98  DEPT CHAIN DETAIL;
    ASCENDING KEY IS S-S-NO;
    DUPLICATES NOT ALLOWED.
98  DEPENDENT CHAIN MASTER;
    SELECT UNIQUE MASTER;
    LINKED TO MASTER.
98  CALC CHAIN DETAIL;
    RANDOMIZE S-S-NO.
```

In this example, EMPLOYEE-REC can be retrieved by a randomizing procedure on field S-S-NO and is a detailed record of the DEPT chain defined previously. Because the DEPT chain has the attribute "LINKED TO PRIOR," each instance of EMPLOYEE-REC includes both "prior" and "next" pointers. In the second example, the defined record is also a master record for a chain named DEPEN-DENT in which all detail records are linked to the appropriate employee record. The three methods of linking in IDS are implied in Figure 16.5 and are summarized as follows:

1. The NEXT pointer is automatically provided by IDS for all detail records.
2. The PRIOR pointer is optional and is provided by IDS for detail records of chains that are specified as being prior processable.
3. The MASTER pointer is also optional and is provided by IDS for detail records of chains that are specified as being LINKED TO MASTER. (This option essentially establishes an inverse mapping as presented earlier.)

The three methods of chain linking, the chain fields in a data record, and chain processing, are integrated through a "chain table" that is built internally by the IDS system for each chain that is processed. Consider the chain structure in Figure 16.6; assume that the chain was entered through its master record, and that the "current" record is detail record #3. Further assume that detail record #3 was accessed by sequencing through the chain and that the chain *does not contain* prior pointers. At this point, the chain table would exist conceptually as follows:

Master	10025
Prior	61397
Current	61351
Next	90001

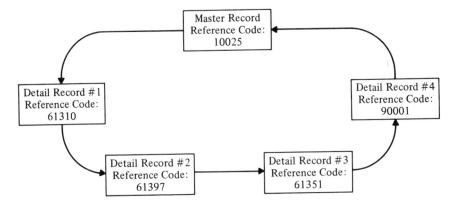

Figure 16.6   Chain structure used for an introduction to chain tables.

If the statement **RETRIEVE PRIOR** of chain-name **CHAIN** were executed, detail record #2 would be accessed and the chain table would exist as follows:

Master	10025
Prior	00000
Current	61397
Next	61351

Thus, the "current record" of the chain is effectively backed up. If the RETRIEVE PRIOR statement were again executed, the IDS system would have to traverse the chain through the master record to arrive at the prior position. If the chain had been given the attribute **LINKED TO PRIOR**, however, traversal would not be necessary and the chain table would exist as follows:

Master	10025
Prior	10025
Current	61310
Next	61397

When records are retrieved directly through the **RETRIEVE DIRECT** statement, the master record of a chain and previous detail records are not referenced. Therefore, the chain table is updated from the detail record providing as much information to the system as possible from the record. Using the chain structure in Figure 16.6 and assuming that detail record #2 was retrieved directly, the following chain table values would be obtained (00000 denotes an unknown pointer):

Master	00000
Prior	00000
Current	61397
Next	61351

No linking other
than NEXT

Master	00000
Prior	61310
Current	61397
Next	61351

Linked to PRIOR

Master	10025
Prior	61310
Current	61397
Next	61351

Linked to PRIOR
and MASTER

The execution of most imperative statements of the IDS/COBOL language cause a chain table to be updated accordingly. In the description of the statements, this information is not provided because the level of detail becomes excessively great; but it is available from IDS reference manuals. Selective information in a chain table can be referenced from an application program and can be used to design and process chains in an efficient manner.

DATA DESCRIPTION

Data description* affects the environment and data divisions of an IDS/COBOL program. The skeleton for the environment division is given in Figure 16.7; the most significant entry from an IDS point of view is the SELECT IDS statement that is used to assign an IDS file name, and to specify the logical device on which it resides. The IDS-SPECIAL-NAMES paragraph is implement-dependent and is not discussed further.

```
ENVIRONMENT DIVISION.
CONFIGURATION SECTION.
SOURCE-COMPUTER.  · · ·
OBJECT-COMPUTER.  · · ·
IDS-SPECIAL-NAMES.  · · ·
INPUT-OUTPUT SECTION.
FILE-CONTROL.
        SELECT IDS file-name ASSIGN TO file-code-1
          .
          .
          .
1-0-CONTROL.
        APPLY  · · ·
```

Figure 16.7   Skeleton of the environment division of an IDS/COBOL program.

*The COBOL syntax notation is used for data description and data manipulation statements. It is given in the "Syntax Notation" section of Chapter 13, DBTG Report.

The description of an IDS file (or data base as it is frequently called) is contained in a special IDS SECTION of the data division, which must be structured in the following manner:

> DATA DIVISION.
> [File Section]
> [Working Storage Section]
> [IDS Section]
> [Constant Section] *
> [Report Section]

The IDS Section is composed of a file description entry followed by one or more record description entries; each record description entry is followed by chain definition (i.e., 98-level items) for chains of which that record is associated. Thus, an IDS Section is structured as follows:

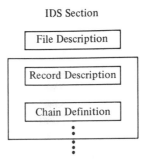

IDS Section

where the vertical ellipses denote an optional repetition of the element that appears directly above. Figure 16.8 gives an example of an IDS SECTION. All other entries in a data division of an IDS/COBOL program have the same syntax and semantics, as in standard COBOL. Skeleton entries for the various data description clauses are given in the following paragraphs and figures. The reader can obtain a notion of what IDS is "all about," even though the entries are not defined in complete detail.

The IDS *file description entry* describes the physical structure of an IDS file and gives the total physical storage requirements. The language skeleton for the IDS file description entry is given in Figure 16.9.

The IDS *record description entry* is used to describe the external format of a logical record and to establish internal working storage areas. Information provided at the 01 level is used to control IDS processing. The language skeleton for the IDS record description entry is given in Figure 16.10 and the function

---

*The Constant Section is no longer used in COBOL; it is included here for completeness.

```
IDS SECTION.
MD DATA-BASE-FILE;
      PAGE CONTAINS 3540 CHARACTERS;
      FILE CONTAINS 20000 PAGES.
01  DEPT-MAST-REC; TYPE IS 20;
            RETRIEVAL VIA DEPT CHAIN.
   02  DEPT-NO PICTURE 9(4).
   02  INFO PICTURE X(25).
   98  DEPT CHAIN MASTER; LINKED TO PRIOR;
       CHAIN-ORDER IS SORTED.
01  EMPLOYEE-REC; TYPE IS 40;
            RETRIEVAL VIA CALC CHAIN;
            PAGE RANGE IS 1 TO 750.
   02   S-S-NO PICTURE 9(9).
   02  NAME PICTURE X(25).
   02  ADDR.
         03  NUMBER X(10).
         03  LOCATION X(15).
         02  ZIP 9(5).
   02  RATE 9(5)V9(2).
   98  DEPT CHAIN DETAIL;
       ASCENDING KEY IS S-S-NO;
       DUPLICATES NOT ALLOWED.
   98  DEPENDENT CHAIN MASTER;
       SELECT UNIQUE MASTER;
       LINKED TO MASTER.
   98  CALC CHAIN DETAIL;
       RANDOMIZE S-S-NO.
01  DEPENDENT-REC; TYPE IS 60;
            RETRIEVAL VIA DEPENDENT CHAIN.
   02  NAME PICTURE X(25).
   02  SEX PICTURE X(1).
         88  MALE VALUE IS 'M'.
         88  FEMALE VALUE IS 'F'.
   02  BIRTH.
         03  MONTH PICTURE 9(2).
         03  DAY PICTURE 9(2).
         03  YEAR PICTURE 9(4).
   98  DEPENDENT CHAIN DETAIL;
       DUPLICATES NOT ALLOWED.
```

Figure 16.8   Structure of a simple IDS section.

MD file-name [;PAGE CONTAINS integer-1 CHARACTERS]
[;FILE CONTAINS integer-2 PAGES] .

Figure 16.9   IDS file description entry skeleton.

01 record-name; TYPE IS integer-1

;RETRIEVAL VIA $\left\{ \begin{array}{ll} \text{field-name} & \text{FIELD} \\ \left\{\begin{array}{l} \text{chain-name-1} \\ \text{CALC} \end{array}\right\} & \text{CHAIN} \end{array} \right\}$

$\left[\text{;PAGE-RANGE IS} \left\{ \begin{array}{l} \text{integer-2 TO integer-3} \\ \text{field-name-1 TO field-name-2} \end{array} \right\} \right]$

[;PLACE NEAR chain-name-2 CHAIN]
[;INTERVAL IS integer-4 PAGES]
[;AUTHORITY IS integer-5]

Figure 16.10   IDS record description entry skeleton.

that is generally performed by each of the subordinate clauses is described in the following list:

1. The TYPE clause is used to define a unique record type for use in several of the IDS/COBOL imperative statements.
2. The RETRIEVAL clause is used to specify the procedures that apply to the storage and retrieval of records.
3. The PAGE-RANGE clause is used for placing records in a designated segment of an IDS file.
4. The PLACE clause is used to facilitate storage and retrieval and indicates that a record is to be placed physically near to the master record of the specified chain.
5. The INTERNAL clause is used to distribute occurrences of the associated record type across an effective page range.
6. The AUTHORITY clause is used for data security and can be used to protect a record against unauthorized access.

The record description entry is oriented more toward operational considerations than toward data base structure, which is inherent in the IDS system. Efficiency is of prime consideration because a record is normally a member of several chains and the "prime" chain, as far as execution time is concerned, is not obvious from the structure of the data base.

The *chain definition entry* is identified by a 98-level number and is used to denote master and detail records, and specify chain membership of the associ-

Format Option 1 (Master);

98 chain-name-1 CHAIN MASTER

;CHAIN-ORDER IS $\left\{\begin{array}{l}\text{SORTED WITHIN TYPE} \\ \text{SORTED} \\ \text{FIRST} \\ \text{LAST} \\ \text{BEFORE} \\ \text{AFTER}\end{array}\right\}$

[;LINKED TO PRIOR]

Format Option 2 (Detail):

98 $\left\{\begin{array}{l}\text{chain-name-2} \\ \text{CALC}\end{array}\right\}$ CHAIN DETAIL

[;RANDOMIZE ON field-name-1 [;RANDOMIZE $\cdots$]]

$\left[\begin{array}{l}\text{;DUPLICATES} \quad \left\{\begin{array}{l}\text{ARE FIRST} \\ \text{ARE LAST} \\ \text{NOT ALLOWED}\end{array}\right\}\end{array}\right]$

$\left[;\left\{\begin{array}{l}\text{ASCENDING} \\ \text{DESCENDING}\end{array}\right\}\text{KEY IS field-name-2} \left[;\left\{\begin{array}{l}\text{ASCENDING} \cdots \\ \text{DESCENDING} \cdots\end{array}\right\}\right]\right]$

[;ASCENDING RANGE KEY IS field-name-3]

$\left[\text{;SELECT} \left\{\begin{array}{l}\text{UNIQUE} \\ \text{CURRENT}\end{array}\right\} \text{MASTER}\right]$

[;MATCH-KEY IS field-name-4 [MATCH-KEY $\cdots$]]

$\left[\text{;MATCH-KEY IS field-name-5} \left\{\begin{array}{l}\text{SYNONYM} \\ \text{SYN}\end{array}\right\} \text{field-name-4 [MATCH-KEY} \cdots\text{]}\right]$

[;LINKED TO MASTER]

Figure 16.11   IDS chain definition entry skeleton.

ated record description (i.e., the preceding 01-level entry). The language skeleton for the chain definition entry is given in Figure 16.11 and the function that is generally performed by each of the subordinate clauses is described in the following list:

1. The *master/detail* clause denotes that the record is either a master record or a detail record. This entry is required for each chain in which the record participates.
2. The CHAIN-ORDER is used to specify the sequencing of detail records in a chain.
3. The LINKED TO PRIOR clause is used to indicate that a prior pointer is required in the detail records of a chain.

4. The RANDOMIZE clause is used to specify the data fields in a data record that are to participate in the randomizing procedure to generate page numbers.
5. The DUPLICATES clause is used to specify how duplicate records, by sort key values, are to be handled.
6. The ASCENDING/DESCENDING clause is used to specify the data fields that control the sequencing of detail records.
7. The SELECT clause is used to specify the procedure to be followed when a detail record is added to the data base.
8. The MATCH-KEY clause is used to denote the fields in working storage or their alternates that are used to uniquely identify a master record.
9. The LINKED TO MASTER clause is used to add a "master pointer" to each detail record of a chain.

One of the major advantages of IDS is the relative simplicity of the data description techniques. The capability in this regard is not as sophisticated as in the DBTG system, for example, but it does provide a means for the COBOL-type user to store interrelated records in an efficient manner, and to avoid redundancy and facilitate update and maintenance

An example of the use of IDS data description methods and a comparison with corresponding DBTG methods are given in the appendix.

DATA MANIPULATION

The data manipulation statements of IDS are an adjunct to the standard COBOL language and are used in the procedure division of an IDS/COBOL program. The only restriction on the use of IDS statements is that, "An IDS sentence must be preceded by the statement

ENTER IDS.

and be terminated with a Period." The scope of the ENTER IDS statement is the sentence that immediately follows it. The format of an IDS sentence is given in Figure 16.12.

Paragraph-name.
ENTER IDS. IDS-statement-1 [IDS-statement-2]···
[IDS-statement-n].

Figure 16.12   Format of an IDS sentence.

As in COBOL, an IDS data file must be "opened" before processing and be "closed" after processing is complete. The close verb serves to transfer IDS pages that have been modified to the assigned external storage device. The format of the OPEN and CLOSE statements is given in Figure 16.13.

$$\text{OPEN} \left[\text{FOR} \left\{\begin{array}{l}\underline{\text{RETRIEVAL}}\\\underline{\text{UPDATE}}\end{array}\right\}\right] [\text{WITH} \underline{\text{AUTHORITY-KEY}} \text{ integer}]$$

$\underline{\text{CLOSE}}$ [WITH $\underline{\text{LOCK}}$]

Figure 16.13   Format of the OPEN and CLOSE verbs in IDS.

The basic data manipulation capability of IDS is associated with the STORE and RETRIEVE statements. The STORE verb is used to place a record into an IDS file and to establish the chain membership that has been defined. The format of the STORE verb, given in Figure 16.14, is deceptively simple. The execution of the STORE statement uses the information provided with the RE-

$\underline{\text{STORE}}$ record-name RECORD

Figure 16.14   Format of the STORE verb.

TRIEVAL VIA, PAGE-RANGE, PLACE NEAR, and INTERVAL clauses in the specified record—which must be defined at the 01 level in the IDS section of the data division.

After the storage operation is complete, the reference code of the stored record is left in the communication cell DIRECT-REFERENCE, and is placed in other data fields that apply. The execution of the STORE statement involves the use of a randomizing technique and/or a linking operation in conjunction with the information provided with the CHAIN-ORDER and other descriptive clauses. The operations are performed automatically by the IDS system using the information supplied by the user in the data division.

The RETRIEVE statement is used to retrieve a record from an IDS data file and make it available for processing in an IDS/COBOL program. The format of the RETRIEVE statement is given in Figure 16.15. The RETRIEVE verb only transfers a data record to a buffer area in main storage; a subsequent DELETE, HEAD, MODIFY, or MOVE statement must be executed before the data in the retrieved record can be used.

The MOVE statement is used to move the current record* or the fields named in the current record to working storage, or to move the contents of the chain table to working storage. The format of the MOVE statement is given in Figure 16.16. The IDS/COBOL translator/compiler system provides working-storage areas for 02-level items in IDS records in the same manner that standard COBOL automatically provides record areas for COBOL records. When data fields are specified in option-1 of the MOVE statement, only those fields specified are

*That is, the record last processed.

Format Option 1:

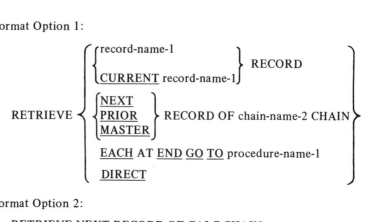

Format Option 2:

RETRIEVE NEXT RECORD OF CALC CHAIN

Figure 16.15   Format of the RETRIEVE statement.

Format Option 1:

;MOVE TO WORKING-STORAGE [field-name-1 [,field-name-2 · · ·]]

Format Option 2:

Figure 16.16   Format of the MOVE statement.

moved to working storage. When no data fields are specified in an IDS MOVE statement, all fields defined in the IDS record are moved to working storage.

The MODIFY statement is used to change the contents of the specified fields of the current record, and to perform any relinking that is made necessary by a change to a control field, such as one used as a sort key or a randomizing field. The format of the MODIFY statement is given in Figure 16.17. The data fields specified in a MODIFY statement must be level-02 entries; the contents of the corresponding fields in working storage are moved to the equivalent field in the current record, which resides in a page buffer.

The DELETE statement is used to remove the current record* from the IDS file and to remove it from all chains in which it is a detail record. The ON clause

*That is, the last record retrieved with the RETRIEVE statement.

Format Option 1:

;<u>MODIFY</u> field-name-1 [,field-name-2 · · ·]

Format Option 2:

;<u>MODIFY</u> <u>CURRENT</u> record-name [field-name-1 [,field-name-2 · · ·]]

Figure 16.17   Format of the MODIFY statement.

;<u>DELETE</u> $\left[\underline{\text{CURRENT}}\text{ record-name-1 RECORD}\left[\underline{\text{ON}}\text{ record-name-2 DETAIL}\right.\right.$

$\left[\underline{\text{MOVE}}\text{ TO WORKING-STORAGE}\right]$

$\left.\left[\underline{\text{HEAD}}\text{ chain-name-1 CHAIN }[\text{HEAD}\cdots]\right]\right.$

$\left[\underline{\text{PERFORM}}\text{ procedure-name-1}\right]$

$\left.\left.\left.\left[\underline{\text{GO}}\ \underline{\text{TO}}\text{ procedure-name-2}\right]\right]\right]\right.$

$\left[\left\{\begin{matrix}\text{OTHERWISE}\\ \underline{\text{ELSE}}\end{matrix}\right\}\underline{\text{ON}}\text{ record-name-3 DETAIL}\cdots\right]$

Figure 16.18   Format of the DELETE statement.

is executed when the specified record possesses dependent records. The format of the DELETE statement is given in Figure 16.18.

The HEAD statement is used to retrieve the master record of the specified chain and move its data fields to working storage. The format of the HEAD statement is given in Figure 16.19.

<u>HEAD</u> chain-name CHAIN[; <u>HEAD</u> · · ·]

Figure 16.19   Format of the HEAD statement.

The IDS/COBOL language includes four program control statements that allow the user to test for specific records or error conditions, to depart from the normal sequence of statement execution, and to designate error procedures. The four control statements are given in Figure 16.20. The IF statement is used to test for the occurrence of a particular record type or for an error condition following a STORE, RETRIEVE, MODIFY, DELETE, or MOVE statement. Option 1 in the IF statement allows imperative statements to be used conditionally; IDS/COBOL statements that may be used in this option are MOVE TO WORKING STORAGE, MODIFY, DELETE, HEAD, PERFORM, or GO TO.

The second IDS/COBOL program control statement is the GO TO statement

Format Option 1:

    ;IF record-name-1 RECORD statement-1 [;statement-2 · · ·]

$$\left[\left\{ \begin{array}{c} \text{OTHERWISE} \\ \text{ELSE} \end{array} \right\} \text{statement-3 } [;\text{statement-4} \cdots] \right]$$

Format Option 2:

$$;\text{IF } \underline{\text{ERROR}} \text{ statement-1} \left[\left\{ \begin{array}{c} \text{OTHERWISE} \\ \text{ELSE} \end{array} \right\} \text{statement-2 } [;\text{statement-3} \cdots] \right]$$

;GO TO procedure-name-1

;PERFORM procedure-name-1 [THRU procedure-name-2]

USE procedure-name-1 [THRU procedure-name-2]
    [WITH TRACE]
    ON $\left\{ \begin{array}{l} \text{error-code-1 } [, \text{error-code-2} \cdots]. \\ \underline{\text{ANY}} \text{ ABORT} \end{array} \right\}$

Figure 16.20   Four formats of IDS/COBOL programs control statements.

that is used to transfer program control to the specified procedure.* The GO TO statement can be used with the IF and USE statements. The third IDS/COBOL PERFORM statement is used to execute an out-of-line procedure and then return to the normal execution sequence. As with the IDS/COBOL GO TO statement, the PERFORM statement can be used with IF and USE statements. The fourth IDS/COBOL program control statement is the USE statement that can be used to supplement the standard error procedures provided by the IDS system. In general, the IDS/COBOL program control statements correspond to standard COBOL statements that cannot be used in IDS sentences.

Two IDS/COBOL statements are particularly appropriate for modern multi-access systems. The INHIBIT statement is used to suspend the sharing of an IDS file until an ENABLE statement is executed. The ENABLE statement is used to

---

*A *procedure* in the COBOL language is a paragraph or a series of successive paragraphs.

INHIBIT

ENABLE

Figure 16.21   Format of the INHIBIT and ENABLE statements.

permit a previously inhibited file to be shared. The format of both statements is given in Figure 16.21. Ordinarily, the INHIBIT statement is used when a shared file is to be updated. Execution of the INHIBIT statement prevents other programs from sharing an IDS file and suspends execution of the program executing the INHIBIT statement (i.e., the program that is updating the file) until all activity on the file has quiesced. Thus, the program issuing the INHIBIT has exclusive use of the file when it resumes execution.

IDS/COBOL also includes CLEANPOINT, SORT, RETURN, DEBUG, and JOURNALIZE statements that are used for buffer control, chain sorting, relinking sorted records, selective dumping and tracing, and transaction recording, respectively. These statements are not discussed further.

An example of the use of IDS data manipulation statements and a comparison with corresponding DBTG statements are given in the appendix.

INTERNAL COMMUNICATIONS

The description of records that comprise an IDS file is included primarily in an IDS-STRUCTURE SECTION that is generated by the IDS translator and included in an IDS/COBOL program. The structure section exists as a list structure of control blocks that represent the interrelationships between master and detail records. The set of control blocks is referred to as a *definition structure* and their relationship is shown in the structure diagram in Figure 16.22. The use of a definition structure is an implementation technique, and is a means of passing information between an application program and the routines of the IDS system. The various control blocks are also used to hold control and operating data during the operation of the IDS system. The functions performed by the control blocks are given as follows:

1. The *communication control block* is the only control block not contained in the IDS structure section. It serves as the "master" of a list of record types and serves as a communications area for data that is passed between and application program and the IDS system. Sample fields in the control block are: reference code of the record last processed by a STORE or RETRIEVE statement, record type, pointer to the first record definition entry, error code, file code, authority value, and a processing mode supplied by the OPEN routine.

2. A *record definition entry* is generated by the IDS translator for each type

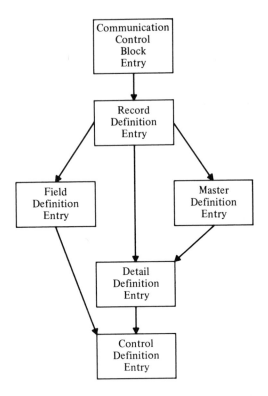

Figure 16.22   Structure diagram of the control blocks
that comprise an IDS definition
structure.

of data record in an IDS file. Sample fields in this entry are: record type, record size, pointers to the first field, master and detail definition entries, page range code, and authority value.

3. A *master definition entry* is generated for each chain occurrence in which a record is specified as a master record. Sample fields in this entry are: reference code of first detail on the chain, pointer to next master definition entry if the record is a master to more than one chain, and reference codes of the chain master, chain prior, chain current, and chain next entries.

4. A *detail definition entry* is generated for each case where a record type is a detail record on a chain. Sample fields in this entry are: record type, an order code (i.e., sorted, first in chain, last in chain, etc.), and the locations in the record of the various reference codes (i.e., for prior records, next records, etc.).

5. A *field definition entry* is generated for each *data* field contained in a record. Sample fields in this entry are: computational mode (i.e., BCD or

binary), arithmetic form, location in the record of the field, and a pointer to the next field definition entry in the definition structure.

6. A *control definition entry* is generated for each control field (i.e., sort key or randomize field) in a record. Sample fields in this entry are: control field type, location in the record of the field, and a pointer to the next control definition entry in the definition structure.

It is probably true that for many applications the structure of the "definition structure" could be more complex than the structure of the data base itself; however, the complexity is necessary because of the dynamically-changing interrelationships in the data base that could not be represented conveniently in any other way.

MAIN STORAGE MANAGEMENT

The IDS system requires buffers and work areas for holding control information and data pages during execution of an application program. The main storage space for these buffers and work areas is specified by an operating system control card and is allocated in labeled common. Most of the details are implementation-dependent and are not of substantial value to a person who is not using the system. The manner in which page buffers are handled, however, provides some insight into the efficiency measures that must be taken into consideration.

The user can specify the amount of buffer space available to the system and, to some extent, can control the efficiency of operation. The objective is to hold several data pages in main storage so that successive references to the same page do not necessarily require subsequent input/output activity. The IDS system uses a set of buffers chained together through a "Page Buffer Activity Table." Figure 16.23 depicts an example of a simple chain of buffers and the corresponding activity table.

The buffer strategy is straightforward and uses the least-recently-used (LRU) principle. The set of page buffers can be regarded as though they were chained together; this structure is defined in the page buffer activity table. There always exists an empty buffer, whose corresponding "next buffer" in the table is the buffer of highest activity and corresponding "prior buffer" is the buffer of lowest activity.

When a page is brought into main storage, it is read into the empty buffer which serves as the top of the list of buffers. To allocate buffer space for a new data page, the page on the bottom of the list (i.e., the prior buffer to the empty buffer) is written out to the IDS data file. However, a data page is only written out if it has been updated since a fresh copy always exists on external storage. When a page that is already in main storage is referenced, its buffer number is placed at the head of the list, so that the most frequently used pages are at the top of the list. Otherwise, the list is ordered on the basis of decreasing use.

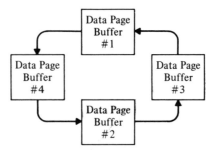

Data Page Buffer Chain

	Prior Buffer	Next Buffer
1	#3	#4
2	#4	#3
3	#2	#1
4	#1	#2

Page Buffer Activity Table

Figure 16.23   Example of a simple chain of data page buffers and the corresponding Page Buffer Activity Table used for buffer management.

A FINAL NOTE

This chapter represents a brief look at the IDS system. Admittedly, it is an overview and if Murphy's law holds, the information that a reader needs *most* is probably not covered. From an overall point of view, however, the material should give some idea of "what IDS is all about." The language formats are given in detail instead of giving simple examples for a specific reason. The options available with many of the statements give insight into many capabilities of the system that would take several pages to describe. In this case, a language format is worth a thousand words.

REFERENCES

CODASYL Systems Committee Technical Report, *A Survey of Generalized Data Base Management Systems*, May 1969. Available from the Association for Computing Machinery.

CODASYL Systems Committee Technical Report, *Feature Analysis of Generalized Data Base Management Systems*, May 1971. Available from the Association for Computing Machinery.

Eriksen, S., "The database concept," *The Honeywell Computer Journal*, Volume 8, No. 1 (1974), pp. 17–32.

Integrated Data Store, Honeywell Information Systems, Inc., Wellesley Hills, Massachusetts, Order No. BR69.

17 | INFORMATION MANAGEMENT SYSTEM

INTRODUCTION

Information Management System (IMS) was initially developed as a joint effort by IBM system engineers and by North American Rockwell in the years surrounding 1965. The system showed great promise and was eventually taken over by IBM as a program product. An introduction to IMS is included here because it is a widely used system and because it incorporates concepts that should be known by a person knowledgeable in data base technology. Because of the current state of the computer industry, the fact that IMS is supported by IBM Corporation is also a contributing factor in its inclusion as a chapter in this book.

This presentation of IMS serves as neither a systems manual nor as a user's manual. The sole objective of the chapter is to present an overview of the system and to give some indication of the design philosophy used.

IMS is a relatively sophisticated system that involves fairly extensive computer facilities and a substantial investment in personnel and development time. The most significant aspect of IMS is perhaps the fact that it incorporates data base technology and data communications facilities in a conventional operating environment. Therefore, the use of IMS constitutes more of a "total systems" approach to the management of data in an enterprise, than it is the use of a new concept in computer technology.

OVERVIEW OF THE SYSTEM

IMS is an interesting combination of technological concepts. First, it is a control program that supports multiple application programs and provides concurrent access to a common data base in an on-line operating environment. This means that the operation of IMS is integrated into the normal functioning of the operating system. Next, IMS is a host-language system, which means that programs are written in a common programming language (such as COBOL or PL/I) and an interface with IMS is achieved through the CALL statement. Lastly, an IMS data base is structured through the execution of utility programs that are executed as normal jobs in a conventional operating environment.

An IMS data base is composed of tree-structured entries from which logical data files are defined by the user of the system. The process of data definition involves four related concepts: segment, logical data record, logical data base, and sensitivity. A fixed-length unit of data that contains one or more data fields is known as a *segment*. The segment is the basic unit of interface data between the IMS system and the user program and it exists as both applications data and as system data. A *logical data record* is a tree structure of segments that can be referenced independently of its physical representation. When an application program accesses the data base, it accesses segments—as compared to the accessing of records in conventional data management, and in some data base systems. A *logical data base* consists of a set of logical data base records stored according to one of the IMS organization techniques and is accessible by one of the defined access methods. During data base definition, a concept known as *sensitivity* is used to establish a subset of the data base that can be accessed by a given application program.

Two methods of storage organization are used to provide data independence: hierarchical sequential and hierarchical direct. Either method can be used by an application program without knowing specifically how the data elements in a data base are physically structured. In *hierarchical sequential organization*, the segments that comprise a physical data base record are organized consecutively and are related by physical location. This means that the segments occupy contiguous blocks or occupy blocks that are linked by an address/location relationship; collectively, the physical data base record occupies a variable number of conventional data management logical records. In *hierarchical direct organization*, the segments that comprise a physical data base record are organized directly and are related by address pointers. Physical segments are linked according to the hierarchical structure of the data base record but the physical blocks are not linked consecutively as in the hierarchical sequential organization.

The hierarchical sequential organization has two access methods: hierarchical sequential access method (HSAM) and hierarchical indexed sequential access method (HISAM), and they provide sequential and indexed sequential access, respectively. The hierarchical direct organization also has two access methods: hierarchical direct access method (HDAM) and hierarchical indexed direct access method (HIDAM), providing "hash addressed" access and "indexed" access to the segments of a data base record that are stored directly. The manner in which data base records are physically stored is introduced in subsequent sections.

SYSTEM STRUCTURE AND BASIC OPERATIONAL PROCEDURES

The IMS system consists of three major functional facilities:

1. A *data base* facility.
2. A *data communications* facility.
3. A set of *utility programs.*

The data base facility is called *Data Language/I*, which provides two interfaces with an application program: (1) a means of describing the logical structure of a data base, and (2) a symbolic program linkage for specifying input and output requests from the application program. The data communications facility consists of telecommunications, message scheduling, checkpoint, and restart support. Data communications is an important component of IMS and a significant aspect of the "total systems" approach to data base management. However, data communications is peripheral to this approach to data base technology and is not discussed further.

Utility programs are divided into three convenient categories: (1) programs concerned with the systems aspects of IMS and its relationship to the operating system; (2) programs concerned with the operational aspects of data base management, such as dump/restore, system log analysis, security maintenance, and data base recovery; and (3) programs concerned with data base description and program specification. The last item is essentially concerned with schema and subschema* definition and is of primary concern to us, along with the data base facility.

The operational flow of the IMS system is suggested in Figure 17.1. The application program communicates with Data Language/I through the use of the CALL statement in a host language program. Changes to the data base are logged on tape to facilitate subsequent recovery in the case where rebuilding the data base is necessary. Before an IMS data base can be used, three preliminary data base operations must be performed:

1. Data base description.
2. Description of data to which a program is sensitive.
3. Program generation.

*The terms *schema* and *subschema* are not used in IMS; however, the concepts are the same.

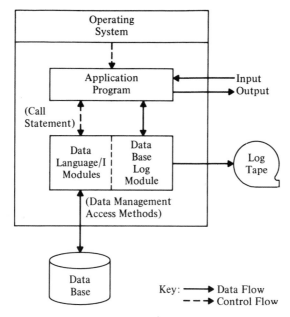

Figure 17.1   Conceptual view of data base operational flow.

The description of a data base must be established before a data base can be used in an application program. The process of generating a *data base description* (DBD) is performed as a normal computer job—i.e., a normal run on the computer. The DBD is specified through the use of a set of DBD macro instructions that place an object code version of a DBD in a DBD library, which is used during IMS execution. DBD generation, depicted in Figure 17.2, includes a specification of the data base name, segment names and attributes, inter-segment relationships, field names and attributes, data base organization, and access methods.

A description of the data (in the data base) to which an application program is sensitive is contained in a *program specification block* (PSB) that is also used during IMS execution. PSB generation, which is depicted in Figure 17.3, is accomplished as a separate computer run in the same manner that the DBD is generated. A PSB includes a definition of the data bases that can be used by an application program, a specification of an operational mode (i.e., retrieve only, update, etc.), and a specification of the segments to which the program is sensitive.

The final operation that must be performed prior to data base operation is preparation of the application program, using the operational conventions necessary for IMS utilization. The object module must be placed in a special

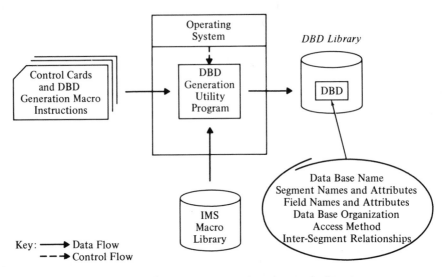

Figure 17.2   Generation of a data base description (DBD).

program library where it can be retrieved by the IMS system during data base operation. The process of application program preparation is suggested by Figure 17.4; the significance of the special IMS application program library is covered in the next section.

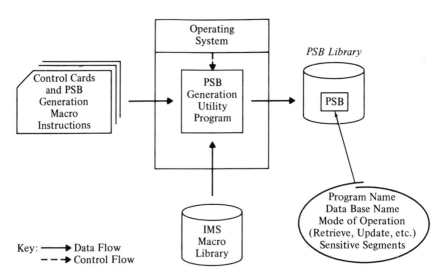

Figure 17.3   Generation of a program specification block (PSB).

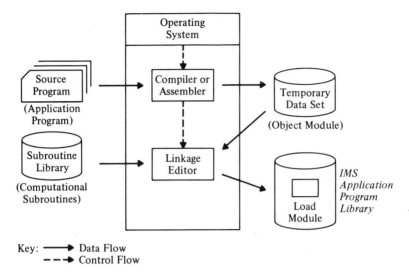

Key: ———▶ Data Flow
     — —▶ Control Flow

Figure 17.4 Application program preparation.

DATA BASE OPERATION

The program elements necessary for IMS operation consist of the following control blocks and load modules: an application program, PSB and DBD control blocks, an IMS region controller, and the IMS modules that comprise the Data Language/I facility. The program elements are employed during the three phases of data base operation: system initialization, readying of the application program and operating environment, and execution of the IMS system and application program.

Data base operation is initiated by an IMS load module, known as a *region controller,* that executes in the user's region* and to which program control is passed by the operating system. The region controller, as the name suggests, controls the execution of IMS for that region. The first step in data base operation is *system initialization* that involves the execution of a "Control Block Loading and Building" program. The loading and building program loads the PSB from the PSB library and required DBDs from the DBD library. (One PSB exists for each application program and is given the same name. Each PSB specifies one or more DBDs, which correspond to data bases accessed by the application program. The relationship between a PSB and associated DBDs is covered later in this chapter.) System initialization is depicted in Figure 17.5.

---

*The term *region* can be interpreted generically as the area of main storage assigned to an application program. For those familiar with IBM terminology, it corresponds to an OS/MVT, OS/VS1, or OS/VS2 region.

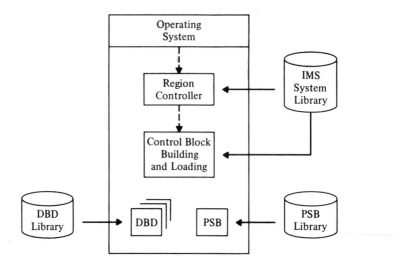

Figure 17.5   System initialization.

After the loading and building of control blocks is complete, control returns to the region controller.

The region controller then readies the operating environment by: loading the Data Language/I and data base log modules, creating a buffer pool for data base operation, and loading the needed data management access method modules. Finally, the application program is dynamically loaded by the operating system from a request by the region controller. The data base operating environment, at this stage, is depicted in Figure 17.6. The parameters necessary for data base initialization are specified with control cards.

After the operating environment is established by the region controller, control is passed to the application program for execution. The application program responds to input and output requests through conventional data management or data communications facilities and the data base is accessed through Data Language/I with the CALL statement—as mentioned previously.

A more detailed description (compared to Figure 17.1) of operational flow of the IMS system in a batch processing environment is given in Figure 17.7. (The numbers in parentheses correspond to those in Figure 17.7.) Control is passed, initially, to the application program (1), and a parameter list that accompanies the call from the region controller provides access to information in the application program's PSB (2). The application program interacts with Data Language/I to access the data base (3). After a call from an application program, Data Language/I references the PSB and DBD control blocks (4 and 5) to verify the validity of the request, and to obtain descriptive information on the data requested by the application program. If the request can be satisfied

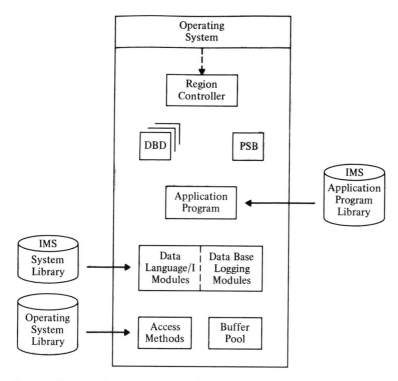

Figure 17.6 Data base operating environment after initialization, and prior to operation.

from a buffer (6), then the requested data is returned to the application program (7). If the request cannot be satisfied from the buffer, then an access method is called (8) to place the requested data in a buffer (9), and the operation is completed as in the preceding description. For a data base insertion operation, the data is transferred from the application program (10), then to a buffer (11), and finally to the data base (12).

To sum up, data requests are satisfied from a buffer whenever possible. Requests requiring an access to the data base utilize the access methods and utilize the buffer pool as storage areas. Program control always passes from the access methods, through Data Language/I, to the application program when a data request is complete.

DATA STRUCTURES

One of the primary objectives of data base technology is the capability of accessing data structures independently of the manner in which they are stored—

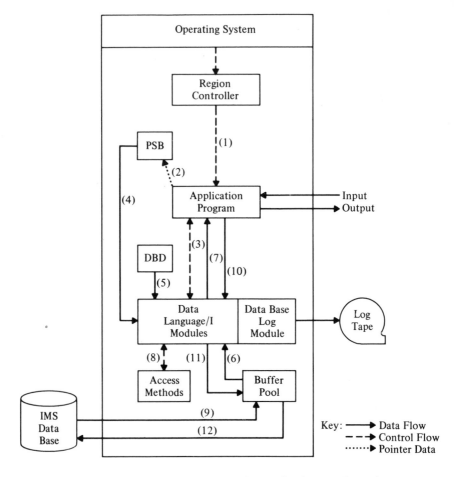

Figure 17.7 Operational flow of data base operation in a batch processing environment.

hence the name *logical data structures*. The end result is that redundancies can be removed from the data base, and that the data base can be restructured without affecting the form of application programs. All of this enables us to deal with a logical data structure, at least from a programming point of view, as though the corresponding physical data structure did not exist. Obviously, a physical data structure must exist and the purpose of this section is to introduce the notion of the kind of physical data structure that is needed to support a logical data structure. This is a difficult task for two major reasons: (1) the topic is complex and generally beyond the scope of this chapter, and (2) the synthesis of effective logical and physical data structures is more of an art than it is a science at this point in the evolution of data base technology.

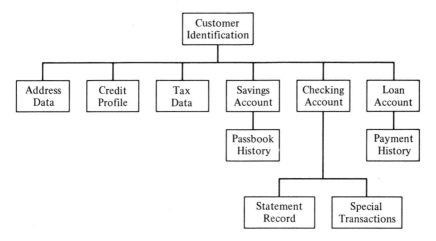

Figure 17.8 Structure diagram of a logical data structure representing a customer account in a bank.

A useful example—although perhaps unrealistic—of customer accounts in a bank is used to demonstrate the concepts. A structure diagram of a logical data structure representing an individual customer account is given as Figure 17.8; the logical data base exists as a set of customer accounts. It is important to mention that the data structure in Figure 17.8 is *not* the physical data structure, nor is it necessarily the logical data structure that is viewed by a given application program. Figure 17.9 demonstrates the concept of sensitivity

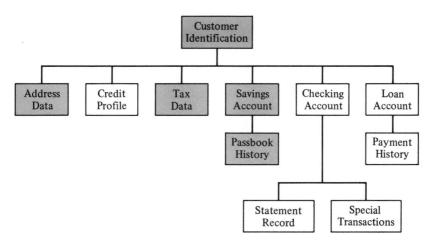

Figure 17.9 An example of *sensitivity* showing the portion of the data base to which the "savings account" application program is sensitive.

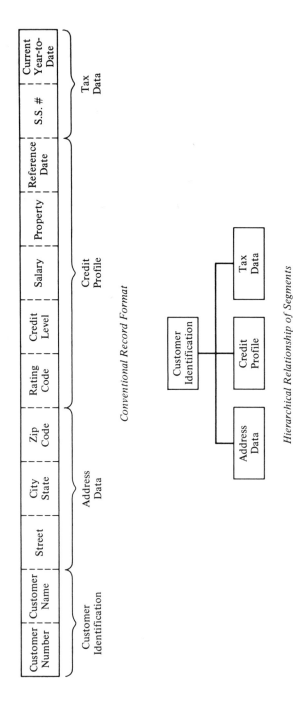

Conventional Record Format

Hierarchical Relationship of Segments

Figure 17.10 A hierarchical structure of segments provides a framework for implementing nonredundancy, independence, and sensitivity.

by showing the portion of the data base to which the "savings account" application program is sensitive. (Recall that sensitivity is specified with the "program specification block (PSB).")

Data independence and nonredundancy are achieved through the use of segments. Conventional record formats include fields that are often unrelated from an application point-of-view and exist at varying levels of sensitivity. However, because of the "packed" form in which conventional records are stored, it is cumbersome, if it is possible at all, to implement nonredundancy and to provide sensitivity. On the other hand, a hierarchical structure of segments, each containing one or more fields, does provide a logical and physical framework in which nonredundancy, independence, and sensitivity can be provided. The correspondence between a conventional record format and a hierarchical structure of segments is depicted in Figure 17.10. In this case, "customer identification" is referred to as a *root segment*; "address data," "credit profile," and "tax data" are *dependent segments* that rely on the root segment for qualification.

The information contained in the customer account logical data structure (i.e., Figure 17.8) can be viewed in several ways; in fact, this is one of the major advantages of using the concept of a logical data structure. For example, Figure 17.11 contains structure diagrams for some possible logical data structures. Structure diagrams (a) and (b) in Figure 17.11 further demonstrate the concept of sensitivity. Structure diagrams (c) and (d) demonstrate data structures that are inverted on the "checking account" segment. The extent to which logical data structures can be inverted is dependent upon the physical data structures over which the logical data structures are defined.

A root segment and all of its dependent segments is defined as a data base record to which certain terminology applies. A structure diagram for a simple data structure is given in Figure 17.12 and an occurrence of that structure is given in Figure 17.13. Three terms are employed: "twin," "parent," and "child." Two or more occurrences of the same segment type within a data base record are referred to as *twins*. Thus, the "customer identification" segments for A. ABLE and B. BAKER are twins, as are the "tax data" segments for 1975, 1974, and 1973. The segment types immediately above and immediately below a given segment type in a hierarchy are called *parent* and *child* segment types, respectively. Thus, for example, the "address data" segment for ABLE is the child of the "customer identification" segment for ABLE, and the "customer identification" segment for ABLE is the parent of the "savings account" segment #1141. The relationships between segments apply in general to both logical and physical data records.

One means of achieving data nonredundancy is to establish a logical interrelationship between physical data structures. The inverted data structure in

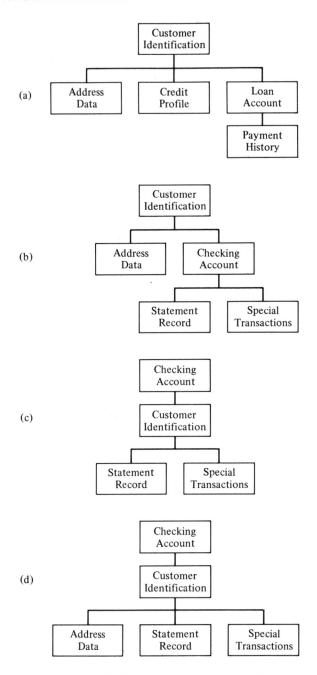

Figure 17.11   Examples of logical data structures.

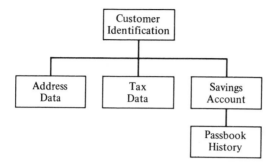

Figure 17.12 Structure diagram for a data structure (used in Figure 17.13).

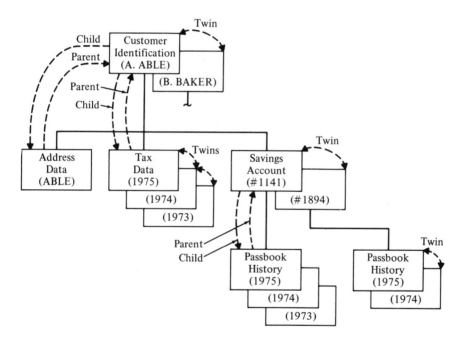

Figure 17.13 An occurrence of the data base structure given in Figure 17.12.

structure diagram (c) of Figure 17.11 is depicted as an interrelated tree structure in Figure 17.14. In this figure, the "customer identification" segment exists only once but participates in two logical data structures. The "customer identification" segment in the checking account data base is replaced by a pointer segment that addresses the unique occurrence of the "customer identification" segment, referred to as a target segment.

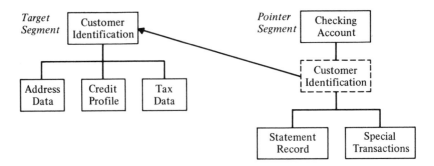

Figure 17.14 Structure diagrams of the logical relationship between physical data structures.

The use of pointer and target segments permits a user to define a logical data base, as in Figure 17.15, over two or more physical data bases, as those given previously in Figure 17.14. A pointer segment may also include data that is unique to the relationship between the pointer segments. Data of this type is called *intersection data* and is maintained in the pointer segment.

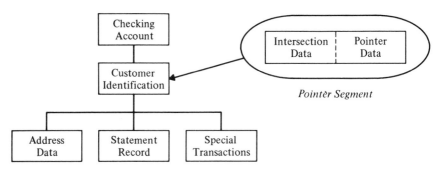

Figure 17.15 Structure diagram of a logical data base defined over two physical data bases.

The relationship between specific logical and physical data structures is necessarily dependent upon the data base descriptions (DBDs) and the program specification block (PSB). The logical data structure in Figure 17.16, for example, is synthesized from two physical DBDs. The logical DBD is used to support a logical data structure described in the PSB of an application program.

Clearly, the precise relationship between logical and physical data structures must be specified somewhere; this is the role of the DBDs and the PSB mentioned previously. The description of logical data structures is dependent upon a physical data base description—which includes a description of data organization and access methods.

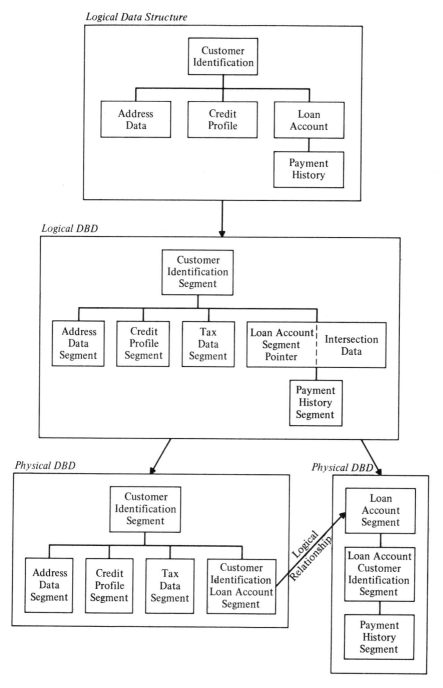

Figure 17.16 Relationship between logical and physical data structures.

ACCESS METHODS

In IMS, a logical data structure and the physical storage of that data structure are both hierarchical, and the system uses two methods of organization: hierarchical sequential and hierarchical direct. Conventional data management access methods do not satisfy the needs of a data base environment, and IMS uses a special access method of its own for the majority of data base operations.

The *overflow sequential access methods* (OSAM) is used in cases where conventional access methods are not appropriate. The IMS interface with OSAM is through macro instructions, such as OPEN, CLOSE, READ, and WRITE; and an application program never uses the OSAM access method directly. The user interface is always with Data Language/I. The operational advantages of OSAM over the use of conventional access methods in a data base environment are listed as follows:*

1. OSAM data sets can be comprised of extents on several direct-access volumes.
2. An OSAM data set can be opened for update-in-place operations and for extensions-to-the-end operations, which may involve acquiring additional extents.
3. It is not necessary to format OSAM data sets prior to use, as in some conventional access methods.
4. Fixed-length blocked or unblocked records can be used with OSAM, and OSAM data sets can be read by conventional *sequential* (such as BSAM or OSAM) access methods.

In general, however, the execution of OSAM is transparent to the user. It is mentioned here because it is used in the description of the hierarchical access methods.

The simple data structure described in Figure 17.17 is used to demonstrate the manner in which data is stored for the various methods of physical storage organization.

In the hierarchical sequential method of storage organization, the blocks used to store the segments of a hierarchical tree structure are organized consecutively, or utilize a linked organization on direct-access storage. The *hierarchical sequential access method* (HSAM) is used for sequential access to a data structure stored on tape or direct-access storage. As shown in Figure 17.18, the segments that comprise an HSAM physical data base record are stored in consecutive order with the root segment followed by dependent segments.

The *hierarchical indexed sequential access method* (HISAM) is used for indexed sequential access to a hierarchical sequential data base record. As depicted in

---

*The OSAM is described in more detail in the IMS reference manual, *System/Application Design Guide*. References are given at the end of the chapter.

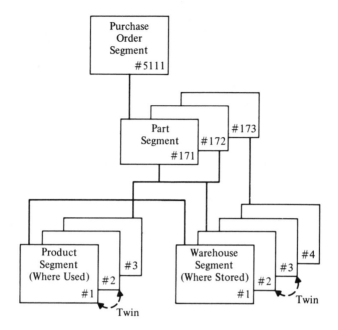

Figure 17.17 Structure diagram of a data structure used to demonstrate the various methods of physical storage
organization.

Physical block #1	PURCHASE ORDER #5111	PART #171	PRODUCT #1	PRODUCT #2
Physical block #2	WAREHOUSE #1	PART #172	PRODUCT #3	WAREHOUSE #2
Physical block #3	WAREHOUSE #3	PART #173	WAREHOUSE #4	

└─ Next data
base record

Figure 17.18 HSAM physical storage structure of the logical purchase order data base
record (Figure 17.17). HSAM data base records can in general be stored on
tape or direct access storage devices.

Figure 17.19, each data base record begins with an ISAM data record* and as
much of the HISAM data base record as possible is placed in the ISAM record.
Additional segments from the data base record are stored as OSAM logical
records. (Apparently, this is the origin of the word "overflow" in the OSAM
acronym.) There are obvious restrictions on the HSAM data sets. Data cannot
be added, deleted, or replaced in an existing HSAM data set and random opera-

*ISAM is an acronym for Indexed Sequential Access Method.

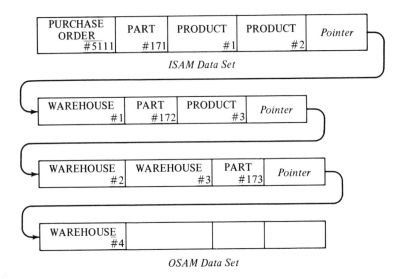

Figure 17.19   HISAM physical storage structure of the logical purchase order data base record (Figure 17.17). HISAM data base records must be stored on direct-access storage devices. (Note that blocks are chained together.)

tions are inefficient since the physical data set must be searched either forward or backward to locate a desired record. If random processing of records is desired, then the HISAM access should be used. To sum up, hierarchical sequential organization provides sequential or indexed access to logical data base records and utilizes storage in an efficient manner since a minimum of control information is stored with the data.

In the hierarchical direct method of storage organization, the segments that comprise a hierarchical tree structure are related by direct-access pointers. The *hierarchical direct access method* (HDAM) uses hierarchical pointers wherein each segment points to the next segment in the hierarchy for that data base record. HDAM uses a user-supplied randomizing technique that is used to locate a root segment in a root-segment addressable area; the root segment points to dependent segments stored in an OSAM overflow area. An example of HDAM storage organization is depicted in Figure 17.20. Dependent segments may also be stored in the root segment addressable area; the number of bytes of a data base record that may be placed in the root segment addressable area is governed by a parameter specified in the data base description.

The *hierarchical indexed direct access method* (HIDAM) provides indexed access to data base records stored using hierarchical direct organization. Each logical record contains an index segment in an ISAM data set. The index segment contains an image of the record key and a direct-access pointer to an

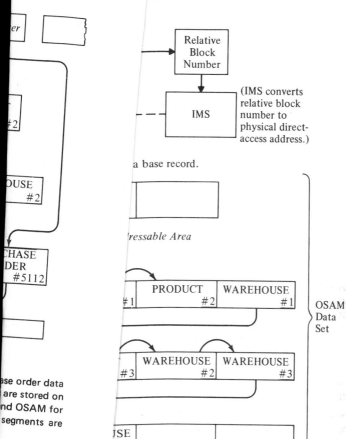

a base record.

ressable Area

OSAM
Data
Set

erflow Area

e structure of the logical purchase order data base
HDAM data base records are stored on direct-
using the OSAM access method.   (Note that
ogether.)

ase order data
are stored on
nd OSAM for
segments are

gram reads and
nsparent to the
tial processing.
e known, how-
nount to saying
ase system and

a DBD library,
s of generating

gical record in the data base. The physical
base record is given in Figure 17.21. HIDAM
ocating the record key in the index segment;
root segment for the data base record. Each
ent in the hierarchy for the record so that after
AM and HIDAM access are the same. The pri-
o methods is that HDAM provides direct access
cess.

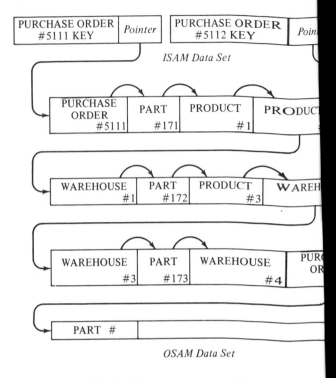

Figure 17.21 HIDAM physical storage structure of the logical purch
base record (Figure 17.17). HIDAM data base records
direct-access storage devices using ISAM for the keys a
the segments that comprise the record. (Note that
chained together.)

It should be pointed out at this point that the application pro
writes segments, and the method of storage organization is tra
user—within the scope of sequential, direct, or indexed sequen
The various methods of data base organization and access must b
ever, when the DBDs and the PSBs are generated. This is tantam
that the control blocks provide the interface between the data b
the application program.

DATA BASE DESCRIPTION

A data base is described in a DBD control block that is stored in
which is maintained as an operating system data set. The proces
a DBD control block consists of two related steps:

1. DBD specification.
2. DBD generation.

DBD specification involves the use of control statements that describe the data base. The control statements exist as assembler language macro instructions that are assembled to form an object module. *DBD generation* creates a DBD control block from the object module and places it in the DBD library.

Table 17.1 contains a listing of the data base description control statements and the functions performed by each. The control statements are entered in assembler language format and a DBD specification takes the following general form:

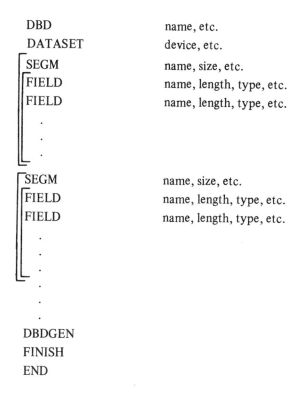

DBD	name, etc.
DATASET	device, etc.
SEGM	name, size, etc.
FIELD	name, length, type, etc.
FIELD	name, length, type, etc.
.	
.	
.	
SEGM	name, size, etc.
FIELD	name, length, type, etc.
FIELD	name, length, type, etc.
.	
.	
.	
.	
.	
.	
DBDGEN	
FINISH	
END	

The various forms of DBD specification are given as examples because a detailed presentation of the various control statements would be meaningless from an introductory point of view. The data base records for which structure diagrams are given in Figure 17.22 are used as a sample data base. Five examples of DBD generation are given: HSAM, HISAM, HDAM, HIDAM, and the index segment.

DBD generation control statements for the *patient record* using HSAM is given in Figure 17.23. The name of the DBD is PATREC. The physical record size is 6320 bytes and the blocking factor within the record is 10. The clause NAME=(SSNO,SEQ,U) in statement numbered 4 denotes a unique sequence field. The TYPE=C clause (the first occurrence is statement numbered 5) speci-

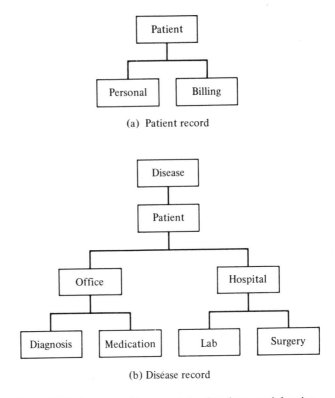

(a) Patient record

(b) Diséase record

Figure 17.22 Structure diagram of the data base used for data base description examples.

fies an alphanumeric field, and the TYPE=P clause in statement numbered 17 specifies a packed decimal field. Clearly, the hierarchy is specified with the SEGM statements and the PARENT keywords.

DBD generation control statements for the *disease record* using HISAM is given in Figure 17.24. The name of the DBD is DISREC. DISFILE is the ISAM data set and DISFLOW is the OSAM data set. The hierarchical structure of the data base record closely resembles its structure diagram and requires no further explanation.

DBD generation control statements for the *patient record* using HDAM with hierarchical pointers is given in Figure 17.25. The name of the DBD is again PATREC. RANMOD is the name of the randomizing module; the number of anchor pointers is one; the maximum relative block number is 3000; and 3160 is the maximum number of bytes that can be inserted into the root segment's addressable area (statement (1)). The block size is 6320; the BLOCK parameter has a different meaning here. The POINTER=H clause in statement (3) specifies

TABLE 17.1   DATA BASE DESCRIPTION CONTROL STATEMENTS.

Control Statement Operation Code	Function	Number of Occurrences per DBD	Optional/Required
PRINT	Causes suppression of assembly listing.	0–1	Optional
DBD	Specifies data base name	1	Required
DATASET	Specifies a data set group within a data base	1–10	Required
SEGM	Defines a segment within the data base	1–255	Required
LCHILD	Specifies logical relationship among segments	0–255	Optional
FIELD	Defines a field within a segment	1–1000	Optional
DBDGEN	Denotes end of DBD specification	1	Required
FINISH	Verifies DBD completion	1	Required
END	Denotes end of source module	1	Required

```
DBD  NAME=PATREC,ACCESS=HSAM                                               (1)
DATASET DD1=PATFILE,DD2=PATOUT,DEVICE=TAPE,BLOCK=10,RECORD=6320  (2)

SEGM  NAME=PATIENT,BYTES=40,FREQ=15000                                   (3)
FIELD NAME=(SSNO,SEQ,U),BYTES=9,START=1,TYPE=C                        (4)
FIELD NAME=NAME,BYTES=31,START=10,TYPE=C                              (5)

SEGM NAME=PERSONAL,BYTES=555,FREQ=15000,PARENT=PATIENT         (6)
FIELD NAME=ADDRESS,BYTES=75,START=1,TYPE=C                          (7)
FIELD NAME=BIRTH,BYTES=15,START=76,TYPE=C                           (8)
FIELD NAME=BLOOD,BYTES=5,START=91,TYPE=C                            (9)
FIELD NAME=ALLERG,BYTES=100,START=96,TYPE=C                       (10)
FIELD NAME=PHYCHAR,BYTES=200,START=196,TYPE=C                     (11)
FIELD NAME=RELIG,BYTES=10,START=396,TYPE=C                         (12)
FIELD NAME=RELAT,BYTES=50,START=406,TYPE=C                         (13)
FIELD NAME=MISC,BYTES=100,START=456,TYPE=C                        (14)

SEGM NAME=BILLING,BYTES=37,FREQ=30000,PARENT=PATIENT           (15)
FIELD NAME=COVAGE,BYTES=25,START=1,TYPE=C                          (16)
FIELD NAME=BALDUE,BYTES=12,START=26,TYPE=P                         (17)

DBDGEN                                                                   (18)
FINISH                                                                    (19)
END                                                                       (20)
```

Figure 17.23   DBD generation for *patient record* using HSAM.

```
DBD  NAME=DISREC,ACCESS=HISAM
DATASET  DD1=DISFILE,OVFLW=DISFLOW,DEVICE=DISK

SEGM  NAME=DISEASE,BYTES=55,FREQ=500
FIELD  NAME=(DISNAM,SEQ,U),BYTES=35,START=1,TYPE=C
FIELD  NAME=DISCODE,BYTES=20,START=36,TYPE=C

SEGM  NAME=PATNAM,BYTES=9,FREQ=5000,PARENT=DISEASE
FIELD  NAME=SSNO,BYTES=9,START=1,TYPE=C

SEGM  NAME=OFFICE,BYTES=35,FREQ=25000,PARENT=PATNAM
FIELD  NAME=DATE,BYTES=15,START=1,TYPE=C
FIELD  NAME=MDNAME,BYTES=20,START=16,TYPE=C

SEGM  NAME=DIAG,BYTES=200,FREQ=25000,PARENT=OFFICE
FIELD  NAME=DESC,BYTES=200,START=1,TYPE=C

SEGM  NAME=MEDIC,BYTES=100,FREQ=25000,PARENT=OFFICE
FIELD  NAME=RX,BYTES=75,START=1,TYPE=C
FIELD  NAME=DOSAGE,BYTES=25,START=76,TYPE=C

SEGM  NAME=HOSPIT,BYTES=70,FREQ=15000,PARENT=PATNAM
FIELD  NAME=DATE,BYTES=15,START=1,TYPE=C
FIELD  NAME=TIME,BYTES=10,START=16,TYPE=C
FIELD  NAME=DAYS,BYTES=5,START=26,TYPE=C
FIELD  NAME=MD1,BYTES=20,START=31,TYPE=C
FIELD  NAME=MD2,BYTES=20,START=51,TYPE=C

SEGM  NAME=LABWORK,BYTES=265,FREQ=45000,PARENT=HOSPIT
FIELD  NAME=DATE,BYTES=15,START=1,TYPE=C
FIELD  NAME=FUNCT,BYTES=200,START=16,TYPE=C
FIELD  NAME=TECHNAM,BYTES=50,START=216,TYPE=C

SEGM  NAME=SURGERY,BYTES=445,FREQ=30000,PARENT=HOSPIT
FIELD  NAME=DATE,BYTES=15,START=1,TYPE=C
FIELD  NAME=TIME,BYTES=10,START=16,TYPE=C
FIELD  NAME=MDNAME,BYTES=20,START=26,TYPE=C
FIELD  NAME=DESCR,BYTES=400,START=46,TYPE=C

DBDGEN
FINISH
END
```

Figure 17.24   DBD generation for *disease record* using HISAM.

```
DBD  NAME=PATREC,ACCESS=HDAM,RMNAME=(RANMOD,1,3000,3160)          (1)
DATASET DD1=PATFILE,DEVICE=DISK,BLOCK=6320                        (2)

SEGM  NAME=PATIENT,BYTES=40,FREQ=1500,POINTER=H,PARENT=0          (3)
FIELD NAME=(SSNO,SEQ,U),BYTES=9,START=1,TYPE=C                    (4)
FIELD NAME=NAME,BYTES=31,START=10,TYPE=C                          (5)

SEGM  NAME=PERSONAL,BYTES=555,FREQ=15000,POINTER=14,PARENT=PATIENT (6)
FIELD NAME=ADDRESS,BYTES=75,START=1,TYPE=C                        (7)
FIELD NAME=BIRTH,BYTES=15,START=76,TYPE=C                         (8)
FIELD NAME=BLOOD,BYTES=5,START=91,TYPE=C                          (9)
FIELD NAME=ALLERG,BYTES=100,START=96,TYPE=C                      (10)
FIELD NAME=PHYCHAR,BYTES=200,START=196,TYPE=C                    (11)
FIELD NAME=RELIG,BYTES=100,START=396,TYPE=C                      (12)
FIELD NAME=RELAT,BYTES=50,START=406,TYPE=C                       (13)
FIELD NAME=MISC,BYTES=100,START=456,TYPE=C                       (14)

SEGM  NAME=BILLING,BYTES=37,FREQ=30000,POINTER=H,PARENT=PATIENT  (15)
FIELD NAME=COVAGE,BYTES=25,START=1,TYPE=C                        (16)
FIELD NAME=BALDUE,BYTES=12,START=26,TYPE=P                       (17)

DBDGEN                                                          (18)
FINISH                                                          (19)
END                                                            (20)
```

Figure 17.25   DBD generation for *patient record* using HDAM with hierarchical pointers.

hierarchical pointers of the general type given in Figure 17.26. The remainder of the data base description is similar to the HSAM and HISAM examples.

DBD generation control statements for the *disease record* using HIDAM with physical child and physical twin pointers is given in Figure 17.27. The name of

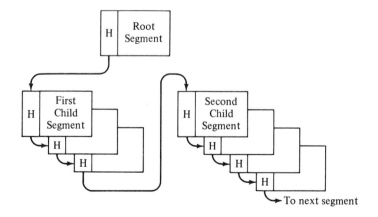

Figure 17.26   Hierarchical pointers.

```
DBD  NAME=DISREC,ACCESS=HIDAM                                              (1)
DATASET  DD1=DISFILE,DEVICE=DISK,BLOCK=1179                                (2)


SEGM    NAME=DISEASE,BYTES=55,FREQ=500,POINTER=T,PARENT=0                  (3)
LCHILD  NAME=(DINDEX,DISDB),POINTER=INDX                                   (4)
FIELD   NAME=(DISNAME,SEQ,U),BYTES=35,START=1,TYPE=C                       (5)
FIELD   NAME=DISCODE,BYTES=20,START=36,TYPE=C                              (6)


SEGM    NAME=PATNAM,BYTES=9,FREQ=5000,POINTER=T,PARENT=((DISEASE,SNGL))    (7)
FIELD   NAME=SSNO,BYTES=9,START=1,TYPE=C


SEGM    NAME=OFFICE,BYTES=35,FREQ=25000,POINTER=T,PARENT=((PATNAM,SNGL))
FIELD   NAME=DATE,BYTES=15,START=1,TYPE=C
FIELD   NAME=MDNAME,BYTES=20,START=16,TYPE=C


SEGM    NAME=DIAG,BYTES=200,FREQ=25000,POINTER=T,PARENT=((OFFICE,SNGL))
FIELD   NAME=DESC,BYTES=200,START=1,TYPE=C


SEGM    NAME=MEDIC,BYTES=100,FREQ=25000,POINTER=T,PARENT=((OFFICE,SNGL))
FIELD   NAME=RX,BYTES=75,START=1,TYPE=C
FIELD   NAME=DOSAGE,BYTES=25,START=76,TYPE=C


SEGM    NAME=HOSPIT,BYTES=70,FREQ=15000,POINTER=T,PARENT=((PATNAM,SNGL))
FIELD   NAME=DATE,BYTES=15,START=1,TYPE=C
FIELD   NAME=TIME,BYTES=10,START=16,TYPE=C
FIELD   NAME=DAYS,BYTES=5,START=26,TYPE=C
FIELD   NAME=MD1,BYTES=20,START=31,TYPE=C
FIELD   NAME=MD2,BYTES=20,START=51,TYPE=C


SEGM    NAME=LABWORK,BYTES=265,FREQ=45000,POINTER=T,PARENT=((HOSPIT,SNGL))
FIELD   NAME=DATE,BYTES=15,START=1,TYPE=C
FIELD   NAME=FUNCT,BYTES=200,START=16,TYPE=C
FIELD   NAME=TECHNAM,BYTES=50,START=216,TYPE=C


SEGM    NAME=SURGERY,BYTES=445,FREQ=30000,PARENT=((HOSPIT,SNGL))
FIELD   NAME=DATE,BYTES=15,START=1,TYPE=C
FIELD   NAME=TIME,BYTES=10,START=16,TYPE=C
FIELD   NAME=MDNAME,BYTES=20,START=26,TYPE=C
FIELD   NAME=DESCR,BYTES=400,START=46,TYPE=C


DBDGEN
FINISH
END
```

Figure 17.27 DBD generation for *disease record* using HIDAM with physical child and physical twin pointers.

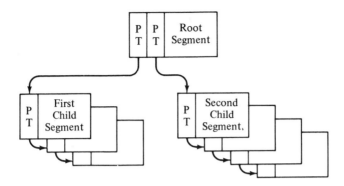

Figure 17.28 Physical twin pointers.

the DBD is again DISREC and the POINTER=T clause in statement (3) denotes physical twin pointers as shown in Figure 17.28. The LCHILD clause denotes that the root segment is the logical child of an index segment, which is given as Figure 17.29. (The reader should note the correspondence between names in Figures 17.27 and 17.29.) The SNGL parameter in statement (7) specifies that the "twin" pointers are unidirectional; bidirectional pointers would have been specified with the parameter DBLE.

```
DBD  NAME=DISDB,ACCESS=INDEX
DATASET  DD1=INDXDS1,DEVICE=DISK,OVFLW=INDXDS2

SEGM    NAME=DINDEX,BYTES=35,FREQ=500
LCHILD  NAME=(DISEASE,DISREC),INDEX=DISNAME

FIELD   NAME=DISKEY,BYTES=35,START=1

DBDGEN
FINISH
END
```

Figure 17.29 DBD generation for the INDEX segment of the HIDAM *disease record* of Figure 17.27.

"Reading" a data base description with a reasonable degree of understanding is relatively easy; "writing" an effective data base description is a completely different matter. This process is actually as much a systems analysis problem as it is one of understanding the DBD generation methods of IMS.

PROGRAM SPECIFICATION BLOCK GENERATION

Each application program that utilizes the facilities of IMS needs a program specification block (PSB) that describes the use of data communication devices and of logical data structures. PSB generation for Data Language/I data bases is introduced here.

One PSB is needed for each application program. A PSB includes a description of each data base accessed by the program; the data base description takes the form of a *program communication block* (PCB). Thus, a PSB consists of one or more PCBs. The process of generating a PSB control block consists of two related steps:

1. PSB specification.
2. PSB generation.

PSB specification involves the use of control statements that describe the logical data base and exist as assembler language macros. As in DBD generation, the macros are assembled to form an object module that is placed in a PSB library by a *PSB generation* program.

Table 17.2 lists the PSB control statements and the function performed by each. A PSB specification takes the following general form:

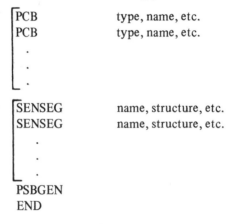

```
⎡ PCB            type, name, etc.
⎢ PCB            type, name, etc.
⎢   .
⎢   .
⎣   .

⎡ SENSEG         name, structure, etc.
⎢ SENSEG         name, structure, etc.
⎢   .
⎢   .
⎣   .
  PSBGEN
  END
```

TABLE 17.2   PROGRAM SPECIFICATION BLOCK (PSB)
CONTROL STATEMENTS.

Control Statement Operation Code	Function
PCB	Describes a Data Language/I data base.
SENSEG	Describes the segments to which an application program is sensitive and specifies the data base processing options.
PSBGE	Specifies the characteristics of the application program.
END	Denotes end of source module.

There must be one PCB statement for each DBD that a program accesses and one SENSEG statement for each segment to which the application program is sensitive.

As with DBD generation, PSB specification is introduced through examples. A PSB for the *patient record* of Figure 17.22 and the HSAM DBD in Figure 17.23 is given in Figure 17.30. The application program, which is named

```
PCB     TYPE=DB,DBDNAME=PATREC,PROCOPT=A,KEYLEN=9   (1)
SENSEG  NAME=PATIENT,PARENT=0,PROCOPT=G              (2)
SENSEG  NAME=PERSONAL,PARENT=PATIENT,PROCOPT=A       (3)
PSBGEN  LANG=COBOL,PSBNAME=ADMIS00X                  (4)
END                                                 (5)
```

Figure 17.30 Program specification block (PSB) for the *patient record* (Figure 17.22) and the HSAM DBD (Figure 17.23). The application program (named AD-MISOOX) is sensitive to only the PATIENT and PERSONAL segments and may not access the BILLING segment.

ADMISOOX, is sensitive to only the PATIENT and PERSONAL segments and may not access the BILLING segment. Statement (1) specifies the following:

1. It is a data base PCB.
2. The DBD name (PATREC).

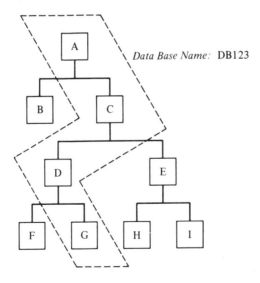

Figure 17.31 Structure diagram of a logical data structure, demonstrating sensitivity.

3. The processing options (PROCOPT), where A is a nominal value that denotes all processing options.
4. The key length for data base accessing.

The processing option of G in statement (2) denotes that only the "get" operation can be executed on the PATIENT segment. In addition, the control statements specify the segments to which the program is sensitive, the hierarchical structure, and the host language.

Figure 17.31 gives a structure diagram of logical data structure with data base name DB123. The example is designed to demonstrate the concept of sensitivity. An application program named AP123 can access segment A with processing option I (insert), segment C with processing option R (replace), segment D with processing option D (delete), and segment G with processing option A (all operations). An appropriate PSB for the application program written in the PL/I language is given as Figure 17.32.

```
PCB      TYPE=DB,DBDNAME=DB123,PROCOPT=A,KEYLEN=XX
SENSEG NAME=A,PARENT=0,PROCOPT=I
SENSEG NAME=C,PARENT=A,PROCOPT=R
SENSEG NAME=D,PARENT=C,PROCOPT=D
SENSEG NAME=G,PARENT=D,PROCOPT=A
PSBGEN LANG=PL/I,PSBNAME=AP123
END
```

Figure 17.32   PSB specification for the structure diagram of Figure 17.31.

IMS has a definite systems orientation, and that fact should be obvious at this point. The traditional programming functions, such as "subschema" definition and data base processing are effectively subordinated to the systems aspects of data base management.

DATA BASE PROCESSING

Data base processing is initiated when the region controller calls the application program; at that time, the PCB addresses are passed as arguments in the same order as they were specified in the program's PSB. Thus, the COBOL entry declaration (from the region controller) would take the general form:

ENTRY 'DLITCBL' USING pcb-name-1,pcb-name-2, . . . ,pcb-name-n.

Similarly, a PL/I entry would take the general form:

DLITPLI: PROCEDURE(pcb_name_1,pcb_name_2,...,pcb_name_n)OPTIONS(MAIN);

The PCB information is used in subsequent input and output calls to Data Language/I.

When making an input or output call to Data Language/I, the host language program specifies the following required and optional parameters:

1. Symbolic name of the desired input or output function.
2. PCB-name.
3. Input/output work area.
4. Option "segment search arguments."

A Data Language/I call from COBOL takes the general form:

ENTER LINKAGE.
CALL 'CBLTDLI' USING [parmcount,] function,PCB-name,
    IO-area,SSA-1,SSA-2,. . . ,SSA-*n*.
ENTER COBOL.

In PL/I, the Data Language/I call has the general form:

CALL PLITDLI (parmcount,function,PCB_name,IO_area,SSA_1,
    SSA_2, . . . ,SSA_*n*)

The parameter count (i.e., "parmcount") is optional in COBOL and required in PL/I.

The *segment search argument* is used by an application program to specify a desired segment by field name and by field names in parent segments leading to the desired segment. The segment search argument is specified as a string of BCD characters and has the structure given in Figure 17.33. The *segment name* field specifies the specific segment type in the hierarchical data base record. The *command codes* augment the input or output operation; they are not discussed further.* The *Boolean statement* exists as a series of relational expressions connected by *and* (i.e., *) or *or* (i.e., +). The relational operators (i.e., RO) that are permitted are:

Operator	Meaning
⌷=	equal to
>=	greater than or equal to
<=	less than or equal to
⌷>	greater than
⌷<	less than
¬=	not equal to

The *field name* must be a key or named field in the specified segment and the *comparative value* must be equal in size and type to the field with which it is

*For a discussion of command codes, the reader should consult the *Application Programming Reference Manual*, pp. 2.21–2.24.

SEGMENT NAME	COMMAND CODES		BEGIN QUAL.	BOOLEAN STATEMENT							
				QUALIFICATION STATEMENT			END QUAL. OR CONNECTOR	QUALIFICATION STATEMENT			END QUAL.
	*	CODES		FIELD NAME	RO	COMPARATIVE VALUE		FIELD NAME	RO	COMPARATIVE VALUE	
			(				) OR * OR +				)
8	1	VAR	1	8	2	1 TO 255	1	8	2	1 TO 255	1

Figure 17.33   Structure of the segment search argument.

being compared. The following segment search argument might be used with the HISAM DBD in Figure 17.24:*

DISEASE(DISNAME=CARCINOMA*DISCODE=KL323R4)

A segment search argument must exist for each parent segment in the path to a desired segment.

The input and output operations that can be specified** in a call to Data Language/I are listed as follows:

Meaning	Call Function
GET UNIQUE	'GUbb'
GET NEXT	'GNbb'
GET NEXT WITHIN PARENT	'GNPb'
GET HOLD UNIQUE	'GHUb'
GET HOLD NEXT	'GHNb'
GET HOLD NEXT WITHIN PARENT	'GHNP'
INSERT	'ISRT'
DELETE	'DLET'
REPLACE	'REPL'

The functions performed by the various input and output operations are listed in Table 17.3. Other than a few operational modes and special conditions, data base processing is as straightforward as the preceding description. Clearly, the biggest problem in data base processing is the design of an application program to utilize the data base effectively and efficiently.

When the application program has completed its processing, it returns to the region controller with the GOBACK statement in COBOL and the RETURN statement in PL/I.

An example of IMS processing is given in the appendix.

A FINAL NOTE

This chapter represents an introduction to IMS, and the reader who is interested in pursuing the subject further will want to study the reference manuals. The material presented here, however, should provide him with an idea of "what IMS is all about."

---

*In this example, the comparative value is not padded with blanks or zeros as would normally be required.

**The IO operation is specified symbolically as four BCD characters whose address is contained in the calling sequence.

TABLE 17.3   FUNCTIONS PERFORMED BY THE DATA BASE
OPERATION CALLS.

Data Base Operation	Function
GET UNIQUE	Retrieve a segment occurrence independent of current position within data base.
GET NEXT	Retrieve next segment in a path of segments by proceeding forward from a previously established position in the data base.
GET NEXT WITHIN PARENT	Retrieve a segment occurrence independent of current position within the data base but limited to dependent segments of an established parent.
GET HOLD UNIQUE GET HOLD NEXT GET HOLD NEXT WITHIN PARENT	Before the contents of a data base can be changed (with a DLET or REPL call) the segment must first be obtained by the application program. The contents are changed and the segment is placed back in the data base. The HOLD option obtains a segment so that it can be returned to the data base.
INSERT	Used to load segments during data base creation and to insert new occurrences of an existing segment type into the data base.
DELETE	Used to delete a segment from the data base after it was first retrieved with a GET HOLD call.
REPLACE	Used to return a modified segment to the data base. The segment must have been first retrieved with a GET HOLD call.

Two topics should definitely be explored further: data communications, and the interrelationship of physical data bases. The latter topic is concerned with logical DBDs which were not covered.

REFERENCES

Curtice, R. M., "Data base design using IMS/360," *Proceedings of the 1972 Fall Joint Computer Conference*, AFIPS Volume 4 (1972), pp. 1105–1110.

Information Management System/360, Version 2 publications:
General Information Manual, Form GH20-0765
System/Application Design Guide, Form SH20-0910
System Programming Reference Manual, Form SH20-0911
Application Programming Reference Manual, Form SH20-0912
Utilities REference Manual, Form SH20-0915.

IBM Corporation, 1133 Westchester Avenue, White Plains, N.Y. 10604.

APPENDIX A. COMPARISON OF DBTG AND IDS PROGRAMS*

*Reprinted by permission, Sven Eriksen, "The Data-base Concept," *Honeywell Computer Journal*, Volume 8, No. 1 (1974), pp. 17–32.

EXAMPLE OF A DATA-STRUCTURE-DESCRIPTION (DBTG)

```
            SCHEMA NAME IS ORGANIZATION-AND-PERSONNEL.
            AREA NAME IS TOTAL.

            RECORD NAME IS COMPANY   LOCATION MODE IS DIRECT ENTRY.
                ENTRY                       PIC 9(8)   COMP-1.

A)          RECORD NAME IS ORG-UNIT
B)              LOCATION MODE IS CALC
C)                  USING UNIT-NO
D)              DUPLICATES ARE NOT ALLOWED.
E)              UNIT-NO                     PIC 9(4).
F)              UNIT-NAME                   PIC X(20).
                BUDG-NO-OF-EMPL             PIC 9(4).
                BUDGET                      PIC 9(7).

G)          RECORD NAME IS RELATIONSHIP
H)              LOCATION MODE IS VIA SUPERORDINATE SET.
I)              SUBUNIT-NO                  PIC 9(4).

            RECORD NAME IS EMPLOYEE   LOCATION MODE IS CALC USING EMPLOYEE-NO
                DUPLICATES ARE NOT ALLOWED.
                EMPLOYEE-NAME               PIC X(25).
                EMPLOYEE-NO                 PIC 9(5).
                JOB-TITLE                   PIC X(20).
                JOB-CODE                    PIC 9(4).
                SALARY                      PIC 9(6).
                SEX                         PIC X.
                BIRTHDATE                   PIC 9(6).

            RECORD NAME IS CAPABILITY   LOCATION MODE IS VIA HAS-EXTRA SET.

            RECORD NAME IS WORK   LOCATION MODE IS CALC USING CAPABILITY-CODE
                DUPLICATES ARE NOT ALLOWED.
                CAPABILITY-CODE             PIC 9(4).
                CAPABILITY-NAME             PIC X(20).

J)          SET NAME IS SUPERORDINATE   MODE IS CHAIN
K)              ORDER IS SORTED
L)              OWNER IS ORG-UNIT.
M)              MEMBER IS RELATIONSHIP   OPTIONAL   AUTOMATIC
N)                  ASCENDING KEY IS SUBUNIT-NO
P)                  DUPLICATES ARE NOT ALLOWED
Q)                  SET OCCURRENCE SELECTION IS THRU LOCATION MODE OF OWNER.

R)          SET NAME IS SUBORDINATE   MODE IS CHAIN
S)              ORDER IS FIRST
T)              OWNER IS ORG-UNIT.
U)              MEMBER IS RELATIONSHIP   OPTIONAL   AUTOMATIC
V)                  SET OCCURRENCE SELECTION IS THRU LOCATION MODE OF OWNER
X)                      ALIAS FOR UNIT-NO IS SUBUNIT-NO.

            SET NAME IS EMPLOYS   MODE IS CHAIN   ORDER IS LAST
                OWNER IS ORG-UNIT.
                MEMBER IS EMPLOYEE   OPTIONAL   AUTOMATIC
                    SET OCCURRENCE SELECTION IS THRU LOCATION MODE OF OWNER.

            SET NAME IS CONSISTS-OF   MODE IS CHAIN   ORDER IS SORTED
                OWNER IS COMPANY.
                MEMBER IS ORG-UNIT   OPTIONAL   AUTOMATIC
                    ASCENDING KEY IS UNIT-NO   DUPLICATES ARE NOT ALLOWED
                    SET OCCURRENCE SELECTION IS THRU CURRENT OF SET.

            SET NAME IS HAS-EXTRA   MODE IS CHAIN   ORDER IS FIRST
                OWNER IS EMPLOYEE.
                MEMBER IS CAPABILITY   OPTIONAL   AUTOMATIC
                    SET OCCURRENCE SELECTION IS THRU LOCATION MODE OF OWNER.

            SET NAME IS CAN-BE-DONE-BY   MODE IS CHAIN   ORDER IS FIRST
                OWNER IS WORK.
                MEMBER IS EMPLOYEE   OPTIONAL   AUTOMATIC
                    SET OCCURRENCE SELECTION IS THRU LOCATION MODE OF OWNER.
                MEMBER IS CAPABILITY   OPTIONAL   AUTOMATIC
                    SET OCCURRENCE SELECTION IS THRU LOCATION MODE OF OWNER.
```

EXAMPLE OF A DATA-STRUCTURE-DESCRIPTION (IDS)

```
        MD ORGANIZATION-AND-PERSONNEL.

        01  COMPANY TYPE IS 70    RETRIEVAL VIA ENTRY FIELD.
            02  ENTRY              PIC 9(8)  COMP-1.
            98  CONSISTS-OF CHAIN MASTER   CHAIN-ORDER IS SORTED.

A)      01  ORG-UNIT TYPE IS 10
B)          RETRIEVAL VIA CALC CHAIN.
E)          02  UNIT-NO            PIC 9(4).
F)          02  UNIT-NAME          PIC X(20).
            02  BUDG-NO-OF-EMPL    PIC 9(4).
            02  BUDGET             PIC 9(7).
L)          98  SUPERORDINATE CHAIN MASTER
K)              CHAIN-ORDER IS SORTED.
T)          98  SUBORDINATE CHAIN MASTER
S)              CHAIN-ORDER IS FIRST.
            98  EMPLOYS CHAIN MASTER    CHAIN-ORDER IS LAST.
            98  CONSISTS-OF CHAIN DETAIL   SELECT CURRENT MASTER.
B)          98  CALC CHAIN DETAIL
C)              RANDOMIZE ON UNIT-NO.

G)      01  RELATIONSHIP    TYPE IS 30
H)          RETRIEVAL VIA SUPERORDINATE CHAIN.
I)          02  SUBUNIT-NO         PIC 9(4).
M)          98  SUPERORDINATE CHAIN DETAIL
Q)              SELECT UNIQUE MASTER   MATCH-KEY IS UNIT-NO
N)              ASCENDING KEY IS SUBUNIT-NO
P)              DUPLICATES NOT ALLOWED.
U)          98  SUBORDINATE CHAIN DETAIL
V)              SELECT UNIQUE MASTER
X)                  MATCH-KEY IS SUBUNIT-NO SYNONYM UNIT-NO.

        01  EMPLOYEE  TYPE IS 50   RETRIEVAL VIA CALC CHAIN.
            02  EMPLOYEE-NAME      PIC X(25).
            02  EMPLOYEE-NO        PIC 9(5).
            02  JOB-TITLE          PIC X(20).
            02  JOB-CODE           PIC 9(4).
            02  SALARY             PIC 9(6).
            02  SEX                PIC X.
            02  BIRTHDATE          PIC 9(6).
            98  CALC CHAIN DETAIL RANDOMIZE ON EMPLOYEE-NO.
            98  EMPLOYS CHAIN DETAIL
                SELECT UNIQUE MASTER MATCH-KEY IS UNIT-NO.
            98  HAS-EXTRA CHAIN MASTER CHAIN-ORDER IS FIRST.
            98  CAN-BE-DONE-BY CHAIN DETAIL
                SELECT UNIQUE MASTER MATCH-KEY IS JOB-CODE.

        01  CAPABILITY  TYPE IS 60   RETRIEVAL VIA HAS-EXTRA CHAIN.
            98  HAS-EXTRA CHAIN DETAIL
                SELECT UNIQUE MASTER   MATCH-KEY IS EMPLOYEE-NO.
            98  CAN-BE-DONE-BY CHAIN DETAIL
                SELECT UNIQUE MASTER   MASTER-KEY IS CAPABILITY-CODE.

        01  WORK  TYPE IS 20   RETRIEVAL VIA CALC CHAIN.
            02  CAPABILITY-CODE    PIC 9(4).
            02  CAPABILITY-NAME    PIC X(20).
            98  CALC CHAIN DETAIL     RANDOMIZE ON CAPABILITY-CODE.
            98  CAN-BE-DONE-BY CHAIN MASTER   CHAIN-ORDER IS FIRST.
```

EXPLANATION OF THE DATA STRUCTURE DESCRIPTIONS

A) This line contains a name declaration of the record-class ORG-UNIT.

B) Specifies that records of the record-class ORG-UNIT are to be stored and subsequently retrieved (when this becomes desirable) according to their membership of a certain set of the set-class CALC.

C) Specifies the name of a data field (UNIT-NO), the contents of which will serve to determine or select a particular set of the set-class CALC for storage or retrieval of a record of the record-class ORG-UNIT.

D) Requires the contents of the field UNIT-NO to be unique (this is automatically assumed by IDS).

E) Describes the first data field in every record of the record-class ORG-UNIT.

F) Describes the second data field in every record of the record-class ORG-UNIT.

G) Names the record-class RELATIONSHIP.

H) Specifies that records of the record-class RELATIONSHIP are to be stored and subsequently retrieved (when this becomes desirable) according to their membership of a certain set of the set-class SUPERORDINATE.

I) Describes the only data field in every record of the record-class RELATIONSHIP.

J) Names the set-class SUPERORDINATE and specifies that the association of records into sets of this set-class should be implemented by means of chaining techniques, i.e., pointers referring from one record of the set to another (this is automatically implied in IDS).

K) Specifies that new member records (of the record-class RELATIONSHIP) are to be logically associated into a set (of the set-class SUPERORDINATE) according to the contents of a certain data field (see line N) acting as a sort key.

L) Specifies that any set of the set-class SUPERORDINATE is owned by a record of the record-class ORG-UNIT.

M) Specifies that any set of the set-class SUPERORDINATE HAS 0, 1, or more member records of the record-class RELATIONSHIP.

N) Specifies the name of a data field (SUBUNIT-NO), the contents of which will serve as a sort key for the logical placement or retrieval of a particular record of the record-class RELATIONSHIP within a particular set of the set-class SUPERORDINATE.

P) Requires the contents of the field SUBUNIT-NO to be unique and prohibits the storage, within the selected set of the set-class SUPERORDINATE, of more than one member record of the record-class RELATIONSHIP having that particular value of the data field SUBUNIT-NO.

Q) Specifies that a particular set of the set-class SUPERORDINATE is to be located through unique identification of its owner record (based upon the contents of its match-key field UNIT-NO).

R) Names the set-class SUBORDINATE and specifies that the association of records into sets of this set-class should be implemented by means of chaining techniques (this is automatically assumed by IDS).

S) Specifies that new member records of the record-class RELATIONSHIP should be stored as the first member record of the selected set of the set-class SUBORDINATE, i.e., logically directly following the owner record.

T) Specifies that any set of the set-class SUBORDINATE is owned by a record of the record-class ORG-UNIT.

U) Specifies that any set of the set-class SUBORDINATE has 0, 1, or more member records of the record-class RELATIONSHIP.

V) Specifies that a particular set of the set-class SUBORDINATE is to be located through unique identification of its owner record (based upon the contents of its match-key field UNIT-NO, which must match the contents of the data field SUBUNIT-NO).

X) Specifies the names of two data fields (SUBUNIT-NO and UNIT-NO) the contents of which will serve to identify two owner records of the record-class ORG-UNIT (one being the owner of a set of the set-class SUBORDINATE and the other being the owner of a set of the set-class SUPERORDINATE) in order to enable the storage or retrieval of one particular member record of the record-class RELATIONSHIP.

EXAMPLE OF A DATABASE CREATION PROCEDURE (DBTG)

```
       PROCEDURE DIVISION.
       BEGINNING SECTION.
          OPEN-IT.
A)        OPEN ALL.
          ACCEPT ENTRY.
          FIND COMPANY USING ENTRY.
B)        IF ERROR-STATUS NOT = 0 GO TO ERROR-COMPANY.
          OPEN INPUT CARD.
          GO TO READ-CARD IN CREATION.
          ERROR-COMPANY.
C)        IF ERROR-STATUS = 0326
             GO TO STORE-COMPANY-RECORD.
          DISPLAY "ERROR FIND COMPANY", ERROR-STATUS.
          GO TO ENDING.
          STORE-COMPANY-RECORD.
D)        STORE COMPANY.
          IF ERROR-STATUS NOT = 0 GO TO ENDING.
          GO TO READ-CARD IN CREATION.
       ERROR-TESTING SECTION.
          ERROR-TEST.
E)        IF ERROR-STATUS = 0 GO TO EXIT-ERROR-TESTING.
             -
             -
             -
             -
          EXIT-ERROR-TESTING.   EXIT.
       CREATION SECTION.
          READ-CARD.
             READ CARD AT END GO TO ENDING.
             GO TO STORE-ORG-UNIT-RECORD,
                STORE-RELATIONSHIP-RECORD,
                STORE-EMPLOYEE-RECORD,
                STORE-WORK-RECORD,
                STORE-CAPABILITY-RECORD
                   DEPENDING ON CARD-TYPE.
             DISPLAY "CARD TYPE INCORRECT", INPUT-CARD.
             GO TO READ-CARD.
          STORE-ORG-UNIT-RECORD.
             MOVE U-NO TO UNIT-NO.
F)           MOVE U-NAME TO UNIT-NAME.
             MOVE B-EMPL TO BUDG-NO-OF-EMPL.
             MOVE BUDG TO BUDGET.
G)           STORE ORG-UNIT.
             PERFORM ERROR-TESTING.
             GO TO READ-CARD.
          STORE-RELATIONSHIP-RECORD.
             -
             -
             -
          STORE-CAPABILITY-RECORD.
             -
             -
             -
       ENDING SECTION.
          CLOSE-IT.
H)        CLOSE ALL.
          CLOSE CARD.
          STOP RUN.
```

EXAMPLE OF A DATABASE CREATION PROCEDURE (IDS)

```
       PROCEDURE DIVISION.
       BEGINNING SECTION.
          OPEN-IT.
A)        ENTER IDS. OPEN.
          ACCEPT ENTRY.
          ENTER IDS.   RETRIEVE COMPANY RECORD
B)           IF ERROR GO TO ERROR-COMPANY.
          OPEN INPUT CARD.
          GO TO READ-CARD IN CREATION.
          ERROR-COMPANY.
C)        IF ERROR-REFERENCE = "R08"
             GO TO STORE-COMPANY-RECORD.
          DISPLAY "ERROR FIND COMPANY", ERROR-REFERENCE.
          GO TO ENDING.
          STORE-COMPANY-RECORD.
D)        ENTER IDS.   STORE COMPANY RECORD.
             IF ERROR GO TO ENDING.
          GO TO READ-CARD IN CREATION.
       ERROR-TESTING SECTION.
          ERROR-TEST.
          ENTER IDS.   IF ERROR  GO TO ERROR-FOUND
E)           ELSE GO TO EXIT-ERROR-TESTING.
          ERROR-FOUND.
             -
             -
             -
          EXIT-ERROR-TESTING.   EXIT.
       CREATION SECTION.
          READ-CARD.
             READ CARD AT END GO TO ENDING.
             GO TO STORE-ORG-UNIT-RECORD,
                STORE-RELATIONSHIP-RECORD,
                STORE-EMPLOYEE-RECORD,
                STORE-WORK-RECORD,
                STORE-CAPABILITY-RECORD
                   DEPENDING ON CARD-TYPE.
             DISPLAY "CARD TYPE INCORRECT", INPUT-CARD.
             GO TO READ-CARD.
          STORE-ORG-UNIT-RECORD.
             MOVE U-NO TO UNIT-NO.
F)           MOVE U-NAME TO UNIT-NAME.
             MOVE B-EMPL TO BUDG-NO-OF-EMPL.
             MOVE BUDG TO BUDGET.
G)           ENTER IDS. STORE ORG-UNIT RECORD
             IF ERROR PERFORM ERROR-TESTING.
             GO TO READ-CARD.
          STORE-RELATIONSHIP-RECORD.
             -
             -
             -
          STORE-CAPABILITY-RECORD.
             -
             -
             -
       ENDING SECTIO.
          CLOSE-IT.
H)        ENTER IDS. CLOSE.
          CLOSE CARD.
          STOP RUN.
```

EXPLANATION OF THE DATABASE CREATION PROCEDURE

A) This line specifies the "opening" of the database, presuming that the "initialization" of the database has already been accomplished (in a previous run).

B) Tries to find an owner record of the record-class COMPANY by "direct addressing", using the contents of the data field ENTRY, which is a data-base-key (DBTG) or reference-code (IDS) values. After the "find" command, a test is made to examine whether it was successful or not.

C) In case the previously "find" command was not successful, a test of the value of the corresponding error status indicator, which is called ERROR-STATUS (DBTG) or ERROR-REFERENCE (IDS), is undertaken in order to find out if this is the first creation run (after initialization), in which case the COMPANY record sought does not yet exist.

D) Storing of a record of the record-class COMPANY using the contents of the data field ENTRY as an actual logical data-base-key (DBTG) or reference-code (IDS) value. After the "store" command, a test is made to examine whether it was successful or not.

E) Subroutines used for evaluating the contents of the error status indicator.

F) Moving input data values previous to the actual storing of a record of the record-class ORG-UNIT; the data field UNIT-NO will be used for the unique selection of a set of the special set-class CALC into which the ORG-UNIT record is to be associated as a member.

G) The actual storing of a record of the record-class ORG-UNIT, with the correct data contents and as a member record of two different and uniquely selected sets of the set-classes CONSISTS-OF and CALC. The record stored is at the same time made the owner record of three empty sets of the set-classes EMPLOYS, SUPERORDINATE, and SUB-ORDINATE. The store operation is checked by an error procedure.

H) The last action is the "closing" of the database.

EXAMPLE OF A DATABASE APPLICATION PROCEDURE (DBTG)

```
WORKING-STORAGE SECTION.
   01  DATE-TODAY.
       02  YEAR          PIC 99.
       02  FILLER        PIC 9999.
   01  DATE-OF-BIRTH.
       02  YEAR-BORN     PIC 99.
       02  FILLER        PIC 9999.
   01  LINE-OF-INFORMATION.
       02  E-NO          PIC 9(4)BB.
       02  E-NAME        PIC X(25)BB.
       02  J-TITLE       PIC X(20)BB.
       02  U-NO          PIC 9(4)BB.
       02  U-NAME        PIC X(20).
       -
       -
       -
   PROCEDURE DIVISION.
       BEGIN-IT.
A)         OPEN ALL.
           ACCEPT DATE-TODAY FROM DATE.
B)         MOVE 3340 TO CAPABILITY-CODE.
           FIND WORK RECORD
C)         IF ERROR-STATUS NOT = 0 GO TO ERROR-WORK.
       NEXT-OF-CAN-BE-DONE-BY.
           FIND NEXT RECORD OF CAN-BE-DONE-BY SET.
           IF ERROR-STATUS NOT = 0
D)             GO TO ERROR-CAN-BE-DONE-BY.
           IF RECORD OWNER OF CAN-BE-DONE-BY SET
               GO TO END-IT.
           IF RECORD OWNER OF HAS-EXTRA SET GET
               GO TO EMPLOYEE-FOUND.
       CAPABILITY-FOUND.
           FIND OWNER RECORD OF HAS-EXTRA SET.
E)         IF ERROR-STATUS NOT = 0 GO TO ERROR-HAS-EXTRA.
           GET.
       EMPLOYEE-FOUND.
           IF SEX NOT = "M" GO TO NEXT-OF-CAN-BE-DONE-BY.
           IF JOB-TITLE = "MANAGER"
               GO TO NEXT-OF-CAN-BE-DONE-BY.
F)         MOVE BIRTHDATE TO DATE-OF-BIRTH.
           IF YEAR-BORN > YEAR - 30 OR < YEAR - 50
               GO TO NEXT-OF-CAN-BE-DONE-BY.
           FIND OWNER RECORD OF EMPLOYS SET.
G)         IF ERROR-STATUS NOT = 0 GO TO ERROR-EMPLOYS.
           GET.
           MOVE EMPLOYEE-NO TO E-NO.
           MOVE EMPLOYEE-NAME TO E-NAME.
H)         MOVE JOB-TITLE TO J-TITLE.
           MOVE UNIT-NO TO U-NO.
I)         MOVE UNIT-NAME TO U-NAME.
J)         DISPLAY LINE-OF-INFORMATION.
           GO TO NEXT-OF-CAN-BE-DONE-BY.
       ERROR-WORK.
           -
           -
           -
K)     ERROR-EMPLOYS.
           -
           -
           -
       END-IT.
L)         CLOSE ALL.
           STOP RUN.
```

EXAMPLE OF A DATABASE APPLICATION PROCEDURE (IDS)

```
WORKING-STORAGE SECTION.
   01  DATE-TODAY.
       02  YEAR          PIC 99.
       02  FILLER        PIC 9999.
   01  DATE-OF-BIRTH.
       02  YEAR-BORN     PIC 99.
       02  FILLER        PIC 9999.
   01  LINE-OF-INFORMATION.
       02  E-NO          PIC 9(4)BB.
       02  E-NAME        PIC X(25)BB.
       02  J-TITLE       PIC X(20)BB.
       02  U-NO          PIC 9(4)BB.
       02  U-NAME        PIC X(20).
       -
       -
       -
   PROCEDURE DIVISION.
       BEGIN-IT.
A)         ENTER IDS. OPEN.
           ACCEPT DATE-TODAY FROM DATE.
B)         MOVE 3340 TO CAPABILITY-CODE.
           ENTER IDS. RETRIEVE WORK RECORD
C)         IF ERROR GO TO ERROR-WORK.
       NEXT-OF-CAN-BE-DONE-BY.
           ENTER IDS.  RETRIEVE
               NEXT RECORD OF CAN-BE-DONE-BY CHAIN.
D)         IF ERROR
               GO TO ERROR-CAN-BE-DONE-BY
           ELSE IF WORK RECORD GO TO END-IT
           ELSE IF EMPLOYEE RECORD  MOVE TO WORKING-STORAGE
               GO TO EMPLOYEE-FOUND.
       CAPABILITY-FOUND.
           ENTER IDS.  RETRIEVE MASTER OF HAS-EXTRA CHAIN.
E)         IF ERROR GO TO ERROR-HAS-EXTRA
           ELSE MOVE TO WORKING-STORAGE.
       EMPLOYEE-FOUND.
           IF SEX NOT = "M" GO TO NEXT-OF-CAN-BE-DONE-BY.
           IF JOB-TITLE = "MANAGER"
               GO TO NEXT-OF-CAN-BE-DONE-BY.
F)         MOVE BIRTHDATE TO DATE-OF-BIRTH.
           IF YEAR-BORN > YEAR - 30 OR < YEAR - 50
               GO TO NEXT-OF-CAN-BE-DONE-BY.
           ENTER IDS.  RETRIEVE MASTER OF EMPLOYS CHAIN
G)             IF ERROR GO TO ERROR-EMPLOYS
           ELSE MOVE TO WORKING-STORAGE.
           MOVE EMPLOYEE-NO TO E NO.
           MOVE EMPLOYEE-NAME TO E-NAME.
H)         MOVE JOB-TITLE TO J-TITLE.
           MOVE UNIT-NO TO U-NO.
I)         MOVE UNIT-NAME TO U-NAME.
J)         DISPLAY LINE-OF-INFORMATION.
           GO TO NEXT-OF-CAN-BE-DONE-BY.
       ERROR-WORK.
           -
           -
           -
K)     ERROR-EMPLOYS.
           -
           -
           -
       END-IT.
L)         ENTER IDS. CLOSE.
           STOP RUN.
```

EXPLANATION OF THE DATABASE APPLICATION PROCEDURE

A) Opening of the database.

B) Moving the capability code value 3340 to the data field CAPABILITY-CODE for subsequence use in making the corresponding WORK record available through this association in a set of the set-class CALC.

C) Finding that particular set of the set-class CALC and, within this set, that particular record of the record-class WORK which uniquely corresponds to the capability code values stored in the data field CAPABILITY-CODE. This is an example of record access by "calculation", and provides at the same time an entry point into a particular set of the set-class CAN-BE-DONE-BY, namely that containing all relevant records of the record-class EMPLOYEE and CAPABILITY.

D) Finding the logically "next" record of the selected set of the set-class CAN-BE-DONE-BY; apart from normal error checking it is tested, if the record found is of the record-class WORK (in which case we have reached the end of the set), or if it is of the record-class EMPLOYEE (in which case its data contents must be explicitly made available by GET (in DBTG) and by MOVE TO WORKING-STORAGE (in IDS)). If these tests are not satisfied, we have found a record of the record-class CAPABILITY, the owner record of the record-class EMPLOYEE we may be interested in.

E) Finding the owner record of a particular set of the set-class HAS-EXTRA, which has been accessed through one of its member records of the record-class CAPABILITY. Apart from normal error checking, the data contents of the EMPLOYEE record found must be explicitly made available by GET or MOVE TO WORKING-STORAGE.

F) Test to see if the employee, whose EMPLOYEE record has been found, is interesting in terms of sex, position held, and age; if not, the next record of the selected set of the set-class CAN-BE-DONE-BY should be found.

G) Finding information of the organizational unit to which an "interesting" employee is currently attached.

H) Moving of information from EMPLOYEE record to LINE-OF-INFORMATION record.

I) Moving of information from ORG-UNIT record to LINE-OF-INFORMATION record.

J) Display of the LINE-OF-INFORMATION record concerning one employee.

K) Subroutines for error checking.

L) Closing of the database.

APPENDIX B.
EXAMPLE OF AN
IMS PROGRAM*

*Reprinted by permission from *Information Management System/360, Version 2, Application Programming Reference Manual*, Form SH20-0912. © 1973, Fifth Edition, by International Business Machines Corporation.

```
IDENTIFICATION DIVISION.
PROGRAM-ID.        DFSSAM01
AUTHOR.            IMS-360 SAMPLE PROBLEM.
       REMARKS.    DATA BASE LOAD PROGRAM.
ENVIRONMENT DIVISION.
CONFIGURATION SECTION.
SOURCE-COMPUTER.      IBM-360  H50.
OBJECT-COMPUTER.      IBM-360  H50.
INPUT-OUTPUT SECTION.
FILE-CONTROL.
     SELECT INPUT-FILE        ASSIGN  UT-S-INPUT.
DATA DIVISION.
FILE SECTION.
FD   INPUT-FILE
     RECORD CONTAINS 80 CHARACTERS
     BLOCK CONTAINS 0 RECORDS
     RECORDING MODE IS F
     LABEL RECORDS ARE OMITTED
     DATA RECORD IS INPUT-RECORD.
01   INPUT-RECORD.
     02 INP-SEG-NAME           PICTURE X(08).
     02 FILLER                 PICTURE X(01).
     02 INP-DATA               PICTURE X(67).
     02 INP-SEQUENCE-NO        PICTURE X(04).
WORKING-STORAGE SECTION.
01   DLI-FUNCTION              PICTURE X(04).
01   PREV-SEG-NAME             PICTURE X(08)             VALUE SPACE.
01   PREV-SEQUENCE-NO          PICTURE X(04)             VALUE SPACE.
01   BUILD-SEGMENT-AREA.
     02 BUILD-DATA-AREA        OCCURS 14 TIMES
                               PICTURE X(67).
01   MISC-ARITHMETIC-FIELDS    USAGE COMPUTATIONAL.
     02 SUB-1                  PICTURE S9(02)            VALUE ZEROS.

01   SEG00010-SSA.
     02 SEG-NAME-00010         PICTURE X(08) VALUE 'PARTROOT'.
     02 BEGIN-OP-00010         PICTURE X(01) VALUE '('.
     02 KEY-NAME-00010         PICTURE X(09) VALUE 'PARTKEY '.
     02 REL-OPER-00010         PICTURE X(02) VALUE ' ='.
     02 KEY-VALUE-00010        PICTURE X(17).
     02 END-OP-00010           PICTURE X(01) VALUE ')'.
01   SEG00060-SSA.
     02 SEG-NAME-00060         PICTURE X(08) VALUE 'STANINFO'.
     02 BEGIN-OP-00060         PICTURE X(01) VALUE '('.
     02 KEY-NAME-00060         PICTURE X(08) VALUE 'STANKEY '.
     02 REL-OPER-00060         PICTURE X(02) VALUE ' ='.
     02 KEY-VALUE-00060        PICTURE X(02).
     02 END-OP-00060           PICTURE X(01) VALUE ')'.
01   SEG02000-SSA.
     02 SEG-NAME-02000         PICTURE X(08) VALUE 'STOKSTAT'.
     02 BEGIN-OP-02000         PICTURE X(01) VALUE '('.
     02 KEY-NAME-02000         PICTURE X(08) VALUE 'STOCKEY '.
     02 REL-OPER-02000         PICTURE X(02) VALUE ' ='.
     02 KEY-VALUE-02000        PICTURE X(16).
     02 END-OP-02000           PICTURE X(01) VALUE ')'.
01   SEG02200-SSA.
     02 SEG-NAME-02200         PICTURE X(08) VALUE 'CYCCOUNT'.
     02 BEGIN-OP-02200         PICTURE X(01) VALUE '('.
     02 KEY-NAME-02200         PICTURE X(08) VALUE 'CYCLKEY '.
     02 REL-OPER-02200         PICTURE X(02) VALUE ' ='.
     02 KEY-VALUE-02200        PICTURE X(02).
     02 END-OP-02200           PICTURE X(01) VALUE ')'.
01   SEG02300-SSA.
     02 SEG-NAME-02300         PICTURE X(08) VALUE 'BACKORDR'.
     02 BEGIN-OP-02300         PICTURE X(01) VALUE '('.
     02 KEY-NAME-02300         PICTURE X(08) VALUE 'BACKKEY '.
     02 REL-OPER-02300         PICTURE X(02) VALUE ' ='.
     02 KEY-VALUE-02300        PICTURE X(10).
     02 END-OP-02300           PICTURE X(01) VALUE ')'.
```

```
01   SEG00010-INSERT-AREA.
     02 FILLER               PICTURE X(050).
01   SEG00060-INSERT-AREA.
     02 FILLER               PICTURE X(61).
     02 RIGHT-MAKE-SPAN      PICTURE S9(03).
     02 FILLER               PICTURE X(06).
     02 WRONG-MAKE-SPAN      PICTURE 9(03).
     02 FILLER               PICTURE X(12).
01   SEG02000-INSERT-AREA.
     02 FILLER               PICTURE X(160).
01   SEG02200-INSERT-AREA.
     02 FILLER               PICTURE X(025).
01   SEG02300-INSERT-AREA.
     02 FILLER               PICTURE X(075).
LINKAGE SECTION.
01   PCB-AREA-1.
     02 DBD-NAME             PICTURE  X(08).
     02 SEGMENT-LEVEL        PICTURE  X(02).
     02 STATUS-CODES         PICTURE  X(02).
     02 PROCESS-OPTIONS      PICTURE  X(04).
     02 FILLER               PICTURE  S9(05)    COMPUTATIONAL.
     02 SEG-NAME-FEEDBACK    PICTURE  X(08).
PROCEDURE DIVISION.
     ENTRY 'DLITCBL' USING  PCB-AREA-1.
     DISPLAY 'START DB LOAD'  UPON CONSOLE.
     OPEN  INPUT  INPUT-FILE.
     MOVE 'ISRT'  TO DL1-FUNCTION.
READ-INPUT-FILE.
     READ INPUT-FILE           AT END
                               GO TO END-INP-FILE.
BUILD-SEGMENT.
     IF INP-SEG-NAME NOT EQUAL TO SPACES
          PERFORM WRITE-BUILT-SEGMENT THRU WRITE-SEGMENT-EXIT
          MOVE ZEROS TO SUB-1
          MOVE SPACES TO BUILD-SEGMENT-AREA
          MOVE INP-SEG-NAME TO PREV-SEG-NAME.
     ADD 1 TO SUB-1.
     IF SUB-1 IS GREATER THAN 14
          DISPLAY 'MORE THAN 14 CARDS PER SEGMENT'  UPON CONSOLE
          DISPLAY 'SEGMENT IS  '  PREV-SEG-NAME   UPON CONSOLE
          GO TO LOCKED-HALT.
     MOVE INP-DATA TO BUILD-DATA-AREA (SUB-1).
     GO TO READ-INPUT-FILE.
WRITE-BUILT-SEGMENT.
     IF PREV-SEG-NAME EQUAL TO SPACES
          GO TO WRITE-SEGMENT-EXIT.
     IF PREV-SEG-NAME = 'PARTROOT'   GO TO SEGMENT-IS-SEG00010.
     IF PREV-SEG-NAME = 'STANINFO'   GO TO SEGMENT-IS-SEG00060.
     IF PREV-SEG-NAME = 'STOKSTAT'   GO TO SEGMENT-IS-SEG02000.
     IF PREV-SEG-NAME = 'CYCCOUNT'   GO TO SEGMENT-IS-SEG02200.
     IF PREV-SEG-NAME = 'BACKORDR'   GO TO SEGMENT-IS-SEG02300.
INVALID-SEGMENT-NAME.
     DISPLAY 'INVALID SEGMENT NAME = ' PREV-SEG-NAME.
     GO TO LOCKED-HALT.
SEGMENT-IS-SEG00010.
     MOVE BUILD-SEGMENT-AREA TO SEG00010-INSERT-AREA.
     MOVE BUILD-SEGMENT-AREA TO KEY-VALUE-00010.
     MOVE SPACE TO BEGIN-OP-00010.
     CALL  'CBLTDLI' USING DL1-FUNCTION, PCB-AREA-1,
                           SEG00010-INSERT-AREA, SEG00010-SSA.
               MOVE '(' TO BEGIN-OP-00010.
     IF STATUS-CODES NOT = SPACES, GO TO SEGMENT-INSERT-ERROR.
     GO TO WRITE-SEGMENT-EXIT.
```

```
SEGMENT-IS-SEG00060.
        MOVE BUILD-SEGMENT-AREA TO SEG00060-INSERT-AREA.
        MOVE WRONG-MAKE-SPAN TO RIGHT-MAKE-SPAN.
        MOVE BUILD-SEGMENT-AREA TO KEY-VALUE-00060.
        MOVE SPACE TO BEGIN-OP-00060.
        CALL 'CBLTDLI' USING DLI-FUNCTION, PCB-AREA-1,
                             SEG00060-INSERT-AREA, SEG00010-SSA,
                                                   SEG00060-SSA.
                 MOVE '(' TO BEGIN-OP-00060.
        IF STATUS-CODES NOT = SPACES, GO TO SEGMENT-INSERT-ERROR.
        GO TO WRITE-SEGMENT-EXIT.
SEGMENT-IS-SEG02000.
        MOVE BUILD-SEGMENT-AREA TO SEG02000-INSERT-AREA.
        MOVE BUILD-SEGMENT-AREA TO KEY-VALUE-02000.
        MOVE SPACE TO BEGIN-OP-02000.
        CALL 'CBLTDLI' USING DLI-FUNCTION, PCB-AREA-1,
                             SEG02000-INSERT-AREA, SEG02010-SSA,
                                                   SEG02000-SSA.
                 MOVE '(' TO BEGIN-OP-02000.
        IF STATUS-CODES NOT = SPACES, GO TO SEGMENT-INSERT-ERROR.
        GO TO WRITE-SEGMENT-EXIT.
SEGMENT-IS-SEG02200.
        MOVE BUILD-SEGMENT-AREA TO SEG02200-INSERT-AREA.
        MOVE BUILD-SEGMENT-AREA TO KEY-VALUE-02200.
        MOVE SPACE TO BEGIN-OP-02200.
        CALL 'CBLTDLI' USING DLI-FUNCTION, PCB-AREA-1,
                             SEG02200-INSERT-AREA, SEG00010-SSA,
                                                   SEG02000-SSA,
                                                   SEG02200-SSA.
                 MOVE '(' TO BEGIN-OP-02200.
        IF STATUS-CODES NOT = SPACES, GO TO SEGMENT-INSERT-ERROR.
        GO TO WRITE-SEGMENT-EXIT.
SEGMENT-IS-SEG02300.
        MOVE BUILD-SEGMENT-AREA TO SEG02300-INSERT-AREA.
        MOVE BUILD-SEGMENT-AREA TO KEY-VALUE-02300.
        MOVE SPACE TO BEGIN-OP-02300.
        CALL 'CBLTDLI' USING DLI-FUNCTION, PCB-AREA-1,
                             SEG02300-INSERT-AREA, SEG00010-SSA,
                                                   SEG02000-SSA,
                                                   SEG02300-SSA.
                 MOVE '(' TO BEGIN-OP-02300.
        IF STATUS-CODES NOT = SPACES, GO TO SEGMENT-INSERT-ERROR.
        GO TO WRITE-SEGMENT-EXIT.
WRITE-SEGMENT-EXIT.    GOBACK.
SEGMENT-INSERT-ERROR.
        DISPLAY  'SEGMENT '
                 PREV-SEG-NAME
                 ' INSERT ERROR, '
                 ' STATUS CODE= '
                 STATUS-CODES                 UPON CONSOLE.

        GO TO WRITE-SEGMENT-EXIT.
END-INP-FILE.
        CLOSE INPUT-FILE.
        PERFORM WRITE-BUILT-SEGMENT THRU WRITE-SEGMENT-EXIT.
        DISPLAY 'END   DB LOAD' UPON CONSOLE.
LOCKED-HALT.
                 GOBACK.
```

APPENDIX C.
DATA BASE
LIBRARY

This appendix lists a collection of books and reports that are readily available on the subject of data base technology. An individual or an organization interested in the technical aspects of the subject matter would probably want to select these publications as an initial effort towards a data base library. A multitude of both general and technical papers on the topic are referenced in the listed publications.

BOOKS

House, W. C. (editor), *Data Base Management*, New York, Petrocelli Books, 1974.

Lyon, J. K., *An Introduction to Data Base Design*, New York, John Wiley and Sons, Inc., 1971.

Rustin, R. (editor), *Data Base Systems*, Englewood Cliffs, New Jersey, Prentice-Hall, Inc., 1972.

REPORTS

CODASYL *Data Base Task Group (DBTG) Report*, April 1971. Available from the Association for Computing Machinery.

CODASYL Systems Committee Technical Report, *Feature Analysis of Generalized Data Base Management Systems*, May 1971. Available from the Association for Computing Machinery. 1133 Avenue of the Americas, New York, N.Y. 10036.

CODASYL Systems Committee Technical Report, *A Survey of Generalized Data Base Management Systems*, May 1969. Available from the Association for Computing Machinery.

Codd, E. F., and A. L. Dean (editors), *Data Description, Access and Control*, 1971 ACM SIGFIDET Workshop. Available from the Association for Computing Machinery.

Dean, A. L. (editor), *Data Description, Access and Control*, 1972 ACM SIGFIDET Workshop. Available from the Association for Computing Machinery.

INDEX

INDEX